CONDEMNED UNHEARD

THE GOVERNMENT OF INDIA AND H. H. THE MAHARAJA OF KASHMIR.

CONDEMNED UNHEARD

THE GOVERNMENT OF INDIA AND H. H. THE MAHARAJA OF KASHMIR.

A LETTER

TO THE

RT. HON. SIR UGHTRED KAY-SHUTTLEWORTH,

BART., P.C., M.P.,

Sometime Under-Secretary of State for India,

BY

WILLIAM DIGBY, C.I.E.

AUTHOR OF

INDIA FOR THE INDIANS—AND FOR ENGLAND,' 'INDIAN PROBLEMS FOR ENGLISH CONSIDERATION,' 'THE FAMINE CAMPAIGN IN SOUTHERN INDIA,' 'NEPAL AND INDIA,' INDIA'S INTEREST IN THE BRITISH BALLOT BOX,' ETC., ETC.

'STRIKE, BUT HEAR'

GYAN

Published by

GYAN

Gyan Publishing House
5, Ansari Road
Daryaganj, New Delhi-110002
Phone: 011-47034999, 9811692060
E-mail: books@gyanbooks.com

Distribution Network
gyanbooks.com
India, USA, Canada, UK, Australia, France

ISBN : 978-81-212-3269-2 (PB)
First Published, July, 1890

2nd Impression 2020

Printed at: Gyan Press, Delhi.

The Vijayanagar Empire Chronicles of Paes and Nuniz
Author: Chronicle of Fernao Nuniz

CONDENDEMNED UNHEARD.

THE GOVERNMENT OF INDIA

AND H. H. THE

MAHARAJA OF KASHMIR.

A Letter

TO THE

RT. HON. SIR UGHTRED KAY-SHUTTLEWORTH,

BART., P.C., M.P.,

Sometime Under-Secretary of State for India,

BY

WILLIAM DIGBY, C.I.E.,

AUTHOR OF

INDIA FOR THE INDIANS—AND FOR ENGLAND,' 'INDIAN PROBLEMS FOR ENGLISH CONSIDERATION,' 'THE FAMINE CAMPAIGN IN SOUTHERN INDIA,' 'NEPAL AND INDIA,' INDIA'S INTEREST IN THE BRITISH BALLOT BOX,' ETC., ETC.

'STRIKE, BUT HEAR!'

Indian Political Agency,
25, CRAVEN STREET, CHARING CROSS,
LONDON.

July, 1890.

'Where Empires towered that were not just:
Lo! the skulking wild fox scratches in a
little heap of dust.'

THE LATE MAHARAJA RUNBIR SINGH'S PROPHECY.

MR. EDWARD E. MEAKIN, in an address delivered at a meeting of the East India Association in August, 1889, said :—I wish particularly to allude to the necessity of maintaining the confidence of the Indian princes in the *justice* of the English Government. Now, I am afraid that the present position of affairs with regard to two or three of the States is not such as to inspire the confidence of the Native Princes. I will relate an incident which occurred in the year 1876. I was one day sitting by the side of the late Maharaja of Kashmir talking over various matters, and his eldest son, the present Maharaja, was seated on the other side of him. The Maharaja suddenly turned to me and said: 'I learned a great many things by my recent visit to Calcutta. Some of my people urged me not to go, saying that no sooner should I leave my territory than I should find myself a sort of honoured State prisoner, something like Shah Shoojah when he visited Ranjeet Singh, who would not allow him to cross the Sutlej until he had left the Koh-i-Noor behind him. They said that it was an open secret that the British Government wanted to annex Kashmir, and that it was only a question of time and skilful manœuvring, and that I should be inveigled into allowing the first step towards the attainment of that object before I should be permitted to return to my own country'; and His Highness concluded with a derisive laugh. I remarked that the safety of His Highness's dominions lay in a good sound administration, and the encouragement of trade and commerce. I also told His Highness that he must be careful not to give any excuse for the British authorities to interfere with him, and that, if they did unjustly interfere, he might always rely upon the English Press to defend his rights. After a pause he said: 'Sahib, what do you call that little thing between the railway carriages? It is like a button stuck on a sort of gigantic needle that runs through the train, and when the carriages are pushed at one end or the other you hear a "houff, houff," and bang they go against the poor little button. I felt very sorry for the poor little button, but it is doubtless useful in its way. What do you call it?' I replied that I believed it was called 'a buffer.' 'Buffer, buffer,' repeated the Maharaja in earnest tones. 'Yes, buffer, that's just what I am, and that shall henceforth be one of my titles;' and he directed Dewan Kirpa Ram to see that it was written down correctly. I was puzzled for a moment to know what to say or do. I felt a fear lest some other European might come after me who might make His Highness think that I had been hoaxing him. I begged to be allowed to explain that in the English language the word 'buffer,' when applied to human beings, had another signification, which could not be applied to His Highness, as it was a term of derision. 'Never mind,' said he, 'it is all the same, I am a buffer; on one side of me there is the big train of the British possessions, and whenever they push northward they will tilt up against me: then on the other side is the shaky concern Afghanistan, and on the other side of it is the ponderous train and engine called Roos. Every now and then there is a tilting of Roos towards Afghanistan, and simultaneously there is a tilting upwards of the great engine in Calcutta, and I am the poor little button between them. Some day, perhaps not far distant, there will be a tilting from the North, and Afghanistan will smash up. Then there will be a tremendous tilt from the South, and I shall be buried in the wreck and lost! It may not come in my time, but it is sure to come when that poor little button is on the pin'—pointing to his son, the present Maharaja, who laughed merrily at the novel idea. At that time the present Maharaja seemed a bright, intelligent young fellow, and I have no doubt that, if he had been quietly and kindly dealt with by the British Government, they might have made a good ruler of him, and even now I do not think it is too late to try what honest and kindly treatment may do to make him all we have any right to expect. I do not think the Princes of India will view with complacency our present doings in

Kashmir. It was clearly wrong for the East India Company to cede Kashmir to Ghulab Singh (grandfather of the present Maharaja) for £750,000 when it was not a possession of theirs, and they had no manner of right to deal with it, but 'a bargain is a bargain.' The East India Company took the money and left Ghulab Singh to annex Kashmir *if he could.* He *did* annex it, and was duly acknowledged as its sovereign, and, logically speaking, his grandson, the present Maharaja, is the lawful ruler of this Naboth's vineyard which seems to be so ardently coveted by certain Indian officials. His right to rule is at least as good as that of the descendants of General Bernadotte to rule Sweden. It is said that the Maharaja is given to excesses. We have heard the same things alleged against other princes, noblemen, and gentlemen before now. Let him that is entirely guiltless amongst them cast the first stone at this unfortunate prince. I regard this as the most despicable excuse that could be invented for high-handed robbery. If this principle of confiscation be allowed, how many of our old noble families are liable to have their vast estates confiscated? I hope that my countrymen possess a sufficient sense of honour to rise as one man and protest against this shocking iniquity being perpetrated in the name of the British nation.

CONTENTS.

APPENDIX.

To

THE RIGHT HON. SIR U. KAY-SHUTTLEWORTH,
BART., P.C., M.P.,
Sometime Under Secretary of State for India.

SIR,

In the debate on the proposed adjournment of the House of Commons, moved on July 3rd by Mr. Bradlaugh, M.P., to enable him to bring forward the grievances of H.H. the Maharaja of Kashmir, you took part. You did so with the view of doing what in you lay to prevent an inquiry being granted into the circumstances under which the Government of India virtually deposed the Maharaja without giving him an opportunity (1) of disproving the charges alleged against him; and (2) of showing that the Indian authorities, in the course which they took, were acting beyond their rights or powers, and wholly in contravention of treaty stipulations.

The Maharaja's position was in some respects (with this exception, that it was on all grounds of high policy infinitely worse) that of a so-called 'criminal' under the Balfour Irish Coercion Act. Wholly on suspicion, and with no evidence but that of Residency 'shadowing,' he has been condemned and punished. To the course pursued by the Removable Magistrates, a course justified by the Chief Secretary for Ireland, you are a most determined opponent. It surely cannot be that your sense of justice is circumscribed by the limits of the United Kingdom, and that, in relation to India, you, who have had so much to do with its administration, and who may again have much to do with its rule, are prepared to regard the commonest and most rudimentary elements of fair-play as of no account whatever.

The issue before the House of Commons on the 3rd of July was this: The Government of India had taken away from the Maharaja of Kashmir the control of his State and a portion of his revenues, on certain grounds alleged in official papers laid before Parliament, while all inquiry into the grounds for the action taken against a great feudatory Prince had been refused. Thereupon it was proposed that a Select Committee of the House, or a Judicial Committee in India, be appointed to make due inquiry. You voted against inquiry. You justified yourself by saying:—

> In this debate we have been placed under this disadvantage, that the papers relating to Kashmir are not yet in the hands of members. But by the courtesy of the right hon. gentleman (Sir J. Gorst), I have had the advantage of perusing these papers for a short time, and it is only fair that I should rise to say that, so far as I can judge from a hasty perusal of the papers and following carefully the speech of the right hon. gentleman, he has stated the case as regards the action of successive Viceroys and successive Secretaries of State, in their relation to the late Maharaja of Kashmir and the present Maharaja, with perfect fairness. I may venture to say one or two words more as to whether the facts which have been laid before us show a necessity for such an inquiry as is asked for. I believe, if hon. members will examine these papers, they will find that there is nothing in them to call for a review, by a Parliamentary Committee, of the patient and

deliberate action of the Government of India, who seem to have hesitated long before taking any strong step, although the misgovernment of the Maharaja has been, I fear, of a very glaring description. I would only venture to make this one remark. It should be a satisfaction to members on this side of the House to find with respect to the Government of India that it has not been drawn into the annexation policy which my hon. friend (Mr. Bradlaugh) deprecates, but that it leaves the government of Kashmir under a council of natives of India, guided by the Resident of India; and, in concluding a despatch addressed by the Viceroy of India to the Maharaja of Kashmir, the Viceroy treats him with the greatest consideration and courtesy, and expresses a hope that it may be possible to give greater power to him in the future. At present the Maharaja is put in an ornamental position. He is not deposed, but simply relieved of the powers of ruler of the country, and these powers are confided to a council. I hope, therefore, the House will pause before voting for this motion.

I venture most respectfully to submit that even if —which I entirely deny, and which denial I will, before I conclude this letter, completely maintain—the papers submitted in proof to you by Sir John Gorst did, in your view, justify the Government of India, in its own opinion, in taking action, seeing that the Prince accused denied those allegations, and that no evidence in support of them was produced, the inquiry asked for ought to have been granted. Further that Liberals were justified in expecting that if you took part at all in the division it would be in support of the prayer of the motion.

There are many things germane to the issue in which the Indian Government played the threefold part of Accuser, Judge, and Executioner, which do not appear in the papers you have seen. Some of them

I produce in the pages of this communication. All that Mr. Bradlaugh asked for was that an opportunity should be given for the Maharaja's case to be stated before a competent authority. The decision of such a tribunal would be accepted as final. There is much more involved in the proceedings, which you appear to have treated with so light a heart, than transpired even in debate. First, there are the rights of the people of Kashmir. Surely the Kashmirian population may be permitted to have something to say about the deposition of their ruler. Mr. Gladstone, your honoured chief and mine, on the cession of the Ionian Islands, laid down the true principle of the rights of peoples in such a regard when he said that it was only with the consent of the people ruled that a change of rulers should be made. At the present moment, probably with your acquiescence, the Liberal party and Liberal journals are taking exception to the proposed cession of Heligoland and the Heligolanders to Germany, without the consent of the island people having been first asked and obtained. What is due and fitting in regard to the two thousand Europeans of Frisian race, on a solitary rock in the North Sea, is not unfitting in regard to the million and a-half Kashmirians living under the shadow of the Himalayas and in valleys renowned in poesy, whose ruler has been deposed against their wishes.[1] As a matter of fact, although the

---

[1] As an instance of the manner in which the action of the Government of India is regarded in Jammu, the following petition addressed to Mr. C. Bradlaugh, M.P., and presented by him to the House of Commons in July, 1889, is of interest:—

'*The humble petition of the following Dogras of Jammu.*

"The Kashmir State is divided into two portions: one is *Kashmir* proper, inhabited by Brahmin Pundits, and the other is *Jammu*, inhabited by *Dogras*.

Government of India has professed to act in the interests of the people of Kashmir in removing their ruler, no complaint whatever has been made by them. They do not declare that they are aggrieved. On the contrary, if a plebiscite were taken, it is believed nine-tenths or more of the people would call for the Maharaja's speedy restoration. No doubt there was misgovernment in Kashmir, as there is misgovernment in many parts of British India, and as there is, you and I consider, in one important part of the United Kingdom. The misgovernment in Kashmir, however, was misgovernment which could have been removed with His Highness, Pertab Singh, on the Kashmir throne, quite as well as with his removal from all power and authority in his own dominions. Indeed, it was in process of removal by the Maharaja, Lord Dufferin being my authority. Mr. Wingate, the solitary witness cited by the Government of India, says, what no doubt the Maharaja's subjects all felt, namely, that 'His Highness has a ready sympathy for the poor, a keen interest in land questions, and a determination to protect the cultivators against the officials.'

These *Dogras* form the fighting portion of the State. The present Maharaja Pertab Singh belongs to their caste, and is loved to devotion by them. He has been by a trickery deposed, and his *gadi* occupied by a few strangers, and these strangers are nothing but tools in the hand of the British Resident. The *Dogras* have never known Foreign domination, and the condition to which they have been just reduced has thrown them into great alarm and distress. At the moment the saying among the *Dogras* is that they would rather prefer to be plundered by their own Maharaja than to be rewarded with gold by the slavish Council. The *Dogras* have always fought for the British Government, and will ever fight for it to their last drop of blood. In India it is said that you are the friend of the people, and, therefore, the petitioners appeal to you for help and protection.'

[Here follow signatures.]

I may here mention a few facts concerning the Prince who has been so cruelly maligned by anonymous slanderers—maligned in a manner which would be scouted as disgraceful if adopted in connection with a European Prince. Sir Lepel Griffin, with the shameless audacity which characterizes his conduct towards the Indian races, people and princes alike, declared the Maharaja to be a 'drunken debauchee.' While in India, last year and the year before, I had special opportunities of ascertaining the real character of the Maharaja and of his rule. I am compelled, in justice to Pertab Singh, to say that all the information I received showed that he ruled his dominions with much kindness and good sense; he was animated by staunch loyalty to the British dominance, highly appreciating British over-rule and its many merits, sincerely anxious to further the objects of the Government of India so far as these were compatible with the maintenance of those sovereign rights guaranteed by the Queen to all Indian princes in 1858. No acts of misgovernment have been proved against His Highness; according to my information none exist. It is true, misgovernment—tested by a European standard—exists in Kashmir as it exists in British India. The Maharaja did his best to remedy the evils which were prevalent, and would have continued his good work if opportunity had been given him. It has not yet been proved that the people of Kashmir are not lightly taxed; it is not denied that justice is dispensed with even-handedness by honest and thoroughly capable and trained judges—barristers in some cases having been raised to the Bench, or that public works are flourishing; while those who know the country well declare that the people are contented and happy, and that in every direction there were, when the Maharaja was deposed, signs of a desire to keep Kashmir in line with the most advanced provinces in the Empire.

I know that vague statements of a contrary character are made. I also know, unfortunately, that it has been the practice of some Anglo-Indians to trade largely on abuses in Kashmir which existed only in their imagination. Writing a year ago on this question, I found occasion to remark that during the reign of the late Maharaja certain Anglo-Indian newspapers were continually writing of the misgovernment of Kashmir, declaring that that misgovernment established occasion for British intervention. The gravest charges of neglect, and even of dreadful cruelty, were brought against the late Maharaja. On one occasion it was declared that His Highness, in order to be saved the expense of feeding his people during a time of great scarcity, actually drowned them by boat-loads at a time in the Srinagar Lake. The Maharaja declined to sit quietly under this calumny, and at his request a Mixed Commission was appointed by the Government of India to inquire into the truth of the story. The Commission found there was no truth in the hideous statement; the people who were said to be drowned were discovered to be living, and were actually produced at the inquiry. Other calumnies of a like kind were circulated, and all, on examination by the British Resident, were found to be false. The late Maharaja was a man of strong will and resolution, and was able to defend himself and his country against the wretched charges brought against him. For a time the land had peace. The present Maharaja, unfortunately, has not the strength of character and indomitable will of his predecessor. He is an exceedingly kind-hearted and good-natured man, fond of work, never sparing himself, and is greatly solicitous for the welfare of his subjects. All who are brought into contact with him speedily learn to love him.

If ever there was an issue in connection with our administration of India in which a Liberal statesman could have no ground for doubt as to the course he should take it was, I respectfully submit, the issue presented by Mr. Bradlaugh on the 3rd of July. Your late colleagues, with a minor exception or two, recognised this. While it is matter for serious regret and even for indignation that none of them supported Mr. Bradlaugh, there is this much of grace in their conduct, that they left you to go alone into the Government Lobby. The barest justice, that of an accused person being allowed to show cause why a particular course should not have been taken, was sought. You, alone (as I beg again to remind you), among Liberal ex-officials, deliberately refused to a feudatory Prince of the British Empire in India what you would insist upon being granted to the most wretched tenant in Connaught or Connemara.

The significance of your action, and the chief justification for the liberty I am taking in publicly addressing you, lies in the fact that you have been the member responsible in a Liberal Government to the House of Commons for the conduct of Indian affairs; you were honoured by a place in an Administration which gave emphatic proof of its desire to act fairly towards India, under the leadership of one who has been most friendly in his feelings and expressions towards the Indian people. Several acts of Mr. Gladstone's Governments of 1880-86 put the English rule of India in an altogether new light. There was then—surprising, nay wonderful, as it may seem—a desire displayed to treat the people of our great Empire with fairness. Nothing more than fairness. But that was a marvel. Such conduct aroused hopes of brighter and better times for the princes and people of India alike. A yet higher position than that you have already occupied towards India may, ere many months are past, be conferred upon you. In the House on Thursday, July 3, you represented the past, and possibly the future, Liberal official relations of your party with two hundred and sixty millions of people. Your vote, therefore, in itself carried great weight. More than that, your conduct must have influenced some of your fellow-members to vote against Mr Bradlaugh's motion. And, as things go in the House of Commons, not surprisingly so. It is easy to imagine hon. members who would shield themselves under the remark: 'Oh! Shuttleworth has looked into the matter: he is satisfied that the Government of India has done rightly'; and who, having satisfied their consciences by allowing you to think for them, followed you into the 'No' lobby. Even if the Government of India had done rightly in the course they took, the Maharaja of Kashmir, I submit, was entitled to the fair and open trial which he desires, and which Mr. Bradlaugh was hindered in securing by *your* vote among others, and by your vote more than by any other. *Your* vote, the vote of a sometime Under Secretary of State for India, a possibly high official in a new

Administration, prevents your reconsideration of the case when, as you must have known, in due course it would in all probability be submitted to you should Mr. Gladstone, as it is reasonable to suppose he will, again ask you to go to the India Office. Loyalty to the Department over which one has presided, and may again preside, is, I venture to urge, carried too far when it permits of the intervention in a debate of an ex-official of your eminence, and the prejudgment by you of a case only a portion of one side of which was before you.

So grievous a wrong has been maintained by the vote of the House of Commons on the 3rd of July that, as one acquainted, to some extent at first hand, and more largely by the possession of many documents from wholly trustworthy parties, and also as a humble member of the political party of which you are an eminent representative and office-holder, I venture to publicly address to you this letter. I endeavour, in the pages which follow, without a particle of passion against members of the Government of India who are responsible for the course which has been taken against the Maharaja of Kashmir, to tell the story of the treatment to which His Highness Pertab Singh has been subjected. The blanks left in the Government papers are, as far as may be, filled up by facts which, if opportunity were given, could be fully established. Some degree of heat may be found in a portion of my remarks. I do not profess to be able to write of such doings as are here portrayed without stirrings of indignation. If passion of any kind be displayed it is directed against the institution known as the Calcutta Foreign Office, and not against any individual. Some day the many wrongs perpetrated by that department of the Government of India may obtain publicity. Should the day ever arrive, Englishmen will hardly credit the statements which must be made if an honest record is forthcoming. The lack of any controlling power over its doings, either in India or in England, has enabled the Foreign Office of India to act in a manner which could not receive sanction in any English Parliament which this century has known. However, that is a matter which, in due time, will come up for settlement. The many wrongs done by the Calcutta Foreign Office, like the proverbial chickens, will one day come home to roost. The reckoning will not be a satisfactory one.

In the succeeding pages I set forth with the utmost fairness all that has been urged for and against the virtual deposition of the Maharaja of Kashmir. I keep back nothing urged on the other side; I do not, consciously, extenuate any wrong done by him for whom I plead, while, most assuredly, I set down naught in malice. I hope my presentation of the facts may be considered worthy of your most attentive perusal, and that it may be read with care by you and by the many other persons to whom this communication, publicly addressed to an ex-Secretary of State for India, will be sent.

THE BEGINNING OF THE END IN KASHMIR.

EARLY in last year much excitement was caused in India and (in a less degree) in England by the announcement that the Maharaja of Kashmir had been discovered to be engaged in treasonable correspondence with Russia. It was stated that the British Resident in Kashmir had proceeded to Calcutta with ample proofs in his possession of the Maharaja's treachery. Further, it was remarked that the Maharaja, conscious of his guilt, had placed the resignation of his rule in the hands of the representative of the British Government. Soon afterwards it was stated that the resignation had been accepted, and that a Council of State, under the control of the Resident, had been appointed. By these means Kashmir virtually passed under the direct control of the Government of India. Another independent State in India was wiped out of existence.

In England it was felt that a danger to the Empire had been removed, and not a little credit, it was agreed, attached to the Viceroy of India for what he had done. At what seemed like a crisis in affairs, Lord Lansdowne had acted with decision and promptitude, entitling him to much honour. Within a very short time, however, a telegram was published in the London papers to the effect that the Maharaja, in an autograph letter addressed to the Viceroy, denied that he had been guilty of treacherous conduct. He asserted that the treasonable letters were forgeries. He protested in strong and pathetic language against the harsh treatment to which he had been subjected, denied that he had resigned his rulership, begged for a further opportunity of ruling his own dominions, and, in a not unnatural frenzy, besought Lord Lansdowne, if he would not restore him and thus save him from present ignominy, to shoot him through the heart, as life had become unsupportable.

It was clear from these circumstances that there were two sides to the matter, and that it would not be fair to rely implicitly upon the *ex-parte* statements which, in great haste, had been forwarded to England. It became certain that, so far as the Maharaja was concerned, there was much to be urged which might put a different complexion upon the affair.

The deposition of His Highness Pertab Singh formed the subject of inquiry in Parliament. In your House, on March 14, 1889, Mr. Webster, the (Conservative) Member for East Saint Pancras, asked whether it was a fact that letters of Lachman Das, late Prime Minister of Kashmir, had been discovered showing a course of treason on the part of the Maharaja towards the Indian Government; whether these letters, amongst other things, revealed a design set on foot by the Maharaja of Kashmir to poison the British Resident; and, if the information was correct, what steps the Government of India proposed to take. Sir John Gorst disposed of the questions in a very easy fashion. 'The Secretary of State,' he said, 'is advised that the Government of India attach very little importance to the intercepted letters.'

A month later Mr. Caine asked for papers relating to the charges against the Maharaja. Sir John Gorst again pooh-poohed, and treated with contempt and as of little importance, the so-called treasonable letters.[1] He, however, now, as on a previous occasion, raised a distinctly false issue by speaking of 'intercepted letters' as though certain communications on the way to an enemy had been discovered. This is a wholly incorrect rendering of the facts.

Two months passed without the India Office or the Government of India being disturbed by questions in Parliament. Mr. Bradlaugh, on the 20th of June, put an important series of questions, covering the whole ground of the action of the authorities in regard to Kashmir. His question was in these terms:—

> I beg to ask the Under Secretary of State for India whether the Secretary of State for India is aware that the Government of India have, virtually, annexed the State of Kashmir to British India, and subjected its ruler to great indignities;
>
> Whether the Secretary of State is aware of the contents of a letter, No. 11 C, of 1889, dated 17th April, from Colonel Nisbet, C.I.E., Resident of Kashmir, to Raja Amir Singh, Prime Minister of Kashmir;
>
> Whether such letter is a violation of the solemn promises made by the Queen on the assumption by Her Majesty of the direct rule of India, that the Native Indian Princes should be safeguarded in

[1] 'Sir J. Gorst: I stated in reply to a question on the 14th of March that the Government of India attached very little importance to the intercepted letters. No official papers have yet arrived in this country, and it is, therefore, impossible to say whether the Secretary of State will lay any on the Table.'—*Indian Hansard*, 1889, 63.

their dominions, and that no annexation of Native territory should be made;

Whether the Maharaja of Kashmir has been removed from the position of an active and responsible ruler of his dominions to that of a mere pensioner on State funds;

Whether the Maharaja has been informed that 'he will be expected to refrain from all interference in the administration,' that 'he will have no power of obtaining the State revenues,' that he is to receive 'an annual sum sufficient to maintain his household in due comfort,' but nothing for what is called 'extravagance,' that he is not to attend meetings of the Council, and that the Council is 'expected' to exercise the powers of administration it possesses 'under the guidance of the British Resident';

Whether the Councillors, three or four of whom (out of five or six who constitute the Council) being 'officials selected by the Government of India,' have also been informed that they are to 'take no steps of importance without consulting the Resident,' and that they are to 'follow his advice whenever it may be offered';

Whether he is aware that, in an autograph letter to the Viceroy, the Maharaja has protested against the treatment to which he has been subjected, begging that if liberty cannot be restored to him his life might be taken;

Whether the Secretary of State will state why the course described has been taken with the Maharaja, without any opportunity being given to him of being heard either by the Government of India or by any other authority;

Whether, in view of the alarm which the course adopted by the Government of India has already caused among the feudatory Princes in India, an opportunity will be given to the Maharaja to apply for a reversal of the decree contained in letter No. 11 C, of 1889, either before a Select Committee of this House or in some other suitable manner; and,

Whether the Secretary of State will, with as little delay as possible, give the House an opportunity of discussing the important step which has been taken by the Government of India, and will lay all papers connected with Kashmir upon the Table of this House.

An answer was given to this series of statements, followed by cross-questioning. As given in the *Indian Hansard* (331, 332), the answer and further questions are as follows:—

Sir J. Gorst: The Government of India has neither annexed the State of Kashmir nor subjected its ruler to great indignities. The Secretary of State has as yet received no information respecting the letter referred to. The Maharaja has voluntarily resigned the administration of his State, and his resignation has been accepted. But he will receive from the revenues of the State a suitable allowance for his maintenance. The answer to this question is in the affirmative. The Secretary of State has as yet received no information respecting the letter referred to. The Secretary of State has no reason to think that recent events in Kashmir have caused any alarm amongst the native chiefs in India, whose rights are, subject to the duties of the paramount power towards the people of the Native States, scrupulously respected by the Government of India. There is no correspondence upon the subject which could, in the opinion of the Secretary of State, be at present laid before Parliament without detriment to the public service.

Mr. Bradlaugh: May I ask if the hon. gentleman is aware that the Maharaja repudiates the voluntary action imputed to him in the hon. gentleman's answer? Will he afford some opportunity of having the matter investigated?

Sir J. Gorst: The Secretary of State has no official information, but I am quite sure that he will not be surprised if that is the fact. If the hon. member knew the Maharaja of Kashmir as well as the Government of India do, I think the hon. gentleman himself would not be surprised.

Mr. Bradlaugh: Does the hon. gentleman mean that, although the Secretary of State has no official information, he is aware, unofficially, that the Maharaja repudiates the voluntary action imputed to him?

Sir J. Gorst: The hon. gentleman is mistaken if he draws that conclusion from my answer.

Mr. Bradlaugh: Then, has the Secretary of State any knowledge, officially or unofficially, that the Maharaja does deny the voluntary action attributed to him, and does he not think that in so grave a matter, affecting so large a question, an opportunity should be afforded for investigation?

Sir J. GORST: My answer was perfectly clear—namely, that the Secretary of State has no information, but I should not be surprised if the statement should turn out hereafter to be true. I should attach no importance to the fact.

Meanwhile, comments were freely made in the Anglo-Indian press as to the alleged badness alike of the Maharaja's character and of his rule. Some of these comments were quoted in English journals.

In the House of Lords the deposition occupied attention. From Hansard's report I quote as follows:—

Lord HERSCHELL: I wish to ask my noble friend the Secretary of State for India whether there is any foundation for the rumour, which seems to have occasioned some alarm in different parts of India, that it is the intention of the Government to take possession of the Native State of Kashmir.

The SECRETARY OF STATE FOR INDIA (Viscount Cross): I can find no foundation for that report, and it is certainly absolutely untrue. It is true that the Viceroy felt bound, with my entire concurrence, to accept the resignation of the ruler of Kashmir for the present, and place the State under a Native Council, a course advised by the Resident who was there; but anyone who has looked into the way in which the State of Kashmir has been governed for some time past can have no doubt whatever that a wise step has been taken. There is not the slightest intention on the part of the Government or of the Viceroy to annex Kashmir to the British Crown. On the contrary, we have every hope that, when the state of things has been remedied in Kashmir, the late ruler will see it to be advisable to re-assume control of his State, and to govern in a way which will be a benefit to his subjects and to neighbouring countries as well.[1]

---

[1] Later, early in September, at Sheffield, Viscount Cross said: 'I have been accused lately of wishing to add to the Indian Empire by the annexation of

It will be seen the charges of treachery, and reliance upon the trustworthiness of the treasonable letters, were speedily abandoned; the so-called evidence of treasonable designs was scouted by the Government of India as unworthy of credence. Other issues were depended upon as justifying the course taken. These, as will be shown later, were as destitute of foundation as were the silly and contemptible letters themselves.

With what was happening in India at this time I need not now stay to trouble you. The proceedings there will appear later on. When those proceedings are recorded it will be seen that the Government of India refused to produce papers to justify the very serious step which they had taken, that they acted in a despotic manner and without the semblance even of that fair-play which is popularly supposed to be a British attribute and, for many hundreds of years, an essential part of British procedure everywhere.

As early as possible in the present session Mr. Bradlaugh pressed for the publication of all documents relating to the 'deposition'[1] of the Maharaja. On the 18th February this happened:—

Kashmir. I had determined to say from my place in Parliament that we had no notion of annexation of any description. It is quite true that we did interfere in the matter of Kashmir, and why? Because the people of Kashmir were so ground down by the tyranny and ill-government of the Maharaja that we were bound as the paramount Power to interfere for the protection of the interests of the inhabitants of that country. We have not annexed it to our Empire: we have placed it under native rule, subject, of course, to the advice of our Resident, and the moment the Maharaja sees the mistake he has made and we can trust him to govern his country as he ought to do, for the benefit of his people and not for his own, we shall be perfectly willing to hand the whole thing back to him.'—*Times* Report.

[1] I have to thank Lord Dufferin for this admirably descriptive word. In his speech before the London Chamber of Commerce in 1889, his lordship used this expression.

Mr. Bradlaugh: I beg to ask the Under Secretary of State for India whether the Government will, at an early date, present to the House the papers relating to the action of the Government of India towards Kashmir since H.H. Pertab Singh became Maharaja. And whether, if the Maharaja of Kashmir, in the words used by the Secretary of State on the 27th August last, 'sees it advisable to resume control of his State, and to govern it in a way which will be a benefit to his subjects and to neighbouring countries as well,' the Government of India will facilitate his doing so.

Sir J. Gorst: The Government is anxious to give full information to the House of Commons respecting the affairs of Kashmir, and papers recently received will be laid on the table. The statement of the Secretary of State quoted by the hon. member was contingent on the existing state of things in Kashmir being first remedied. The Government are anxious to show every consideration to the rights of the Maharaja consistent with a due regard to the still more sacred rights of the people of Kashmir.

Months passed and no papers were produced. In June—on the 10th—Mr. Bradlaugh returned to the charge. He inquired for the papers which had been promised and were not produced. The record of what passed is as follows:—

Mr. Bradlaugh: I beg to ask the Under Secretary of State for India when the papers relating to Kashmir, stated on the 18th February to have been recently received from India, and early publication of which was then promised, will be presented to the House; and, whether the Secretary of State will state what condition he wishes to insure in Kashmir before he gives the Maharaja the opportunity of governing his State 'in a way which will be a benefit to his subjects and to neighbouring countries as well,' which it was stated the Government of India would be prepared to facilitate.

Sir J. Gorst: The papers relating to Kashmir are now before my noble friend the Secretary of State, and will be immediately presented to the House—I have little doubt before the expiration of the week. The hon. member asks me what condition the

Secretary of State wishes to insure in Kashmir before he gives the Maharaja the opportunity of governing his State in a way to benefit his subjects and neighbouring countries. The condition which the Secretary of State wishes to insure in Kashmir is one of just and upright government in the interest of the people of the State.

Mr. BRADLAUGH: Is the right hon. gentleman aware that the majority of the people of Kashmir are of opinion that the only way to secure the state of things which the Secretary of State desires is the restoration of their lawful ruler and the withdrawal of all improper interference?

Sir J. GORST: No, sir, there is no reason to suppose that the majority of the people of Kashmir entertain any such opinion.

Even then the papers were not forthcoming. Never was greater difficulty experienced by learned counsel in a criminal court in extracting facts from a hostile witness than the hon. member for Northampton had to face in his efforts to get the papers he repeatedly asked for. One opinion—and one only—could be cherished regarding the conduct of the Government. It could only be because their case was very bad, would so little bear scrutiny, that the authorities were reluctant to place information in the hands of hon. members so as to enable them to judge for themselves as to the course which the Government had taken. Mr. Bradlaugh once more returned to the charge, and on this occasion (June 26th) succeeded in getting the papers. Hansard's report gives the particulars of what occurred as follows:—

Mr. BRADLAUGH: I beg to ask the Under Secretary of State for India whether the repeatedly promised papers relating to Kashmir will be presented to this House; and whether, in view of the present painful position of His Highness the Maharaja, the Secretary of State will at once authorize a judicial inquiry into the grave charges made by the Government and solemnly denied by His Highness.

Sir J. GORST: I have to-day laid the papers on the table. The action of the Government in Kashmir has been based, not upon grave personal charges made against the Maharaja, but upon the long-continued misgovernment of Kashmir, which rendered it necessary in the interests of the people to put an end to chronic oppression and misrule. Neither the Secretary of State nor the Government of India, as I have several times stated in Parliament, has ever attached any importance to certain treasonable and criminal correspondence attributed to the Maharaja. It is obvious that the conduct of the Government, in making such arrangements as involve the withdrawal of the Maharaja for a time on political grounds from certain participation in the government of the State, cannot be made the subject of investigation by a judicial officer.

Mr. BRADLAUGH: I will ask when the papers are likely to be circulated to members, and whether, if they disclose a state of things different from that which has just been stated, the Government will afford any opportunity for this unfortunate gentleman to repel accusations which he declares to be absolutely without foundation.

Sir J. GORST: The distribution of papers does not rest with me. It depends on the printing authorities of the House, over whom I have no control. With regard to the second part of the question, I think the hon. member had better wait until he sees the papers.

Mr. BRADLAUGH: In view of the excessive gravity of the matter, as I understand the papers, I shall avail myself of such opportunities as the forms of the House permit, unless the Government afford some opportunity to this unfortunate gentleman to answer the charges made against him.

The papers are now in the hands of hon. members. An attentive perusal of them makes it perfectly clear why the Secretary of State for India was so reluctant to publish them. The surmise that the Government of India really had no case is now made perfectly clear. Viscount Cross and his advisers must have been satisfied as to the weakness of the pleas on which they proceeded to deprive one million and a-half of people of their rightful ruler, and sensible of the gross injustice to which they had resorted in their treatment of Maharaja Pertab Singh. Assertions, in these papers, are plentiful; proofs are, with one exception which cuts both ways, entirely wanting. The papers, among other things, show :—

1. A breach of treaty stipulations;

2. A complete effacement of promises made by the Queen-Empress of India, promises which were proffered as a buttress to treaties and engagements—those treaties and engagements having been found undeniably weak so far as the inferior parties to them were concerned;

3. The deposition of an independent ruler on vague charges for which, only in the latest communication, is there a shred of evidence, and that evidence is accompanied with observations which wholly cut away the ground from under the feet of the Government;

4. An independent ruler, secured in his position by treaty stipulations, condemned and deprived of all power, wholly on the unsupported statements of interested parties, and without any opportunity whatsoever being given him of defending himself;

5. The ignoring of evidence which, had it been fairly considered, would have proved there were no grounds for proceeding against the Maharaja;

6. An assertion of voluntary resignation of power by the Maharaja against his explicit denial of this act; and

7. While misgovernment and the alleged unhappy condition of the people of Kashmir were described

as necessitating the action taken, these were not the whole, and there is grave reason to believe not the real, motives: the real motive being that fear of Russian aggression India-wards, which has led to the commission of so many questionable acts from time to time by the Government of India of the day, while it seems clear there was a desire to obtain complete control over, if not the actual possession of, the Kingdom of Kashmir.

These various propositions it will be my duty to establish, very largely from the Government papers themselves. The duty is a distasteful one. My personal respect for some of the eminent men now ruling India is very great. Opportunities have been vouchsafed to me of seeing the admirable manner in which certain among them have laboured for the good of the Indian people. No one is more ready than I am to bear testimony to the many excellent qualities of Indian administrators generally. My writings abound with such testimonies. But a recognition of worthy doings must not blind me to the real character of acts which are contrary to justice, acts which are the outcome of policies with which the leading men in India at the present time have themselves had little or nothing to do. There is a bad side, an exceedingly bad side, to Indian bureaucratic rule. That it is which I condemn, and not the executive officers for the moment in charge of the respective departments, or the Viceroy who has control of all.

The Kashmir incident, like scores of others affecting Indian Princes and their States, happened because the Government of India is in no way subject to that embodied conscience of present-day civilization—an enlightened public opinion possessing punitive power. Without meaning it, and doubtless working, as it considers, with a single eye to the maintenance of British supremacy in India, the Indian Foreign Office is frequently guilty of grievous injustice. That Office, more than other departments in the Indian Government, is in a position which neither man nor institution is good enough, or free enough from liability to error, to bear. There is no one to call it to account, no one to check its (maybe inadvertent) over-zeal, no one to suggest that there is, perhaps, another side to a matter than that which has fixed itself in the Foreign Secretary's mind; not a whisper is ever raised, or is likely to be ever raised, by any one possessing power in India, suggesting that the traditions of The Office might with advantage be at times broken; it is prosecutor, judge, and executioner; in its hands an Indian Prince is between the upper and nether millstones. The healthy criticism, the more or less adequate knowledge, and the sense of responsibility to Parliament and the Press, which keep the Foreign, Home, and Colonial Departments in Britain in touch with the nation, and which prevent any gross injustice or wide deviation from righteousness, are wholly wanting in India. They are not supplied by the British Parliament, the ultimate ruler of India. As a consequence, the Indian Foreign Office, without possibly knowing it, and certainly in many instances without meaning it, has been and is responsible for a vast number of acts of injustice, which, if set forth in detail, would hardly be credited. The Kashmir incident is one of them.

I now proceed to establish, from the papers published by Parliament and from another official document, admitted—in its most material portion—by Lord Lansdowne to be authentic, and from other evidence, the truth of my several contentions. In an Appendix—for the purpose of easy reference—I republish all the documents, save a long one from Mr. A. Wingate. Of the latter, however, the subject of each paragraph is stated, and the few paragraphs which bear, even incidentally, on the main point, and which are alluded to by the Government of India, are given in full. In all instances, where practicable, sources of information will be stated.

It may be noted in passing that, with the exception of certain unimportant despatches by various Secretaries of State—unimportant inasmuch as they simply echo the observations of the Government of India, and display a mere automaton mind, seemingly incapable of independent judgment—only extracts from despatches and other documents are published by Viscount Cross. The authorities have had the opportunity of preparing their own case. How they understand their duty, and perform it, is shown by their giving just so much of a despatch or minute as will, they think, establish their position. There may be, in other portions of the respective documents much that would tell in another direction, possibly against the main contentions put forward. These are carefully eliminated. Indeed, when one observes the large amount of irrelevant matter published in Mr. Wingate's report, it is perfectly clear that the suppressed parts of the correspondence would not support the action which has been taken. The case before us, then, may be regarded as the best which can be produced. Anything and everything which would be calculated to weaken the course adopted, and to strengthen the contention of the Maharaja and his friends, have been withheld. That is the way in which an Imperial Government, a *British* Imperial Government, marks its sense of right-mindedness and of justice. Even then, out of their own mouths, from their own carefully compiled record, is full condemnation to be found. Time was when there was chivalry enough in the British character to ensure to an opponent fair-play. If there was not the Quixotism which said, 'Gentlemen of the Guard, fire first,' there was a strong desire not to unduly take advantage of an opponent. That time is not wholly past, so far as individuals are concerned. There never, perhaps, was a time when such characteristics were displayed by a bureaucratic administration or by an Office as such. With neither a soul to be saved nor a body to be kicked, Departments sin against justice most grievously, and have no compunctions regarding gross injustice. History bears no record of a time when official nature as official nature—especially such official nature as the bureaucratic government of India develops—even gave so much as a moment's 'law' to the pettiest creature in its toils. Certainly no Indian Prince, with whom a difficulty has arisen, has ever been fairly treated by the Foreign Office of Calcutta. On the other hand, many of our feudatories have been most unjustly dealt with.

(1) *A Breach of Treaty Stipulations.*—The Treaty by which Kashmir[1] came under the rule of Ghulab Singh contained the following articles :—

I.—The British Government transfers and makes over for ever, in independent possession, to Maharaja Ghulab Singh and the heirs male of his body, all the hilly and mountainous country, situated to the eastward of the river Indus and westward of the river Ravee, including Chamba and excluding Lahoul, being part of the territories ceded to the British Government by the Lahore

[1] Kashmir was under Afghan sway until 1819, when it was conquered by the Sikhs. From that time it was ruled by a governor appointed by the Maharaja of the Punjab, until the Sikh War in 1845. Ghulab Singh, who had begun life as a horseman under the Maharaja Runjit Singh, but by distinguished conduct had raised himself to independent command, was presented with the principality of Jammu, whence, nominally on behalf of the Lahore State, he soon extended his authority over his Rajput neighbors, and eventually into Ladakh and Balkistan. In the revolution which preceded the outbreak of the Sikh War, he was elected Minister of the Khalsa, and he took an important part in the negotiations which followed the battle of Sobraon. The results were, that he was enabled to secure his power by a separate treaty with the English at Armitsar, in March, 1846, by which, on payment of 75 lakhs of rupees, or £750,000, he was confirmed in possession of the territory he held as feudatory of the Sikhs, and also obtained the Province of Kashmir. By treaty he bound himself to acknowledge the supremacy of the British Government, to refer all disputes with neighbouring States to its arbitration, to assist British troops when required, and never to take or retain in his service any British subject, or the subject of any European or American State, except with the consent of the British Government. The Maharaja sent a contingent of troops and artillery to co-operate with the British forces against Delhi during the Mutiny of 1857. Ghulab Singh died in August, 1857, and was succeeded by his eldest son, Maharaja Runbir Singh, G.C.S.I., who is by caste a Dogra Rajput, and was born about 1832. The Maharaja of Kashmir is entitled to a personal salute of twenty-one guns, and has received a *sanad* giving adoptive rights. On the occasion of the Delhi Durbar, in January, 1877, he was gazetted a General in the British Army, and created a Councillor of the Empress. Maharaja Runbir Singh died in 1885, and was succeeded by his son, Pertab Singh.—*Gazetteer of India.*

State, according to the provisions of Article IV of the Treaty of Lahore, dated 9th March, 1846.

II.—The eastern boundary of the tract, transferred by the foregoing article to Maharaja Ghulab Singh, shall be laid down by Commissioners appointed by the British Government and Maharaja Ghulab Singh, respectively, for that purpose, and shall be defined in a separate engagement after survey.

III.—In consideration of the transfer made to him and his heirs by the provisions of the foregoing articles, Maharaja Ghulab Singh will pay to the British Government the sum of rupees (Nanakshahi) fifty lakhs to be paid in ratification of this treaty, and twenty-five lakhs on or before the 1st October of the current year A.D. 1846.

IV.—The limits of the territories of Maharaja Ghulab Singh shall not, at any time, be changed without the concurrence of the British Government.

V.—Maharaja Ghulab Singh will refer to the arbitration of the British Government any disputes or questions that may arise between himself and the Government of Lahore or any other neighbouring State, and will abide by the decision of the British Government.

VI.—Maharaja Ghulab Singh engages for himself and his heirs to join, with the whole of his military force, the British troops when employed in the hills, or in the territories adjoining his possessions.

VII.—Maharaja Ghulab Singh engages never to take or retain in his service any British subject nor the subject of any European or American State without the consent of the British Government.

VIII.—Maharaja Ghulab Singh engages to respect, in regard to the territory transferred to him, the provisions of Articles V, VI, and VII of the separate engagement between the British Government and the Lahore Durbar, dated 9th March, 1846. [These clauses in the Lahore Treaty referred to the Jagirdars, to arrears of revenue, and to the property in the forts thereby transferred.]

IX.—The British Government will give its aid to Maharaja Ghulab Singh in protecting his territories from external enemies.

X.—Maharaja Ghulab Singh acknowledges the supremacy of the

British Government, and will in token of such supremacy present annually to the British Government one horse, twelve perfect shawl goats of approved breed (six male and six female), and three pairs of Kashmir shawls.

'In independent possession.' The condition of things existent at the time the treaty was made was intended to continue. Under the treaty no Resident was appointed to the Kashmir Court. The position of Maharaja Ghulab Singh was different to that of the Nizam or of any other Indian Prince. In the *Statistical Abstract of British India*, Population Returns, where every State in alliance with, or in subordination to, the Government of India appears, Kashmir is conspicuous by its absence. Only in late years has a reference even been made to it in a foot-note. When the Indian Government had any communications to make to the Maharaja, an agent ('officer on special duty' was the official designation) stationed at Srinagar or Jammu, as the case might be, was employed. His business was of a comparatively unimportant character and was strictly defined. Meanwhile the most friendly relations existed between the rulers of Kashmir and the Government of India. During the Mutiny of 1857, the son of Ghulab Singh, father of the present Maharaja, rendered inestimable service, and did his part both unselfishly and ungrudgingly. The Maharaja refused even to take rations for his troops, and when offered an increase of territory, in recognition of what he had done, refused to accept it. He proudly remarked that he had helped the Indian Government out of his loyalty and good-will, and not with the sordid object of receiving remuneration. That spirit was manifested by

Runbir Singh and Pertab Singh, the past and present Maharajas. At no time has the Government of India been placed in a position of difficulty without the Kashmir ruler proffering the full resources of his State in aid of the maintenance of British power. This has been the case alike in regard to internal enemies and external foes.

Until about fifteen years ago the possession or virtual control of Kashmir does not appear to have been regarded by the British authorities as a matter of much importance. After the ill-starred Afghan war of 1878, however, a desire seems to have been cherished for the possession of the fertile valleys and the strong mountain-passes of Kashmir. Under the Treaty of 1846, what might be called effective control, was not possible. Everything, nevertheless, that a self-respecting and honestly-minded Government should desire, save actual control or possession, was at the service of the Viceroy. A courteous and friendly bearing towards the Maharaja, followed by kindly counsel and assistance in good administration, would, in any crisis that might have arisen, have ensured the last energy of the last man in the State. The Power which received such assistance would have been honoured in accepting it, as the State proffering it would be proud to give it. Such a mode of obtaining allies, however, is foreign to the conception of Indian civilians. Another course, that of forcing a Resident on the Maharaja, was preferred. It is, unfortunately, the fact that of two courses—friendly co-operation by a semi-independent ally or the absorption of every square mile of land possible into British territory—the Foreign Administration of India always prefers the latter, but cannot, in every instance, secure it. The modes adopted to secure the desired end are not always, are not often, honest or straightforward.[1]

In 1884, so far as the published Papers show, the Government of India—Lord Ripon being Viceroy—in a despatch addressed to the Secretary of State (Lord Kimberley), describe what they call the disorganization of the administration of Kashmir, and, because of

> 'The increasing importance to the Government of India of watching events beyond the North-Western frontier of Kashmir,'

(these words are especially noteworthy), it was determined to force a Resident on the State. I say 'force' advisedly. Any resistance by the Maharaja, beyond a verbal protest, would have led to his non-recognition as ruler and the setting of him aside for a more pliable individual. The Government of India, in this same despatch, add :—

> 'Any disturbances which continued misgovernment might create in Kashmir would be acutely felt on the frontiers of Afghanistan; the connection of Kashmir and its dependent chiefships would, in all probability, be severed, and grave political complications might easily ensue.'

---

[1] Sir Edwin Arnold, K.C.S.I., Editor of the *Daily Telegraph*, in his book on Lord Dalhousie's Administration, says: In 1853 'the Nizam came into our power by a process which has been often and successfully repeated in our Indian annals. There is a curious phenomenon in the insect world where an egg is deposited in the body of a living creature, which nourishes itself upon the substance of its unwilling nurse, gradually taking up all the fat, flesh, and tissues of the victim, till it dies, or drags on a futile existence. Our Government in India has frequently laid such an egg in the shape of "a Contingent," within the confines of friendly States. Oudh, Gwalior, and the territories of Scindia were thus treated, and by no other means were the dominions of the Nizam brought within the grasp of Lord Dalhousie.'

The doctrine is unexceptionable, as much of the preachéd doctrine of the Indian authorities is. Disturbances in Kashmir might be mischievous. But, as a matter of fact, there have never been any disturbances. The practice in this, as in so many other instances in Indian experience, was to make opportunities which should, in the opinion of the Foreign Office, justify overt action. Leave was asked of the Secretary of State to post a Resident at Srinagar when the then Maharaja died.

It goes without saying that the Secretary of State of the day gave the Viceroy the authority he asked for. Except where questions of Home patronage arise, the functions of the Secretaries of State for India seem to be confined to echoing the observations addressed to them by the Viceroy for the time being. Of independent judgment and action they are innocent. Resistance, independent review of circumstances, a determination that when a mistake has been made it shall be rectified, —these things are never seen in a Secretary of State's despatch on any matter concerning which the Viceroy of the day cares anything, always, of course, excepting, as has been remarked, matters of the Horse Guards', or other, patronage. Consequently, when, in the autumn of 1885, the Maharaja Runbir Singh died, and his eldest son, Pertab Singh, succeeded him, the Agent of the Governor-General, Sir Oliver St. John, informed His Highness that a Resident would be appointed to his Court.[1] In his report to the Government of India on

[1] Previous to this there used to be only an 'officer on special duty,' who was located for eight months at Srinagar, to look after the Europeans sojourning in the 'Happy Valley' during the summer season. He also sat in a mixed

16th September, 1885, Sir Oliver St. John describes the consternation with which the Maharaja received what 'was evidently an unexpected blow.'

The Maharaja protested against the appointment. In his thanks to the Viceroy (Lord Dufferin), for a kindly letter of condolence, Mian Pertab Singh said:—'It has, however, pained me exceedingly to learn that exactly at the time when I had made up my mind to deserve and win your Excellency's approbation and encouragement, by proving myself equal to the onerous and responsible duties of a good ruler, your Excellency has been thinking of changing the status of the British Officer on Special Duty in Kashmir to that of a Political Resident, and thus lowering me in the eyes of my subjects and in the estimation of the public. It is fully known to your Excellency that I have only just now acquired the power of showing to the world that without any interference from any quarter or any, the smallest,

---

court, consisting of himself and an official of the Maharaja's, which heard and decided litigation between these European sojourners and the Maharaja's subjects. He never used to be the medium of communication between His Highness and the Government of India. The appointment of a Resident put a stop to this practice. The Maharaja objected to the appointment, but to no purpose. The objection was not groundless. Firstly, direct communication with the Government of India is a great desideratum with the Native States. It often happens that a Prince and the Resident are not on the best of terms, and in such a case it becomes difficult for the former to lay before the Government his complaints against the proceedings, however unjust and oppressive, of the latter, through whom, under existing rules, those complaints are to be forwarded. Secondly, the 'officer on special duty' had nothing to do with the internal affairs of the State. But a Resident, by the very tradition of his office, interferes in such affairs, and if the Prince, at whose Court he is posted, fail to please him or to fall in with his views of government, he becomes a positive stumbling-block in the way of good and effective administration. Thirdly, the appointment of a Resident was in violation of the treaty engagement entered into with Maharaja Ghulab Singh in 1846.—*Kashmir and its Prince*, by Jogendra Chandra Bose.

diminution of the long-enjoyed rights and dignity of this State, I am able and willing of my own accord to introduce and maintain such reforms as are calculated to entitle a ruler to the lasting gratitude of his subjects, and the encouraging approbation of the Paramount Power as well as the public at large.'

It was, of course, stated in reply that the Resident would simply advise His Highness and in no way interfere with the administration of the State. With the sarcasm of which he is so accomplished a master, Lord Randolph Churchill, then Secretary of State for India, in acknowledging the despatch describing what had been done, told the Indian Government that they had shown 'the utmost consideration. . . . to the susceptibilities of Maharaja Pertab Singh.'

The story in the 'Arabian Nights' of the camel and the householder has found exemplification in Kashmir. The Resident arrives. He is not to interfere, he is merely to advise; then he does interfere; and, finally—as is now the case—he becomes virtual ruler of the country. The *arrière pensée* which foretold all this, is to be found in Lord Ripon's despatch of 1884, already referred to and quoted. Under the stress of a North-Western frontier scare the early and complete control of Kashmir became a 'fixed idea' in the Calcutta Foreign Office in 1884. Probably, had Lord Ripon, or a Viceroy with his characteristics, remained in power, Pertab Singh would have been differently treated and his country have maintained its independence. Viceroys come and Viceroys go: the Foreign Office, with its yearly-hardening intentions, traditions, and ideals, remains.

(2) *A Complete Effacement of Promises made by the Queen-Empress, Promises which were Proffered as a Buttress to Treaties and Engagements.*

The Indian authorities, under the Treaty of 1846, it may be repeated, had no right or power (save the power which Might gives) to send a Resident to Kashmir, and certainly none to force him upon the State against the Maharaja's wishes. Twenty-eight years before this high-handed step was taken, the Queen, on assuming control of India, told the Maharaja of Kashmir, among others,

> 'That all treaties and engagements made with' [the native Princes of India] '. . . WILL BE SCRUPULOUSLY MAINTAINED. . . . *We shall respect the rights, dignity, and honour of Native Princes as our own.'*

In the letter to Lord Derby, instructing him as to the tenour of the Proclamation, the Queen, in her own handwriting, referred to her remarks as 'pledges which her future reign is to redeem'.

The representative of the Sovereign who spoke such gracious words and so emphatically expressed her determination to do right and right only, approaches the Maharaja of Kashmir with a letter of sympathy, in which the new ruler is informed by the Viceroy that 'in all difficulties,' of whatsoever kind, 'he may rely with confidence upon the good-will of the British Government.' That 'good-will' is displayed in breaking the provisions of a treaty, and in forcing a foreign official upon a friendly feudatory and ally.

As Sir Edwin Arnold, in a passage quoted in a footnote on p. 47 has told us, there is nothing new in this sort of thing. The annals of India are full of such incidents. Our course is strewn with them. Fewer instances have occurred since 1857 than occurred before, but many a promise and pledge have been 'cast as rubbish to the void' in recent times. If Parliament and the powers that be generally could only realize the effect which such flagrant contradiction between promise and performance has upon British dominion in India, there are no exigencies in the history of our administration which would prevent the Indian house being instantly set in order.

(3) *The Deposition of an Independent Ruler on vague Charges for which, only in the latest communication, is there a show of evidence, and that evidence is accompanied with observations which wholly cut away the ground from under the feet of the Government.*

In this connection allegations 4, 5, and 6 may be taken. They are as follows:—

(4) *An independent ruler, secured in his position by treaty stipulations, condemned and deprived of all power, wholly on the unsupported statements of interested parties, and without giving him any opportunity whatsoever of defending himself;*

(5) *The ignoring of evidence which, had it been fairly considered, would have proved there were no grounds for proceeding against the Maharaja;*

(6) *An assertion of voluntary resignation of power by the Maharaja against his explicit denial of this act.*

In their despatches to the Secretary of State, of April 3, 1889 (signed, I believe, only by Lord Lansdowne, Sir Charles Elliott, and Sir David Barbour),[1]

[1] This does not appear from the published papers. The despatch in question, however, found its way into the Indian newspapers last year, and had the signatures of the officials mentioned, and of them only, attached.

the Government of India give the following reasons for deposing the Maharaja :—

(1) 'The condition of things in Kashmir was by no means satisfactory.'

(2) 'The discovery of certain letters alleged to be of a treasonable character.'

(3) 'Other circumstances of the case.'

This, in sober truth, is all the Government of India allege! And Lord Cross, in whom Indian Princes should find a trustworthy Court of Appeal, humbly states that Her Majesty's Government 'fully approve your proceedings!'

In his letter (Simla, June 28, 1889) to the Maharaja himself, Lord Lansdowne gives the following reasons for the deposition of Pertab Singh :—

a. 'Extremely unfavourable reports' as to 'the manner in which the affairs of your Highness were administered by your Highness;'

b. 'The finances of the State were in disorder,' 'a disorder which, there could be little doubt, was increased by your own extravagance, squandering of the revenue of the State in a most reckless and improvident manner;'

c. Neglect to act upon the advice given by Lord Dufferin to carry out reforms;

d. Certain treasonable letters alleged to have been written by the Maharaja;

e. Offer by the Maharaja to resign the rule of the State.

The Maharaja's own statement as to the circumstances under which his government was carried on will be found set forth in his own letter to Lord Lansdowne. (See Appendix B.) Briefly, His Highness declares he did all he could in the way of reform; that he never had a free hand with which to do all he desired; that he was persistently thwarted by the Resident; that his younger brother was encouraged to intrigue against him; that he had never resigned his position in the sense alleged, but that what he did do in this direction was the result of 'many-sided pressures,' which he was powerless to resist, and from which he expected a just Government in India would relieve him. A letter of a more pathetic character, or one calling more loudly for consideration on the part of a friendly Paramount Power, is not to be found in the whole range of Indian history. Lord Lansdowne was not altogether unmoved by it. He answered it, but could not find himself called upon to do more than to reiterate stale charges, and to make promises of which, it is clear, the Foreign Office, if it can control matters, will never permit the fulfilment.

A complete answer can be given to every accusation made against the Maharaja, whether those accusations be political or personal. Before, however, furnishing these answers it may be well to note the manner in which the Resident was performing his duties at the time when the deposition took place. The story has been well told by Mr. Jogendra Chandra Bose, M.A., B.L., of the Punjab Chief Court Bar, at one time himself an official in Kashmir, from whose pamphlet entitled 'Kashmir and its Prince: An Authentic Exposition of the Recent *Imbroglio* in Kashmir,' I quote as follows:—

'The Maharaja visited Calcutta in the cold season of 1885-86. Shortly after his return to Jammu, Sir Oliver St. John was transferred from the Kashmir Residency and succeeded by Mr. Plowden. Sir Oliver, though not on very cordial terms with the Maharaja for the reasons mentioned above, did not set himself in opposition to the Maharaja's Government at every step, nor withdraw every sympathy with its aims and objects. Mr. Plowden, however, from the moment he took over charge of his office, assumed an attitude unfavourable to His Highness. He seems to have joined his post with a foregone conclusion against the Maharaja. He affected a lofty, supercilious air, and treated the Durbar with almost undisguised contempt. On occasions, he went so far as to insist upon the Ministers retiring before he would condescend to speak to the Maharaja. Latterly, after the dismissal of Dewan Luchman Das, he somewhat relaxed the stiffness of his behaviour, but, at the time of which I am now speaking, every one could perceive that his appointment was a misfortune to the Maharaja. His Highness had just ascended the *gadi*, and, anxious as he was to reform the administration, he wanted a friend and a sympathizer rather than an adversary, in the person of the Resident. Mr. Plowden soon began to make himself obnoxious. He joined his post about March, 1886. Shortly afterwards, the summer season setting in, he went to Srinagar and became anxious that the Maharaja also should go there. His Highness himself had entertained a desire of visiting Kashmir, but the Maharani fell ill, and he had to put off his departure from day to day. On this, the Resident grew impatient. He began to telegraph to His Highness in a somewhat imperative tone, and hinted the displeasure of the Government of India in case of delay. The Maharaja, always loyal and obedient to the wishes of the Paramount Power, was thus in a manner dragged away from his bed-ridden wife—a paragon of a Hindu lady. Some ill-feeling was generated in consequence. Nevertheless, when the Maharaja reached Srinagar, he did not show any unfriendliness towards Mr. Plowden, but treated him with the courtesy and consideration due to the Representative of the British Government.

'The Maharaja stayed at Srinagar about a month on this occasion. During all this time, Mr. Plowden, who had been so solicitous for His Highness's arrival in Kashmir, had not many improvements to suggest in the administration. His visits to the Maharaja were rare and formal, and he seldom discussed State matters with the Durbar at these visits. There was one thing, however, which attracted his particular notice. The Maharaja was anxious that his subjects should receive a liberal education. This seemed to excite Mr. Plowden's worst alarms, and he did not rest until he had secured possession of the Educational Rules which the Durbar had framed.

'The Maharaja had been thinking of an equitable land settlement in Kashmir. To carry out this object, he had written a letter to his friend Sir Charles Aitchison, late Lieutenant-Governor of the Punjab, who used to take a great interest in the welfare of the State, for a well-qualified Native Settlement Officer. Sir Charles Aitchison, after the needful inquiry, recommended a couple of men, and asked the Maharaja to make a selection between them. His Highness, in reply, requested Sir Charles himself to make the selection, and expressed preference for a Muhammadan, the population of Kashmir being mostly Muhammadans. On this, Sir Charles made a selection which was forwarded to the Government of India for sanction, as is necessary in all cases of transfer of services from British India to a Native State. But Mr. Plowden expressed a wish to His Highness that it would be better to appoint an Englishman for settlement work in Kashmir. The Maharani's illness at this juncture having taken a serious turn, and the season for the performance of the annual *shradh* of the late Maharaja having also arrived, His Highness started for Jammu before the matter could be settled. On his way he received a telegram from the Resident, advising the appointment of Mr. Wingate as settlement officer. By this appointment both the

Maharaja and Sir Charles Aitchison were placed in a delicate position, and the latter even got a little offended with His Highness for having readily submitted to it.

'Soon after the Maharaja's return to Jammu, Mr. Nilambar Mookerjee resigned his post. It may not be out of place to say a few words here regarding this gentleman, who cut a prominent figure in Kashmir politics for a period of nearly twenty years. One of the most distinguished graduates of the University of Calcutta, he went to Lahore in 1867 to join the bar of the Punjab Chief Court. In the following year, Dewan Kripa Ram, the late able and liberal-minded Prime Minister of Kashmir, who had heard of Mr. Mookerjee's talents and learning, recommended him to Maharaja Runbir Singh, who appointed him Chief Judge of Kashmir. While working in that capacity, he was deputed by his master to make arrangements for His Highness's property in Lahore. This work, as well as his work as Chief Judge, was so satisfactorily performed that the Maharaja, in token of approbation, almost doubled his remuneration. Shortly after this, the silk industry was started in Kashmir, and Mr. Mookerjee was placed in charge of it. The industry rapidly developed and expanded, and Mr. Mookerjee was favoured with the commendatory notices of the Government of India and the Secretary of State. He rose very high in the estimation of his master, but his brother officials now began to eye him with jealousy, and to whisper ill-natured reports against his management of the silk concern. This disgusted him, and he prayed his master to be allowed to retire from his charge. Maharaja Runbir Singh, while granting his prayer, showed a due appreciation of his valuable past services by promoting him to the rank of a Minister, which he held till the date of His Highness' death. Prince Pertab Singh had not been very favourably inclined towards Mr. Mookerjee in his younger days. But, as he grew up, he came to understand Mr. Mookerjee, whom the late Maharaja also, on his death-bed, enjoined upon him to regard as his most faithful servant and trusted councillor. Maharaja Pertab Singh, on ascending the *gadi*, appointed Mr. Mookerjee his Finance Minister. Mr. Mookerjee worked with the zeal, honesty, devotion, and single-mindedness that characterize him, for a period of twelve months. But finding that, far from receiving any help, he was treated with coldness and suspicion, and seeing that he could do little good to the State, he tendered his resignation in September, 1886, which the Maharaja thrice declined to accept, but which His Highness accepted, when pressed a fourth time, with great reluctance.

'Different men take different views of Mr. Mookerjee's resignation. For my part, I think matters had been driven to such a crisis that it became impossible for a highly honest and conscientious man to continue in office any longer. It must, however, be admitted that his resignation intensified the difficulties of his master's position, and rendered His Highness an easy prey to the machinations of his designing opponents.

'On the departure of Mr. Nilambar Mookerjee from Jammu, Dewan Gobind Sahai was removed and Dewan Lachman Das made Prime Minister in his place. Mr. Plowden had longed for this consummation, and felt glad that it had been brought about. Dewan Lachman Das was his special favourite, and he moved heaven and earth to raise him to dignity and power. But the Dewan, though not devoid of intelligence, never possessed business habits, and soon after his elevation to the Premiership, gave himself up to enjoyment, leaving the affairs of State to be mostly taken care of by his subordinates. He was, besides, a staunch advocate of everything that was old, and, from inclination as well as from self-interest, had never looked upon the reforms, introduced by his master during the previous year, with favour. The abolition of vexatious imposts and cesses had the effect of reducing the income of the State; and Dewan Lachman Das, who, according to an arrangement entered into by Maharaja Ghulab Singh with his father, was entitled to a payment of Rs. 4 on every

Rs. 1,000 of revenue, resented the loss which it caused him. So, on assuming the reins of office, he swept away with little scruple or hesitation most of the reforms that had been introduced during the preceding twelve months, and the Maharaja, rendered powerless by Mr. Plowden, could not save them from total wreck. Neither did Lachman Das's method of work nor his action in this particular call forth the slightest disapproval of his patron. He had been appointed with the sanction of the Government of India, Raja Amar Singh siding with him at the outset, and the Maharaja was reduced to a nullity. But Nemesis was near at hand. The Plowden-*cum*-Lachman-Das *régimé* fell through on account of its own weakness, in spite of the support accorded to it. Its inconsiderate bearing towards the Maharaja and its apathy to the best interests of the State became more and more apparent, till even the Anglo-Indian Press, which a few months before had glorified it, pronounced it "a phenomenal failure." About this time, Raja Amar Singh, who was closely watching his opportunity, came over to join the Maharaja, and moved His Highness, already exasperated, to be rid of his Minister, Lachman Das, who was accordingly dismissed. This was in the spring of 1888. Mr. Plowden continued in Kashmir for a few months after the dismissal of his *protégé*. He was grieved to see the toils which he had so elaborately woven around the Maharaja torn into shreds, and he maintained a sullen dignity. But Lord Dufferin was aware of the overbearing manner in which he conducted himself towards the Maharaja, and His Excellency found it necessary to order his transfer. This was done on the happening of a vacancy for his promotion.

'After the dismissal of Dewan Lachman Das, the Maharaja telegraphed to Mr. Nilambar Mookerjee to return to Kashmir and to resume his duties. Mr. Plowden, getting intimation of this, immediately sent a counter-telegram, forbidding Mr. Mookerjee to join without the permission of the Government of India in the Foreign Department. By what right he did this does not appear, but the Maharaja's idea of forming a Ministry of his choice was thus frustrated. Then the formation of a Council under His Highness's Presidentship was conceived, and the Maharaja again made an attempt to get back his trusted and faithful servant as Financial Member, Mr. Mookerjee possessing an intimate acquaintance with the finances of Kashmir. But this was disallowed, on the ground that Mr. Mookerjee was not a good financier! Then His Highness suggested that Mr. Mookerjee, an experienced and practical lawyer, might serve him at least as Judicial Member, proposing, in the alternative, the name of Mr. P. C. Chatterjee, of the Punjab Chief Court Bar, for long the Legal Adviser of the State, in case Mr. Mookerjee's services were refused. But neither the one nor the other was permitted to be employed by His Highness. It would appear that even an eminent lawyer like Mr. Chatterjee, who has filled with credit the post of a Chief Court Judge, was held disqualified for working as Judicial Member in the Kashmir Council. I mention these facts to show how, in the face of an existing treaty engagement and in spite of the most cordial relationship, His Highness's wishes were, without any justifying cause, ruthlessly over-ridden. In place of men whom the Maharaja knew and wanted, others, perfect strangers to His Highness, were thrust upon him as Members of his Council.'

Independent and most competent authorities, whose communications are in my hands as I write, fully confirm all Mr. Jogendra Chandra Bose has set forth.

The occasion for all this intrigue will appear later on.

I may now return to the charges preferred by the Government of India. In their letter of August 1, 1884, to Sir Oliver St. John, the Government indicated the reforms which the new Maharaja, upon succeeding to power, must carry out. It nowhere appears that the officer on special duty put them specifically before His Highness. They are thus described in the letter:—

1. The introduction of a reasonably light assessment of land revenue, collections to be in cash, if practicable;

2. The construction of good roads;

3. The cessation of State monopolies;

4. The revision of existing taxes and dues, especially transit dues, and the numerous taxes upon trades and professions;

5. The abolition of the system of farming the revenue, wherever it is in force;

6. The appointment of respectable officials, and their regular payment in coin;

7. The establishment of a careful system of financial control;

8. The removal of all restrictions upon emigration;

9. The reorganization and regular payment of the army; and

10. The improvement of the judicial administration.

In a word, the ruler of Kashmir was called upon to reorganize the government of an Oriental State, governed after an Oriental fashion with the general acquiescence of the population, and produce a standard of perfection according to the Western ideas. There was a lifetime's honest work in the complete realisation of the various points of the programme. Before four years had passed the Maharaja was deposed because he had not accomplished thirty years' results. Yet the Maharaja had a good record. Had he been called upon to show cause why he should not be deposed, had he been permitted to defend himself before an impartial tribunal, he would have been able to prove that, in spite of the adverse influences (to be described in detail hereafter) arrayed against him, he had made great progress in good government. He could have shown that important changes had been accomplished and that certain great improvements had been made in his administration. For example, against the ten demands made upon him he could have proved that in sixteen important respects he had achieved excellent results:—

1. Payment of all civil and military salaries monthly instead of at irregular intervals, thus avoiding accumulation of arrears.

2. Abolition of export duties.

3. Abolition of numerous vexatious duties on manufacturers and traders.

4. Abolition of the *harkarabashi*, the *sewai*, and other heavy taxes levied on the cultivators of the soil.

5. Stoppage of the inhuman practice of punishing the innocent relatives of deserters from the army when the deserters themselves could not be found.

6. Partial abolition of the pernicious practice of farming the land revenue by letting it to the highest bidder.

7. Abolition of the practice of buying ghee, horses, wool, and other articles, through the revenue officials, from cultivators, at nominal prices fixed by Government.

8. Abolition of the tax on Muhammadan marriages.

9. Increased allotment of funds for public works.

10. Stringent orders issued to prevent high officials

and influential men influencing the decisions of courts of justice.

11. Equalization of the customs duty on salt.

12. Establishment of high schools at Jammu and Srinagar.

13. Municipal constitution granted to the cities of Jammu and Srinagar.

14. Equitable adjustment of import duties.

15. Leave Code, Educational Code, and other rules calculated to promote public interests, provided. And,

16. Corruption checked among civil and revenue officials by the introduction of a system of strict supervision as well as by the importation of an honest and educated element into the service.

In the face of all this the Maharaja was deposed because, forsooth, he had shown *no* disposition to improve the condition of things in his dominions! Indian Government procedure towards Feudatory Princes is an advance on Jedburgh justice which hanged a man and then proceeded to inquire whether he was guilty. In India condemnation takes place, sentence is carried out, and no attempt is made to ascertain whether occasion for condemnation really did exist, or whether a sentence ought to have been pronounced.

The charges in the two communications (the despatch to the Secretary of State, and the letter to the Maharaja himself) may now be examined in detail. The facts submitted will show how flimsy and untenable were the reasons given for this last step in reprobation of a misgovernment which may or may not have existed, but of which no adequate proof had been given by any one, neither to the Government of India, nor to the Resident, nor to the Maharaja himself. Nothing in the shape of 'evidence' good enough to satisfy a London Police Magistrate in a case of petty larceny is forthcoming to justify the deposition of a monarch from the rule of his dominions.

(1) 'The condition of things in Kashmir was by no means satisfactory'; *a.* 'Extremely unfavourable reports' as to 'the manner in which the affairs of your Highness were administered by your Highness.' The Government of India are on their defence. Driven at last by Mr. Bradlaugh's Parliamentary pertinacity to justify their conduct, they submit the papers now in the hands of hon. members as their justification. Will the statement be believed? Only one piece of evidence is forthcoming. Meanwhile, before that evidence is submitted, an admission had been made by the Government of India which puts Lord Lansdowne and his colleagues

in the wrong. Lord Dufferin himself (July 28, 1888, Letter to Maharaja) admitted these facts: 'Considerable progress has been made in the direction of reform; useful work has been done with regard to the Revenue administration, and in the reorganisation of the Public Works and Medical Departments.' Surely, if so much could be said in July, 1888, things cannot have gone so completely wrong in eight months as to justify—without an opportunity of defence—the extreme step of deposition. Even if there were occasion for interference it by no means follows that His Highness was alone to blame.

The Indian Government, however (despatch of July 26, 1889), have, as I have several times remarked, one piece of evidence which, they declare, contains abundant proof of the misgovernment they allege existed in Kashmir. It is a Report addressed by Mr. A. Win-

---

[1] The Maharaja himself, in his letter to Lord Lansdowne, indicates how greatly he was thwarted in all his efforts. He says: 'Now, to put it very plainly, I have never up to this time enjoyed complete independence of action in State affairs. Some sort of pressure or other has always been put upon me since my accession to the throne, and I have never been free to administer the State according to my internal satisfaction. Under such circumstances it has been very cruel indeed to hold me personally responsible for any maladministration, and punish me severely as a criminal. By the above order of your Excellency it is plain enough to understand that matters have been so represented as to prove that only my interference has brought about this state of affairs, for which the Government of India has been obliged to pass such strictures. Whereas the case is quite the contrary. The man whose disloyal interference is the chief cause of all mismanagement, and who should have been severely punished, has got not only scot-free, but has been placed over my head, enjoying perfect satisfaction of having been successful in his wicked design. Had there been any other loyal and faithful Prime Minister of mine than Raja Amar Singh he would have been expected to send in a suitable reply to the Resident's communication, and to save me from the deadly disgrace which I have been put to; but my brother, the present Prime Minister, quietly submitted to it, and was extremely satisfied to see me thus disgraced, as it was really his own hearty intention to see me so.'

gate, C.I.E., land settlement officer to the Maharaja, in August 1888, shortly after the time that Lord Dufferin declared that 'considerable progress' had been made in the direction of reform. Mr. Wingate's report is a long one, and is mainly of a technical character. The only parts which can, by any torturing, be held to support the statements of the Government of India are paragraphs 27, 28, 31, 32, 34, 35, and 76. Most important among these are paragraphs 27 and 28. These I proceed at once to quote; the others mentioned are given in full in Appendix A. In paragraphs 27 and 28 Mr. Wingate says:—

From the above it will be remarked that floods are rare, and, occurring as they usually do in the spring, the damage is not serious, whilst the fertility of the soil is increased. Severe earthquake has occurred twice in the present century, and, so far as I know, not at all in the previous century. Severe famine has also occurred twice, caused each time by the heavy and continuous autumn rains of 1831 and 1877, and on each occasion producing a scarcity that lasted till the reaping of the second *shâli* harvest after the failure. The visitations of cholera have not been numerous and have seldom been severe. The general result of the last seventy years appears to be that the population is now little more than half of what it used to be. That it is considerably less there can be little doubt. Traces of disused irrigation and of former cultivation, ruins of villages or parts of villages, of bridges, &c., local tradition—all point to a greater prosperity, which by the end of the Sikh rule in A.D. 1846 had well-nigh disappeared. Since that date, progress has been made, though arrested by the famine of A.D. 1878, but that the present revenue management and system of government seriously hinder progress there will be little difficulty in showing. To maintain the population, two devices have been resorted to, both I believe of old date. The first, prohibiting export of rice, is still in existence; at least, last year I understand rice was prevented going to the Punjab. The second, prohibiting any Kashmiri crossing the passes, was removed during the last famine. The door of hope was, however, opened too late, for of the numerous refugees few succeeded in reaching the open country, and consequently few came back. Since then, numbers of Kashmiris visit the Punjab every winter, where they find employment and save on their wages, returning in the early spring to cultivate their fields, generally bringing with them some cloth or other trifle for their wives, but getting frequently roughly handled by the customs clerks for their pains. Doubtless some remain in the plains, but, as on their return they would find their lands given away, few of the regular cultivators overstay the winter. And besides, the Kashmiri cultivator says he cannot live in the plains. Difficulty of getting food during the winter is quite as strong a cause of the annual exodus as the desire of gain. As the families of Kashmiris are decidedly large and the emigration from the valley is not, I should say, considerable, the gaps made by famine would quickly be filled up were it not for the winter mortality from insufficient clothing and food which must take place among the children. The Kashmiri requires more and more frequent nourishment and warmer clothing than his brother of the plains. Not only does the climate necessitate more, but the Kashmiri has the body and strength of an elephant. The collectors of *shàli* often pay insufficient attention to this point, and, as the aim is to collect for the use of the city all that can be safely taken, they are apt, acting on the experience of what a family consume in the plain, to leave too little to properly support and multiply the agricultural population.

In a valley where during the last nine years there have been seven good harvests and only two indifferent ones, and where the ruler is averse to raising the price of *shàli* lest the poor should suffer, it seems strange to speak of chronic scarcity affecting the population, and yet last year, and from reports I have read, the same thing has more or less been going on for years; I saw mobs struggling and fighting to secure a chance of getting a few seers of the Government *shàli*, in a way that I have not witnessed since the great famine of Southern India. I have found it impossible to obtain any record of bazaar prices, but I believe I am correct in saying that before A.D. 1846 the normal price of *shàli* was about eight annas per kharwár, and that it varied with the harvests. For example, during the famine of A.D. 1831–33, the price rose greatly, and even after A.D. 1833 it remained for some time as high as Rs. 1½ per kharwár. Whether the kharwár was reduced to 15 traks instead of 16 traks then, I have not ascertained. Shortly after Maharaja Goláb Singh assumed the control, the present system of collecting *shdli* in large granaries in the city and selling it by retail through Government officials appears to have been introduced, and the price of *shdli*, with a brief interval about A.D. 1879 when it was raised to Rs. 1½, has remained stationary at Rs. 1¼ per kharwár of 15 traks = two maunds and one seer of standard weight at 80 tolas per seer. For over forty years the system has been sufficiently profitable to support a large body of the pandit population of the city in idleness, and the Government has gradually become on the one side a farmer working with coolies under a management closely approximating forced labour, and on the other side, a gigantic bannia's shop doling out food to the poor in exchange for their coppers, and keeping with every cultivator an account showing what is taken from him whether in the way of grain, oil, wool, ponies, cows, etc., and what is given to him in the shape of seed, plough-cattle, cotton or wool to spin and weave, and a hundred other petty details. There are neither grain shops in the bazaar, nor bannias nor bankers anywhere.[1] I do not know whether it is an offence to sell *shdli*, but I do know that the cultivators are afraid to do so, and in tehsils nominally under a cash settlement, and with an abundant harvest, my establishment have once and again been literally starving, and the only way they can get food is by having it sent out, rice, atta, dall, etc., etc., from the Government storehouses in Srinagar to the tehsildars, who thereupon sell to my men for cash. My men still find difficulty in procuring the necessaries of life, and only very urgent representations at head-quarters have secured the supplies necessary to stop the angry, and to me humiliating, clamour of my subordinates to be allowed to buy food for ready money. Doubtless this annoyance has been partly due to the feeling of hostility with which my department is regarded by every official, from the

---

[1] Cultivators, however, do get advances from people in the city.

highest to the lowest,[1] but the scenes I have described in the city convinced me that the widow and the orphan, the weak and the sickly, must fare badly when it comes to physical wrestling for the daily bread. In Kashmir the tehsildar is the bannia, and he is a branch of the great official firm in Srinagar, where the chief business is conducted.

In noting the statements made by Mr. Wingate, it must be remembered that they are merely the observations of a stranger sent to the country for the very purpose of showing that all was wrong, that he was in active hostility towards the officials, that his statements are unchecked, and that, probably, close examination of the various points urged might minimize some of the harsh judgments expressed.

This is all the Government have to go upon in defending their deposition of the ruler of a great State, a ruler of whom their solitary witness himself said, in paragraph 71 of the same Report: 'I have been impressed during my interviews with your Highness with the belief that *your Highness has a ready sympathy for the poor, a keen interest in land questions, and a determination to protect the cultivators against the officials*."[2] Only one witness is called, and he testifies to the good faith and energy of the alleged criminal in securing the good of his people, those very people in whose behalf the Government of India have interfered. Yet not one of those people—so far as the Papers show—has made a single complaint against his ruler. It is

---

[1] This season several of the circles are able to supply themselves in the villages by paying rather more than the fixed price.—A. W.

[2] In para. 71, which I quote in the Appendix, there is much more to the same effect, all showing how zealous the Maharaja was in his desire to reform the abuses of a bad system of land revenue administration.

not as if when Mr. Wingate saw the Maharaja his Highness had contemptuously thrust him aside, and had said he did not care what became of the people. In such a case the Paramount Power might rightfully have intervened. But here was a sympathetic, tender-hearted, kindly despot, who was extremely anxious for the happiness of his people, and who might have secured that happiness if only British influence had allowed to him a measure of fair-play.

Mr. Wingate puts in the forefront of his charges a belief that population has decreased during the past seventy years. No doubt a diminution of population in any district does argue some degree of misgovernment. I will say nothing of the argument as it applies to Ireland. I will confine myself to India. One of the members of the House of Commons, Sir Edward Watkin, in a book he wrote last year on India, said that where population decreased the Government stood discredited. It may be well to see where the Government of India, the very party who make this one of their most important charges against the Maharaja, themselves stand. Can it possibly be that if the same measure were meted out to Lord Lansdowne and his colleagues, to Lord Cross and his councillors, to the present Under Secretary and to the right hon. gentleman who preceded him in office, as they have not scrupled to mete out to Maharaja Pertab Singh, a Power stronger than themselves would be justified in taking away from them the Empire which they administer or have administered? There are certain facts which, founded as they are on the tables published in the *Statistical Abstract of British India*, issued from the India Office, cannot be gainsaid or impugned. An examination of the records reveal these startling figures:—

POPULATION RETURNS: CENSUS OF 1881 COMPARED WITH 1872.

Presidencies or Provinces.	Districts. Increase.	Districts. Minus.	Remarks.
1. Bengal	43	8	Increase considerably more than 1 per cent. per annum.
2. N.-W. Provinces and Oudh	33	16	Nearly two millions decrease. In the districts showing increase that increase is often infinitesimal.
3. Panjab	27	5	1,415,019 minus. Thirteen years have passed between the respective Censuses.
4. Central Provinces	18	—	Increase more than 2 per cent. per annum. The purely Indian States show an increase of nearly 75 per cent., viz., from 1,049,710 to 1,709,720, chiefly on the Bengal side.
5. Madras	13	8	2,000,000 deficient, or, at 1½ per cent. p.a., over 4,000,000.
6. Bombay	16	8	Nearly 1,500,000 deficient.
TOTALS	150	45	

POPULATION FIGURES—ALLOWING 1 PER CENT. PER ANNUM INCREASE.

	Minus.		Plus.
N.-W. Provinces and Oudh	2,000,000	Bengal	6,200,000
Panjab	1,415,019	Assam	760,000
Madras	3,000,000	Ajmere, Berar, etc.	520,000
Bombay	1,500,000	Central Provinces	1,564,967
Mysore	1,250,000	TOTAL	9,144,967
TOTAL	9,165,019		

That is not a very satisfactory record. The loss more than balances the gain. If I take the rate of normal increase which the Indian Government declare, under their administration, ought to accrue, the minus total would be nearly 14,000,000.

Is anybody prepared to say that a like record can be compiled of Kashmir? No one has yet done so.

More than that. While of Kashmir there is merely allegation, in regard to British India there is solid fact. Mr. Wingate hazards the opinion that the population in Kashmir has decreased by one-half during the past seventy years. That is merely a guess of his. I can take you to districts under British administration, which have been under such administration for nearly the whole of this century, where, in the course of two years, the population was reduced by one-third. That is not a matter of opinion, but of absolute fact—fact ascertained by the Government of India itself. It ill becomes us to talk of decreased population.

In Kashmir there has only twice been severe famine in the present century. As much cannot be said of British India; in eighteen years twelve millions of people have died of starvation in the Provinces under English government.

Then, as to the allegation of excessive assessment of the land revenue in Kashmir, and the increasing difficulty of the cultivators to pay the same, if such a state of things is to justify deposition, then ought the present administration of India to be impeached. The burden of life in British India is not easier now than it was. On the contrary, the burden has become heavier, and is much harder to bear. Assessments in some cases are four times higher than they were wont to be: salt is much more heavily taxed; rights over grazing lands have been abolished; fuel is harder to get, with the result that the labouring classes can barely provide sustenance for themselves and their families, even in the most hand-to-mouth fashion.[1] Sir Charles Alfred

---

[1] Look to what a Member of Council said the other day, in the light-hearted fashion in which people speak of sufferings which they do not share: 'Our survey assessments have been lower than those of former rulers.' True in one sense, utterly false in reality, just as a clothier might urge that he charged less than a former dealer, because he only charged Rs. 2 for a suit and the other asked Rs. 3. But when you look into it and find that for Rs. 3 the former man supplied not merely coat and trousers, but pugree, waist-belt, over-cloth, shoes, and that the new man now charges Rs. 1 extra for each of these over and above Rs. 2 for the coat and trousers, you don't think much of his pretended liberality and fair dealing. Now, that is just our case, and if Mr. Peile did not know it, he ought to have known it. A particular number [every field in Bombay has its official number] may be pointed out which pays a lower assessment than it did under former rulers, though I doubt even this. But if you take the landholders, the cultivators as a body, you will find that with no more land to live on—and it is the land and the land only on which they live—they are made to pay one way and another at least four times what they ever paid under any previous rulers, no matter how grasping and unmerciful. Take my own lands in Ratnagiri; they have been assessed at the late survey at not less than ten times what they were assessed at under the Arba Saman survey under the Mahommedan Government. People may ask why we are now pressing for a Permanent Settlement—why did we never ask for it in former times? I will tell you, gentlemen. It is because in former times we could easily pay for the suit, even a little more than what is now nominally asked for; for in those former days we got the shoes, and the pugree, and the kummerbund, and the over-cloth and everything else free, and now we have to pay separately for everything and heavily for everything. Our means of subsistence, *i.e.*, the produce of the land, is the same, or even less. There is the same amount of water in the pot, but there are now six holes by which it runs out, when before there was but one. Gentlemen, we got our salt, life's first necessary, at a nominal price for ourselves and for our cattle. Now it is so dear that the latter cannot have it at all. We had our cattle in plenty, lots of grazing free, and salt to keep them healthy. Now the land is all taken up by the Forest Department and we have no grazing, and, if the starving herds stray where there is food, they are run into the pound and we are fined. And, day by day, cattle, the first necessity of agriculture here, are decreasing in number and deteriorating in quality. We had plenty of fuel free, both for our own purpose and to make the *rab*, or ash manure, without which our rice will not grow; but the forests have absorbed all the woodlands and our warkas lands are assessed, and we must buy our fuel and buy it dear. We had plenty of wood for our houses, our ploughs, for every agricultural purpose; now it is all under the lock and key of the Forest Department, and if we touch it without leave we are run in, and if we want a stick we have a week's running about from one official to another before we get it, and we have to pay, pay, pay! We had arms, and we could shoot or destroy the wild beasts that ravage our crops, but now we have an Arms Act that allows

Elliott, one of the three members of the Government of India who signed the deposition despatch, is currently reported in an official document to have remarked: 'I do not hesitate to say that half our agricultural population never know, from year's end to year's end, what it is to have their hunger fully satisfied.' 'Half our agricultural population' means considerably more even than the forty millions of our Indian subjects who, according to Sir William W. Hunter, 'go through life on insufficient food.' Nothing so bad as this has been said, or could be said, by any one of Kashmir. Yet it is, so they say, on account of the suffering caused to the people by misgovernment that the Maharaja has

---

a basketful of arms to every negro rascal who lands on our shores, but takes good care that we poor cultivators who need them to protect our subsistence from wild animals are practically debarred from any. We had such simple liquor as our people absolutely need at the cost of making it. But now a grand system has been introduced, which, while it makes the population drunken, involves considerable expenditure, and that for a hurtful mixture, to provide what our cultivators, in the damp, low-lying lands of Ratnagiri, really require for their health in the way of stimulant. We could borrow money on reasonable terms, for the land and the crops could not run away, and people were willing to trust us. There was a profit in those days in the land, and we could get what we wanted for seed or what not. But now, when the next turn of the screw may so reduce the value of the land that the surplus may be, as it already is in many places, *nil*, no one will give credit except for very short periods at very high interest. The usurers care nothing for the welfare of the people; all they care for is to exact interest at a penal rate. And yet, gentlemen, Mr. Francis's assessment, which was a fair one, and one that men could pay and live, when all these advantages were ours, has now been largely enhanced when not one of them remains to us. The Deccan Agricultural Relief Act, the reports of Collectors, of the Agricultural Department, all show what the real position of our cultivators is. Why do the cultivators not abandon the hopeless task? Because, unfortunately, they must either cultivate on, they and their families half-starving, or die themselves at once with their wives and little ones. Every one here knows that outside the Presidency towns, where the mills and other works give some relief, our cultivators and labouring classes can barely provide sustenance for themselves and families, even in the most hand-to-mouth fashion.—*Speech delivered by Rao Saheb Janaidin Raghunath Nimi Kar, of the Deccan, at the Indian National Congress, Dec.* 28, 1889. Every sentence nearly was heartily cheered, thus showing how clearly the speaker was expressing the general sentiment.

been removed. 'Misgovernment,' as Colonel Malleson has remarked,[1] 'is a relative term.' He proceeds to say: 'There can be no question but that in the English sense of the term there had been no good government in Oudh. But a kind of administrative system had, nevertheless, prevailed which induced the Sipahis, after the term of their service under the British flag had expired, to settle in their native country. More than that, after the natives of Oudh had had one year's experience of British government, as administered by Mr. Coverley Jackson and Mr. Martin Gubbins, they, one and all, evinced a strong preference for the native government which had been superseded.' There can be little doubt that the one year's experience of Colonel Nisbet's rule, if the opinion of the people were ascertained, would be followed by a like expression of condemnation.

Again, British rule in India has not unfrequently been marked by such incidents as the following—described by Sir H. S. Cunningham, K.C.S.I., a member of the Famine Commission—to be placed to its discredit. The Lieutenant-Governor for the North-Western Provinces in 1878 described the state of certain districts in Jhansi, as one of overwhelming 'indebtedness and ruin.' His Honor enumerated among the causes the following, which are given in Sir H. S. Cunningham's own words, he, as a member of the Famine Commission, having written a Memorandum on the subject:—

(1.) The British Government obliged the

[1] Vol. v., p. 287, Kaye and Malleson's History of the Indian Mutiny. Edition 1889.

people to pay a second time the revenue which had already been exacted from them by the Orchha State during the Mutiny.

(2) A series of bad seasons combined with unrelaxed revenue demand:—'The crops of 1867 were a failure. The year 1868-69 was one of famine; one-fourth of the whole stock of cattle in the district died, and the poorer classes emigrated to Gwalior or Malwa, or perished from starvation or disease. *In the midst of this distress the British officials were inexorable in demanding payment of the revenue, and, in order to pay it, the people were obliged to commit themselves to written contracts of the most one-sided and ruinous character. They thus fell an easy prey to the money lender, whose exactions the Civil Courts have not been slow in supporting. The famine and the injudicious action of the Revenue authorities had reduced the people to a state of absolute poverty.*' [1]

This poverty is summarised thus—The ascertained debts of the revenue-paying proprietors in three pergunnahs are reported as 16½ lakhs, and their annual profits fall short of their annual liabilities by some Rs. 80,000 a year, which is running on at compound interest. A specimen of the way in which debt accumulates is given in the case of some zemindars, who ten years ago borrowed Rs. 3,600 of 'the most respectable firm in the district.' They have since paid Rs. 6,999, and the account, when last balanced, showed the debt to be Rs. 9,766.

[1] The italics are *not* mine; they are Sir H. S. Cunningham's.

'The Zemindars, it is needless to add, "are quite destitute;" population is diminishing, cultivation has decreased from 258,000 to 231,000, and an area of 37,800 acres is infected with a weed (kans) which only capital can eradicate.'

'What,' continues Sir H. Cunningham, 'seems to be wanted is some machinery for bringing the best ability of the Government to bear forthwith upon these acknowledged failures, which the Government of India has described, in the case of Jhansi, "as a blot upon the administration." The state of things in Jhansi, apparently, has been known for many years, yet the machinery for improving it is extraordinary slow in getting into motion; the Senior Member is six months before he can write his Minute upon the Report; the Junior Member takes another six months with his; the North-Western Provinces Government takes another six or seven months to frame its letter to the Government of India; meanwhile the compound interest debt, which increases at the rate of Rs. 80,000 per annum, is running on, and the condition of the patient becoming hourly more desperate, while the doctors at their leisure are discussing the most appropriate remedy.'

Yet once again. On the unimpeachable authority of the *Times of India* it may be stated that the revision of Indapoor taluk enhanced rates by 53 per cent., of Sholapoor by 77, of Medeh 77, of Bhimthuree 69, of Punderpoor 67, of Barsee 66, of Heveli 66, of Pabul 48, of Soopa 36, and of Tharmal 32 per cent. These enhancements of rates were considered moderate at the time they were announced. As, however, they were made at a time when the reaction in prices had set in in full force, Government was compelled, in sheer justice to the complaints of the peasantry, though against the inclination of survey officers, to offer a concession of rates in a resolution dated the 29th October, 1874, in which it was laid down that in no case was the increase of revenue by the re-assessment of a taluk or a group of villages to exceed 33 per cent.: that in case of an individual village the enhancement was not to go beyond 66 per cent.; and in case of a single holding beyond 100 per cent.

To this may be added one piece more of evidence. The *Times*, on August 23, 1885, published a letter in which it was remarked :—'As a rule in India, rents, on estates where the Government is or represents the landlord, are not moderate but the reverse. When the Durbhunga estates were under Government management, some 5,000 ryots, unable to pay the increased rents demanded of them, abandoned their farms and homesteads and fled into Nepaul. In Madras, where the bulk of the land belongs to the State, evictions and sales in realizing the Government demand on land have been increasing in an alarming ratio since 1865. In Bombay, Sir Auckland Colvin's Minute, embodied in the report of the Deccan Riots Commission, states that the excessive enhancements made, in the Government demand on the land held by the cultivators, were among the special causes of the distress and serious disturbances of 1874-75. Many other instances of a similar nature might be cited, the most recent being the cases of the Midnapore ryots, which came up last year on appeal before the High Court of Bengal, and from which it appeared that 75,000 ryots complained of excessive and illegal enhancements having been made in their rents—a complaint which the Court found to be well-grounded in the case selected for the trial.'

Things *may* have been as bad in Kashmir, but no proof has been vouchsafed by the prosecutor that such is the case; there is nothing beyond bare assertion unaccompanied with evidence. And if deposition from power is to follow for such misconduct as that of which the Maharaja is assumed to have been guilty, where will the Government of India itself stand?

Delay in carrying out urgent land reforms in Kashmir is regarded as the worst of crimes as, in fact, justifying the deposition of a ruler. Again, I ask, what then shall be done to the Government of India itself? More than two years have elapsed—eight months only elapsed in the matter of Maharaja Pertab Singh—since the Chief Commissioner of the Central Provinces informed the Viceroy that indebtedness was everywhere increasing in the districts under his rule, and that, unless a measure like that of the Deccan Agriculturists' Relief Act of 1879, or the Jhansi Encumbered Estates Act of 1882, were speedily passed, the inevitable result would be the transfer to the money-lending classes of a very large portion of the land of those provinces. Notwithstanding that the memory of the Government of India was refreshed by action taken in Parliament by Mr. Bradlaugh on August 23 in last year, the late legislative session in Calcutta was allowed to pass without anything being done. It does not appear that legislation of an important character in connection with Indian affairs prevented attention being directed to this matter in the cold season of last year. Were the British Parliament, which is the supreme ruler of India, as much wanting in consideration for the Government of India as that Government was for the Maharaja Pertab Singh, his fate would have been their fate also.

Much more might be said on this point, but enough has been cited to prove the untenableness of the official charge. At the same time it has been shown that even if the charges were true it did not lie with the Government of India, *on the grounds stated*, to take such drastic action. The *tu quoque* argument is not a dignified one, and is often offensive. From the time, however, when the man who having a beam in his own eye was exhorted not to be rude to him who had only a mote in his eye, it has often been found necessary to use the argument.

The next charge against the Maharaja runs thus :—

(*b.*) 'The finances of the State were in disorder,' 'a disorder which, there could be no doubt, was increased by your own extravagance,' 'squandering of the revenues of the State in a most reckless and improvident manner.'

So far as the published documents go there is not one word to show that the Treasury at Srinagar was empty, or that, if it were empty, the Maharaja was in any degree to blame. But there is much evidence available which should make the Government of India ashamed of its conduct in bringing such a charge. What, if—notwithstanding the alleged emptiness of the Treasury—the Government of India should itself have been instrumental in draining the Treasury of an 'independent' prince?

First, as to the Maharaja's own alleged extravagance. Mr. Jogendra Chundra Bose is a competent witness. At pages 46-48 of his pamphlet already referred to, he says :—

'I shall now take up the third charge, namely, that of extravagance. If by this charge is meant waste of public money, it is utterly groundless. In respect of public funds, far from being extravagant, the Maharaja is rather cautious and economical. Following his father's practice he, from the commencement of his reign, fixed a monthly allowance for his private and domestic expenses, and latterly reduced the amount of that allowance. Of course, this allowance, which, in itself, is not a very big sum for a prince of his dignity and position, being only Rs.43,000, or less than £3,000 per month, he spends in any way he thinks proper, but no one can possibly object to his doing so. Then, since his accession, he has incurred six or seven big items of expenditure. The first of these was on the occasion of the late Maharaja's *shradh*[1]; the second was in undertaking a trip to Calcutta to meet Lord Dufferin; the third was to pay off arrears due to the civil and military establishments; the fourth was on the occasion of the formal installation of His Highness; the fifth was for the purpose of paying some debts which the Maharaja had incurred as heir-apparent; the sixth was for performing the first annual *shradh* of the late Maharaja; and the seventh for celebrating the re-marriage of Raja Amar Singh on the demise of his first wife.

'No reasonable mind can raise any objections with regard to the first, second, third, fourth, and sixth of these items. These were spent for necessary State ceremonies or State purposes, and should be allowed to pass perfectly unchallenged. The fifth item may admit of some question, and much discussion took place between His Highness and his Ministers at the time it was disbursed. If the Maharaja had been inclined to defraud his creditors, he could have easily done so. The only courts where they could sue him were his own, and he might have, if so minded, influenced his courts in his own

[1] Religious ceremonies necessary, under the Hindu religion, to ensure the salvation of the departed.

favour, thereby rendering it impossible for his creditors to obtain decrees or to execute the same. But his instincts are too generous for such a subterfuge. He spurned the idea of depriving his creditors of their just dues. He argued with his Ministers, he expostulated with them, he assured them that the debts had been really incurred, he laid stress upon the iniquity that would rest upon his head if he withheld payment, he portrayed the consequent uneasiness to which he would be subject, and he quoted the authority of the *shastras* to show that it was his bounden duty to discharge these debts in order to escape infamy in this world and retribution in the next. His Ministers were overpowered, and His Highness satisfied his conscience and his keen sense of honour by keeping his promises with his creditors. The seventh item was unavoidable, though its amount might have been somewhat less than what it is reported to have been. It is not customary to perform re-marriages with extraordinary *éclat*, but Raja Amar Singh was quite young, and, besides, the Maharaja was at that time very fond of him and wanted to show that he looked upon him as his son. This item also, therefore, cannot be regarded as very heinous. The expenditure was not altogether unwarranted, and to base upon it the charge of extravagance is to lay the foundations of a stone bridge upon a floating straw.'

So much for a ruling monarch's personal extravagance!

Next, the Treasury was empty. If it were, who had a large part in emptying it? I reply, the Government of India. Items which were incurred under the direct influence of the Indian authorities, follow :—

	Items.	Rs.
1.	Loan to the Government of India ...	25,00,000
2.	Annual expenditure on the Jhelum Valley cart road	6,00,000
3.	Jammu - Sialkote Railway, one year's payment only	13,00,000
4.	Jammu waterworks	3,00,000

Worst of all, at the very time when the Viceroy (Lord Dufferin) was warning the Maharaja to look better after the finances of his State,

> 'The Lady Dufferin Medical Fund Committee received Rs. 50,000 from Kashmir, while Rs. 25,000 was accepted as a contribution to the Aitchison College at Lahore.'

If the Kashmir Treasury was in an enfeebled condition, why did Lord Dufferin permit so large an amount to be paid to a fund under the control of his wife? Here are more samples of a like kind:—'Last winter (1888-89), about Rs. 50,000 were lavished upon a European pig-sticking party near Sialkote. A new Residency is being built at Gulmarg and another new one at Jammu, for which last alone the estimate is Rs. 1,00,000, besides Rs. 25,000 for furniture, though the Resident stays there little now and will stay less when the railway line to Sialkote is completed. Was the Maharaja anxious for all this heavy expenditure? Was not, on the contrary, all this expenditure incurred at the instance of the British Government and of its agent at His Highness' Court, and are not they alone answerable for it? At a time when the treasury, to use Lord Lansdowne's own expression, "was empty," was it proper and opportune to lay out thirteen lakhs of rupees on a railway which is not a necessity, and which will serve very little to enhance the prosperity of the people of Jammu? The trade of the place is not considerable and is not susceptible of much development—so the line will prove but an expensive luxury after all. . . . There is another big item I have omitted to mention. It is the lakh of rupees spent on the recent visit of the Commander-in-Chief of the Indian Forces to the Happy Valley. Every man who accompanied His Excellency, from the Aide-de-Camp down to the grass-cutter, was treated at the State expense. The Maharaja of Kuppurthala's recent sojourn cost the State more than Rs. 50,000. Did Maharaja Pertab Singh invite him to Kashmir? Last year (1888) Lord Dufferin intended to travel in the State, and the preparations for His Lordship's reception cost a lakh of rupees. He gave up his intended tour, and so a couple of lakhs more were saved. But these are only the bigger items, and the list, too, as given here, is far from exhaustive. If a detail of the smaller items were attempted, it would occupy pages. So, considering the limited space at my command, it is better to refrain from the attempt. What I have said above will give some idea of the reckless extravagance that is going on under the auspices of the British Government and the British Resident.

'But that is not all. I ought to give here a few samples of the Council's work, which, the Government of India may be under the impression, has been managing affairs very economically. (1.) The *Vakil* with the Resident used to get Rs. 66 a month; the present man, a *confidant* of Raja Amar Singh's, is paid Rs. 400 a month. (2.) The monthly pay of the officer over the *Toshakhana*

(Treasure-house) used to be Rs. 200. Raja Amar Singh's private servant's father has been appointed on Rs. 600. (3.) A photographer, who has no public duty so far as one can ascertain, but who constantly dances attendance upon Raja Amar Singh, has been employed on Rs. 500 per month. (4.) Dhunjibhoy, a favourite of Colonel Nisbet's, gets a monthly payment of Rs. 500, because he is said to have established a Tonga *Dak* along the Murree Route, though he has nothing whatever to do with the carrying of the mails, which come *via* Jammu. (5.) A headman for the reception of European visitors has been appointed on Rs. 500 per month. (6.) Formerly there was a Native doctor on the Murree Road on a pay of Rs. 50 or thereabouts, but a European has now been retained on Rs. 300 a month. (7.) Spedding & Co. have got a contract on the whole of the Murree Road at double the rates formerly allowed to Native contractors. (8.) It is in contemplation to lay out a few lakhs on Water Works at Srinagar, where there is already a plentiful supply of wholesome water, while the conservancy of the city is in a lamentably neglected condition. (9.) Lands are being measured for European settlements at Gupkar near Srinagar, and at Gulmarg, and also plans are being made for gardens, pleasure walks, &c. All this will entail a vast expenditure, besides other things, in the payment of compensation to those poor men who will have to be turned out of their holdings. (10.) A continual round of festivities, including racing, picnics, &c., is going on in Kashmir at the expense of the State. This has been costing large sums of money.'[1]

[1] Pp. 72, 73 of Jogendra Chandra Bose's pamphlet.

The same game is still being merrily carried on. '"Nunky" pays for all,' as the Indian byeword of two generations ago was apt to put it. From a copy of the *Statesman* (Calcutta), published in April last, I quote the following :—

'A correspondent, whose information is unquestionable, writes to say that on the departure of Colonel Nisbet, the Resident, for Srinagar, all his baggage was sent by the Maharaja's private route at State expense, though that gentleman himself went *via* Murree. Now, when we come to consider that the *begar* system[1] flourishes in Kashmir in its worst form, and that the carriage of a whole houseful of furniture means the impressing of hundreds of poor unoffending peasants all along the route, not for a day or two, but for weeks together, it is, to say the least, inexplicable how an officer of Colonel Nisbet's standing could be induced to accept such assistance. That he should draw any help at all is contrary to the best traditions of English rule, but that he should do so at the expense of a lot of miserable villagers—for State expense virtually resolves itself into that—is scandalous. Were the people employed on Colonel Nisbet's work paid by him? Nor is this the only point on which Colonel Nisbet's doings in Kashmir are challenged—doings which, though not without precedent, are none the less regrettable. It has often been a reproach to the British administration that political officers of high merit and integrity should place themselves under indirect pecuniary obligations to the Princes whose interests they are supposed to watch. Thus it is well

[1] Impressment of country people as carriers, etc., without pay.

known that at Sialkote—for he never resides at the Maharaja's capital, where there is a residency—our gallant Colonel lives in a house belonging to the State; the whole of this is furnished at State expense, and certainly a quarter of the expenditure is defrayed from the selfsame source. Even in distant Lahore he is provided with a finely furnished house and carriages, while at Srinagar it is impossible to estimate the amount expended for residency purposes. Not that Colonel Nisbet is alone to blame in this matter. His predecessors have all more or less been guilty of it; but, as he is said to be a man of high spirit, and as moreover his appointment to Kashmir was accompanied by trumpet blasts of applause, he might have been more careful in thus risking exposure.' That so far Colonel Nisbet has not been a success we shall see later on.

I ask you, sir, whether it is not unnecessary to produce more facts on this point. An empty Treasury? Yes; emptied by those who make its emptiness an excuse for what, if done by others than Englishmen, would lead Englishmen to stigmatize it as brutal high-handedness, accompanied with robbery of a neighbour's territory. Probably the worry and anxiety to which he has been wantonly subjected will kill the Maharaja. If they do, the parallel with King Ahab's acquisition of Naboth's vineyard will be complete. Already the parallel is uncomfortably close, so close that it is a marvel that the men of high spirit and tender conscience who constitute the Government of India are not alive to the stain upon character which the transaction is causing.

c. Neglect to act upon the advice given by Lord Dufferin to carry out reforms.

Lord Dufferin himself may be cited to appear in the witness-box in this connection. I observe that Mr Munro-Ferguson voted against Mr. Bradlaugh's motion. Probably, in the passage I am about to cite, he may find reason for regret that he should have taken part in a denial of justice. In July, 1888, Lord Dufferin, as Viceroy of India, had under examination a scheme of government propounded by the Maharaja, in respect to which he sought the advice of the Government of India. Having expressed himself upon these various proposals (Appendix A), Lord Dufferin proceeded to remark:—

'In making these observations I do not overlook the fact that, since the appointment of the Council of which Diwan Lachman Das was a member, *considerable progress has been made in the direction of reform; useful work has been done with regard to the revenue administration, and in the reorganization of the Public Works and Medical Departments.* But much remains to be done, and it is because I am deeply conscious of the importance of the Kashmir State, and of the responsibilities of the British Government in regard to it, that I have so carefully examined the proposals which your Highness has put forward.'

Clearly, Lord Dufferin's memory must have failed him when he so ostentatiously approved, in the city of London, the course which his successor had taken. Further, the production of Lord Dufferin as a witness in this instance is surely a mistake. He has become even as Balaam the son of Peor, when that prophet was called to testify for Balak, King of Moab, against his enemies.

d. Certain treasonable letters alleged to have been written by the Maharaja.

Two witnesses may be called to testify as to this point. They are Lord Lansdowne himself and Sir John Gorst.

Lord Lansdowne to the Secretary of State: 'We were not disposed to attach any excessive importance to these letters.'

Sir John Gorst, in the House of Commons, March and April, 1889: 'The Government of India attach very little importance to the intercepted letters."

e. 'The discovery of the letters was immediately followed by a voluntary resignation of power on the part of the Maharaja.'

The so-called 'voluntary resignation' is contained in the following document, namely:—

Dear younger brother, possessed of much good manners, Raja Amar Singhji.

Whereas for the good of the State, its better administration on the model of the great British Government is desired by us, we do hereby entrust all the administrative matters of the State of Jammu and Kashmir to Members of Council, detailed below, for a period of five years—

Raja Ram Singh.

Raja Amar Singh.

An experienced European to be appointed in consultation with the Government of India on a salary of Rs. 2,000 to Rs. 3,000 per month, who shall be a servant of the State.

Rai Bahadur Pundit Suraj Koul.

Rai Bahadur Pundit Bhag Ram.

The above-mentioned Council shall exercise administrative powers in all departments of the State for a period of five years. In case of any vacancy occurring within the said period of five years in the post of the above-mentioned last three members only, the vacancy will be filled up at our desire by the Government of India.

After the expiry of the said period of five years, we shall have power to adopt such administration for the State as may to us appear proper. The said period of five years will commence from the date of this *purwana*. All matters, great or small, 'private' or connected with 'private', and the Mahalat (the palace), both inner and outer, shall not be liable to interference of any sort by the Council, nor shall the Council have any concern with them.

Such cash and kind for our own expenses, and for those of the Mahalat (the palace) or connected with 'private,' as are fixed and allowed up to this, and are taken from the State, shall, in future, be received as heretofore. The Council shall on no account have the power of causing any reduction in the same.

Such Jagirs and properties, movable and immovable, as are attached to the Mahalat (the palace) or are 'private,' shall not also be subject to interference by the Council. These shall be entirely under the personal control of ourselves.

Such expenses as will be incurred on occasions of marriage and death, and in the observance of other temporal and religious rites, shall be defrayed by the State.

The President of the Council shall be appointed by the order of ourselves from among our full-brothers.

For the period of the above-mentioned five years we shall not interfere in the management of the State. But in other respects the honour and freedom due to our rank shall rest with ourselves.

The above-mentioned Council shall not have the power, without our sanction, to enter into any new treaty or agreement with any State, or the Government of India, or to modify, rescind, or renew any treaty or agreement of our ancestors or our own.

The Council shall not have the power of granting or giving, without the sanction of ourselves, any Jagir, or proprietary rights and *pottas* of land, or of selling any immovable property of the State or public, or alienating any movable property or any other beneficial rights of the State.

Dated the 27th Falgun, Sambat 1945.

The Maharaja himself, in a letter addressed to the Viceroy, declared that he was, against his will, compelled to sign this document. 'With the information of these letters and with the full confidence and strength of being supported by my own brother and his now strong party,' says the Maharaja, 'Colonel R. P. Nisbet dashed into my room at a fixed time and brought such great and many-sided pressures in all solemnity and seriousness that I was obliged to write what was desired by him in order to relieve myself for the moment—having full faith that your Excellency's Government would never accept such one-sided view of the case, and that opportunity will be given to me of defending myself.'

The story as to how the so-called letter of abdication was extracted from the Maharaja is worth telling with somewhat of detail. I will, therefore, quote particulars placed in my hands by parties residing in Kashmir, who were in a position to know intimately what actually transpired. This narrative, I may add, has been in my possession for more than twelve months. It was written at my request, while the circumstances were fresh in the minds of all concerned. Pandit Soorajkole, the Revenue Member of Council, says my informant, arrived at Jammu on 1st January, 1889, but did not do anything of practical importance, as the Judicial Member had not arrived. Whatever proposals were made by the Revenue Member to His Highness were promptly sanctioned, and the man was so well pleased with his situation that more than once he expressed his great satisfaction to His Highness. Prince Amar Singh, Prime Minister, was in secret communication with the Resident. The Judicial Member arrived and took charge of his office on 16th February. The Council, however, did not commence its sittings formally, because the rules of business had not been framed. It appears there was a hint from the Resident to delay their preparations; His Highness himself asked twice or thrice why the rules were not ready, but the Prime Minister satisfied him by saying that they would be ready soon. A fortnight passed, when, all of a sudden, the Revenue Member was summoned to Sialkote and kept there for eight days. What happened at Sialkote can be easily imagined. He was called to advise what use could be made of the incriminating letters which had been sent to the Resident with his knowledge and that of the Prince (Prime Minister).

His Highness made inquiries from Pandit Surajkole on his return from Sialkote, but the Pandit did not warn him of the trap prepared for him.

When the plot was matured between the Resident, the Revenue Member, and the Prince, His Highness was asked to send down the Prince to Sialkote. He readily assented. The Prince remained there for two days, and, leaving his baggage behind, came up to Jammu and presented a letter from the Resident asking his Highness to permit him to accompany the Resident to Calcutta. His Highness asked why the Resident was going to Calcutta, to which the Prince replied, 'The honour of our house is at stake; we are ruined. Certain letters have been found which prove the Jammu family to be in league with Russia and Dhulip Singh;' and, with tears in his eyes, he begged the Maharaja to let him go with the Resident. The Maharaja, being surprised at this mysterious business, refused to let him go, and made a formal request to the Resident to see him at Jammu. The Resident did not give a reply for two days, and, to add to the extreme embarrassment of His Highness, his councillors, including the Prince, depicted in horrible colours his future fate; some said he would be sent to Rangoon as a close prisoner, another that he would be tried for mutiny and hanged, a third that he would be kept a close political prisoner and his State would be confiscated by the Government. He solemnly denied the genuineness of the letters, but this was to no purpose. The Prince told him to his face that he had already told the Resident that the writing appeared to be that of his Highness, though the signature was doubtful. On this the Maharaja, with great composure of mind, declared that, if his own brothers were determined to ruin him with false accusations, he would submit to his fate. His Highness did not take his meals for two days, he was so much overpowered; and in his frenzy he saw no room for escape except to give his consent to such arrangements as were proposed to him. Not favoured by the Resident with a reply to his call, in his despair he said, 'Let them locate a cantonment and take any portion of my territory, but why do they trouble me in this way and put me to all sorts of disgrace?' The triumph was complete, and there could be no doubt that the Resident was apprised of it. Without giving previous notice he went to Jammu, and, before favouring His Highness with a visit, had a long talk with the Prime Minister at the Residency. Thus armed with the necessary weapons, he visited His Highness and was most offensive to him. He distinctly told him that the Viceroy was very much displeased, and that if His Highness's life was saved, he might consider himself lucky.

The Maharaja swore that the letters were forgeries, and begged to have a look at them. The Resident replied imperiously that he was satisfied they were genuine, and would not hear anything more about them.

He further said that he had told the Prime Minister how the matter could be squared, and that, if His Highness was anxious to save himself from the indignity of a prosecution, he must act as he was told. The Resident left a draft of an 'edict' written by the Resident himself. This was laid before His Highness by the Prime Minister, and pressure was put on him from all sides to prepare an 'irsad'[1] on its terms. His Highness persistently refused to do so. Meetings of the Council were held three or four times that day. The members lent from India distinctly refused to have anything to say in the matter; while their other colleagues, who were all Raja Amar Singh's creatures, were trying to induce His Highness by threats and menaces to sign the document. The Resident was still at Jammu, waiting for the documents; and the Prime Minister, finding that the Maharaja did not yield, threatened His Highness with a report to the Resident if the document was not executed. Next morning a vernacular translation of the Resident's draft was made out, and His Highness's signature obtained; it was then delivered to the Resident, who paid the Maharaja a visit and promised to do all he could to save him from the danger that awaited him.

There does not seem much of voluntary resignation in this incident.

[1] Edict.

I now come to a part of the subject where I can, ith one notable exception, no longer rely upon the ıpers presented to Parliament, thanks to the care with hich those papers have been edited. I have to deal ith what seems to be the underlying reason for ıe cruel, unjust, and wholly unjudicial and arbitrary, roceedings taken against the Maharaja of Kashmir. .s I have already shown, in the first Paper published y Government a reference is made to 'the increasing nportance to the Government of India of watching vents beyond the North-Western frontier of Kashmir.' f the Government of India had been really honest with ıemselves, if Lord Lansdowne and his colleagues had not ersuaded themselves that they were actuated by a deep ympathy for the people of Kashmir, this object would ave been stated in so many words. Such a course 'ould have commanded respect for its honesty, however ttle the reason might have been approved in itself. ndian diplomacy, however, is not often afflicted with a esire to run a straightforward and candid course, specially when feudatories or neighbouring kingdoms re concerned.

In October last, on the eve of the Durga Poojah .olidays, a newspaper published in Calcutta, known as he *Amrita Bazar Patrika*, printed an official document, he appearance of which caused intense excitement throughout India. The *Patrika* has an honourable record for its devotion to the interests of the Indian people and the Indian princes, combined with a sincere and deep-rooted loyalty to the maintenance of the British connection with India. The editorial paragraphs in the *Patrika* to which I have referred are as follows:

'To-day we shall publish a document which will startle India—probably Lord Lansdowne himself. Lord Lansdowne, we are credibly informed, has been very much disgusted with the Kashmir business. We have a very high authority for stating that His Excellency was actuated by the best of motives in accepting what he calls the Edict of Resignation by the Maharaja. But when he accepted this responsibility of governing Kashmir through a Resident, he had no notion that there was so much intrigue, to put the matter mildly, surrounding the business. His Excellency's heart now recoils at what he is obliged to do to defend a measure which is wholly untenable. A noble Englishman of high principles, His Excellency is not willing to stick to a measure which his conscience does not justify. And therefore he is only seeking an opportunity to restore Kashmir to its legitimate owner. Our information, incredible as it may appear, is derived from such a high source that we cannot help putting faith in it.

'In the following document, the original of which His Excellency will find in the Foreign Office, the Viceroy will find the real reason why the Maharaja of Kashmir has been deposed. It will be seen that His Highness was deposed not because he resigned, or oppressed his people, but because Gilgit was wanted for strategical purposes by the British Government. Mr. Plowden proposed that the principalities of Gilgit should be occupied by the British Government at once, and this proposal of Mr. Plowden was the main cause of his downfall. Sir H. M. Durand, the Foreign Secretary, however, condemned Mr. Plowden's proposal, and him as Resident, in the following memorandum which was submitted to the then Viceroy, Lord Dufferin :—

'OPINION OF FOREIGN SECRETARY ABOUT THE OCCUPATION OF GILGIT.

'To His Excellency.

'I do not agree with Mr. Plowden, the Resident in Kashmir, in this matter. He is too much inclined to set Kashmir aside in all ways, and to assume that if we want a thing done we must do it ourselves.

'The more I think of this scheme the more clear it seems to me that we should limit our overt interference as far as possible to the organization of a responsible military force in Gilgit. So far we can hope to carry the Durbar thoroughly with us. If we annex Gilgit or put an end to the suzerainity of Kashmir over the petty principalities of the neighbourhood, and, above all, if we put British troops into Kashmir just now, we shall run a risk of turning the Durbar against us and thereby increase the difficulty of the position. I do not think this is necessary. No doubt we must have practically the control of Kashmir relations with those principalities, but this we already have. Indeed, the Durbar has now, since the dismissal of Lachman Das, asked Mr. Plowden to advise the Gilgit authorities direct without reference to them. If we have a quiet and judicious officer at Gilgit, who will get the Kashmir force into thorough order and abstain from unnecessary exercise of his influence, we shall, I hope, in a short time have the whole thing in our hand without hurting any one's feelings.

'Altogether, I think our first step should be to send up temporarily and quietly a selected Military Officer (Captain A. Durand, of the Intelligence Department) and a Junior Medical Officer. Both of them will have the support of the Durbar when and where it will be necessary, and they will not display any indiscretion, so that the Durbar may not have any hint of the work they are about to undertake, and they will have to obtain the consent of the Durbar in matters concerning military difficulties. Once we can establish a belief that our undertaking is nothing but the welfare of the Durbar, we are surely to attain our object. Time will show that my view is not a wrong one. In it lies, I venture to hope, the safe realization of that object which was once contemplated in Lord Canning's time, and afterwards was abandoned after deliberation.

'Eventually Major Mellis should go to Kashmir on the part of the Durbar and submit a mature scheme for the better administration of the State, which is at present very badly managed indeed. This scheme should include the outline of our arrangements for strengthening the Government policy.

'After the expiry of six months we will be in a position to decide whether the permanent location of a Political Agency at Gilgit, also a contingent of troops for the defence of the frontier,

for which the Durbar have already agreed to put their resources and troops at the disposal of the British Government.

'(Sd.) H. M. DURAND.
'6th May.'

'Very well.
'(Sd.) DUFFERIN.
'10th May.'

'All the suggestions contained in the above have been carried out. Captain A. Durand is just now in the neighbourhood of Gilgit, with "a junior medical officer"; the political agency has been established; and "eventually" Major Mellis has gone to Kashmir on the "part of the Durbar ... to submit a scheme ... for strengthening the Government policy." Sir H. Durand's suggestions have been disregarded only on one point, and that, we believe, by himself. He says, "We already have the control over the Gilgit principalities," and we can "have the whole thing without hurting anyone's feelings". Being one of the wisest men in India, why did not Sir H. Durand stick to this wise suggestion of his own, of controlling the affairs of Kashmir without hurting anyone's feelings? So it will be seen that, when Sir John Gorst said that he would not be surprised if a feeble-minded man like Pertab Singh would withdraw his resignation; or when Lord Cross declared that the Maharaja cruelly oppresses his subjects; or when Lord Lansdowne wrote to the Maharaja that His Highness was an extravagant and bad ruler, they were not aware of the real reason of the Maharaja's deposition. It was Gilgit that the Government wanted.

'One of the rumours very current in India is that, when the Viceroy comes to Lahore, the Foreign Office will invite the Maharaja to meet his Excellency there. The Maharaja would, of course, come, and then he would be persuaded to pen a real Edict of Resignation. We notice this rumour at all to show how people are prone to attribute all sorts of motives to the Government. We have, however, very little doubt that there will be a meeting at Lahore, and we hope everything will be satisfactorily settled. If there be any talk of Gilgit, of course the Maharaja should cordially co-operate with the Government for the defence of the Empire."

The key of the whole situation was felt to be in the pregnant words: 'It was Gilgit the Government wanted.'

For a time the journals in India—Anglo-Indian and Indian alike—could not bring themselves to believe the document was authentic. The authenticity of the more important portions of it was not long left in doubt. At the time the publication occurred the Government of India had before the Leglislative Council, sitting in Simla without the non-official members,[1] a Bill intended to make penal the publication of official secrets. During the progress of the measure Lord Lansdowne referred to the publication in the *Amrita Bazar Patrika* of a document alleged to refer to the occupation of Gilgit and the virtual annexation of Kashmir. Lord Lansdowne's remarks were as follows:—

I may, perhaps, be permitted to enforce what I have said by referring to a recent case in which a particularly scandalous disclosure of official information has taken place. A Calcutta journal, the *Amrita Bazar Patrika*, in a recent issue, published what professed to be the text of a document described as one 'the original of which his Excellency will find in the Foreign Office,' and as containing 'the real reason why the Maharaja of Kashmir has been deposed'.

The document purpôrts to be a memorandum submitted to the then Viceroy, Lord Dufferin, by Sir H. M. Durand, the Foreign Secretary, in May 1888, and runs as follows:—

'To his Excellency,—I do not agree with Mr. Plowden, the Resident in Kashmir, in this matter. He is too much inclined to

---

[1] A too frequent practice in India, leading to evils which will be obvious on a moment's thought. Half the Acts passed in India during the last twenty-four years have been carried in the seclusion of Simla, far away from the influence of even the feeble public opinion which exists in India.

set Kashmir aside in all ways, and to assume that if we want a thing done we must do it ourselves.

'The more I think of this scheme the more clear it seems to me that we should limit our over-interference as far as possible to the organization of a responsible military force in Gilgit. So far we can hope to carry the Durbar thoroughly with us. If we annex Gilgit, or put an end to the suzerainty of Kashmir over the petty principalities of the neighbourhood, and above all, if we put British troops into Kashmir just now, we shall run a risk of turning the Durbar against us, and thereby increase the difficulty of the position. I do not think this is necessary. No doubt we must have practically the control of Kashmir relations with those principalities, but this we already have. Indeed, the Durbar has now, since the dismissal of Lachman Das, asked Mr. Plowden to advise the Gilgit authorities direct without reference to them. If we have a quiet and judicious officer at Gilgit, who will get the Kashmir force into thorough order and abstain from unnecessary exercise of his influence, we shall, I hope in a short time, have the whole thing in our hand without hurting any one's feelings.'

Up to this the document is a substantially accurate reproduction of a Minute actually written upon the above date by Sir Mortimer Durand, so much so that there can be no doubt whatever that it must have been communicated to the press by a person who had had an opportunity of copying or committing to memory a part, at all events, of Sir Mortimer Durand's Minute. A few words only have been mis-quoted, but they are not of material importance. I think the Council will agree with me in considering that there is nothing in the passage which I have read which could be legitimately construed as revealing iniquitous designs upom the State of Kashmir on the part of the Government of India. It will no doubt be within the recollection of hon. members that, at the time when the Minute was written, there had been considerable disturbances on the Gilgit frontier, that the Chiefs of Hunza and Nagar were in revolt against Kashmir, that Chaprot had been captured, and other places within the territories of the Maharaja threatened by the insurgents, who had defied the Kashmir authorities.

These events had shown in so striking a manner the insufficiency and weakness of the frontier administration of the Kashmir Durbar, that proposals were submitted by the then Resident for the purpose of coming to its assistance. With this object, Mr. Plowden advised the appointment of an English Political Agent at Gilgit, and he was further of opinion that it might be desirable to send British troops into Kashmir. These were the proposals to which the Foreign Secretary, in the document of which I have just read a part, took exception, and in the passages which follow in the original Minute, which I have lately examined, I find that his objections to the Resident's proposals were throughout based upon the reason which he assigned at the outset, namely, that Mr. Plowden was disposed to rely too much upon British intervention, and not enough upon the efforts of the Durbar. Sir Mortimer expresses his belief that we should 'be able to improve and strengthen the position of the Kashmir authorities'; that any officer whom we send up 'should act with the consent and assistance of the Durbar'; that 'he should not take command of the Kashmir troops or get up any military expeditions'; and he was to 'give advice to the Governor in his present military difficulties' only 'if the Durbar wishes it'.

Will it be believed that the whole of the portion of the Minute from which I have taken these extracts has been omitted, or suppressed, and that in lieu of it has been inserted the passage which I shall now proceed to read?—

'Altogether, I think our first step should be to send up temporarily and quietly a selected military officer (Captain A. Durand, of the Intelligence Department) and a junior medical officer. Both of them will have the support of the Durbar when and where it will be necessary, and they will not display any indiscretion, so that the Durbar may not have any hint of the work they are about to undertake, and they will have to obtain the consent of the Durbar in matters concerning military difficulties. Once we can establish a belief that our undertaking is nothing but the welfare of the Durbar, we are surely to attain our object. Time will show that my view is not a wrong one. In it lies, I venture to hope, the safe realization of that object which was once contemplated in Lord Canning's time, and afterwards it was abandoned after deliberation.'

This extract, with the exception of the first line and a-half, in which it is recommended that an officer should be sent up temporarily to Gilgit, is a sheer and impudent fabrication. Not only is it not to be found in Sir Mortimer Durand's Minute, but it misrepresents him in all the most essential particulars. It has thus come to pass that, on the one hand, important passages of Sir Mortimer Durand's Minute have been altogether suppressed, and, on the other, words have been ascribed to him which he not only never used, but which convey a meaning absolutely inconsistent with those which he actually wrote.

I have already called attention to the suppression of those parts of the Minute which most strikingly illustrate the moderation of the policy which found favour with the Foreign Secretary, and which was approved by the Viceroy. When we come to the passages for which the writer has drawn upon his own imagination, we find a series of unfounded statements expressed in language which those who are familiar with Sir Mortimer Durand's style would not for a moment mistake for his, and abounding in suggestions to the effect that our policy in regard to Kashmir was governed by motives of the most sinister kind. Of such a description are the passages in which it is said that the officers sent to Gilgit are to conduct themselves 'so that the Durbar may not have any hint of the work they are about to undertake,' and the statement that, 'once we can establish a belief that our undertaking is nothing but the welfare of the Durbar, we are surely to attain our object'—an object which is subsequently described as that 'which was contemplated in Lord Canning's time, and afterwards it was abandoned after deliberation'.

The newspaper version of the Minute ends with the following words:—

'Eventually Major Mellis should go to Kashmir on the part of the Durbar, and submit a mature scheme for the better administration of the State, which is at present very badly managed indeed. This scheme should include the outline of our arrangements for strengthening the Government policy.

'After the expiry of six months we shall be in a position to decide whether the permanent location of a Political Agency at Gilgit [is necessary], also a contingent of troops for the defence of the frontier for which the Durbar have already agreed to put their resources and troops at the disposal of the British Government.

'(Sd.) H. M. Durand, 6th May.'

'Very well.—(Sd.) Dufferin, 10th May.'

Upon these passages I have only to observe that the earlier portion is rendered with complete inaccuracy, Sir M. Durand never having recommended that Major Mellis should submit a scheme for the administration of the State, but merely that that officer should at a later date go to Kashmir in order to confer with the Durbar in regard to its offer of aid for the defence of the frontier. The concluding sentence is a pure fabrication, none of the words after 'policy' appearing in the original Minute. The latter, I may add, received the Viceroy's approval, although not in the terms mentioned in the fabricated version.

I have shown already what were the objects with which the Government of India proposed, in 1888, to intervene in the affairs of Kashmir, and within what narrow limits Sir Mortimer Durand, with the Viceroy's approval, was prepared to restrict that intervention; and it is unnecessary for me to point out how full of mischievous and misleading suggestion are the passages which I have quoted from the spurious portions of his supposed Minute.

The responsibility which rests upon those who are ready not only to give to the public documents which they are well aware could not have been obtained except by a distinct and criminal breach of trust, but who are not even at the pains to satisfy themselves that these documents are genuine, is a very serious one.

In the present instance the spurious information can have been published with no other object than that of persuading the people of this country that the recent action of the Government of India in Kashmir has been prompted by motives which have been repudiated in official documents of the first importance, as well as by the public statements of the Secretary of State in the British Parliament. Not content with persistently misrepresenting the Government of India, the publishers of the article have not scrupled to present to the public a garbled version of a confidential note, written more than a year ago, in order to give an entirely distorted account of the then views and actions of the Government. Neither then nor at the present time has it been the desire of the Government of India to promote its own interests at the expense of those of the Kashmir State; then, as now, it was our desire to see that State well and wisely governed, with a minimum of intervention on our part, and without any ulterior designs upon its independence. I am not without hopes that the sincerity of our motives will in process of time come to be understood even by those who have been misled by the persistent misrepresentation which has taken place in connection with these matters, and I believe that an exposure of the practices to which our critics have not scrupled to resort in the present instance may have the effect of, in some degree, opening the eyes of the public as to the

methods which have been adopted for the purpose of prejudicing its judgment in regard to this important case.[1]

No one can read the words spoken with so much of honest conviction and sincerity by Lord Lansdowne without feeling that, to his mind, the action taken was inevitable, and was justified by the circumstances reported to him. I most cheerfully and most readily admit

---

[1] The *Statesman*, alluding to this speech, remarks: 'Since the receipt of the full text of the Viceroy's speech on the Official Secrets Bill, which we publish in another column, we have been at some pains to compare carefully what is therein stated with the suggestions contained in Sir M. Durand's alleged minute as published by the *Amrita Bazar Patrika* three weeks ago. As the result of this comparison we feel bound to say that the Viceroy's repudiation of the authenticity of all but the first two paragraphs of that document, as it appeared in the columns of the *Patrika*, is scarcely borne out by the admissions in His Excellency's own speech. As regards the first two paragraphs, Lord Lansdowne says: "Up to this the document is substantially an accurate reproduction of a minute actually written by Sir M. Durand. . . . A few words only have been misquoted, but they are not of material importance.' The inference to be drawn from this admission is that the remaining paragraphs of the minute are not 'substantially accurate.' But it will be presently seen that, however much their wording may vary in respect to details, the substance of two at least of the subsequent paragraphs has been correctly retained in the copy published by the *Amrita Bazar Patrika*. Thus as regards Captain Durand's deputation to Gilgit, which is suggested in the third paragraph, the Viceroy remarks: 'This extract with the exception of the first line and a half, in which it is recommended that an officer should be sent up temporarily to Gilgit, is a sheer and impudent fabrication.' It can not be denied, however, that this recommendation was subsequently carried into effect, and that Captain Durand did go to Gilgit. Again, as to the paragraph referring to Major Mellis's proposed employment in Kashmir, the Viceroy remarks: 'Upon these passages I have only to observe that the earlier portion is inaccurately rendered, Sir M. Durand never having recommended that Major Mellis should submit a scheme for the administration of the State, but merely that that officer should at a later date go to Kashmir in order to confer with the Durbar in regard to its offer of aid for the defence of the frontier. The concluding sentence is a pure fabrication, none of the words after "policy" appearing in the original minute.' The main allegations of the *Patrika* are thus practically admitted, and it seems to us only fair to say that the inaccuracies which have been found in the published version of Sir M. Durand's minute must be due rather to the circumstances under which, apparently, the copy was made, than to any wilful garbling or manipulation of the document on the part of the *Patrika*, for the purposes of misrepresenting the motives and intentions of the Government, as the Viceroy's speech would seem to imply.'

that the Viceroy acted with perfect sincerity and fully in the spirit of the words he used. But a belief in the good faith of Lord Lansdowne is not sufficient. Complete trust in his *bona fides* does not close the incident. In India, especially in dealings with the feudatory States of the Empire, there must not only be a sense of right in the mind of the Viceroy, there must also be so much of the appearance of right-doing in the course adopted as to command the acquiescence of those affected and of all who are in a similar position. Lord Dalhousie both felt and spoke, in 1856, of what he, during the six years of his Governor-Generalship, had done, as Lord Lansdowne felt and spoke in October last. But Lord Dalhousie's consciousness of rectitude, and firm belief in his own powers of statesmanship, did not prevent the dreadful deeds of 1857. Nor has this viceregal consciousness of rectitude, certainty of meaning to do well and belief that well had been done, prevented the historian connecting the outbreak of 1857 with certain of the actions upon which Lord Dalhousie greatly prided himself.[1] So, in like manner, while yielding to Lord Lansdowne the fullest respect due to his position and to his known most estimable qualities of mind and heart, it must be urged that his

[1] 'The real cause of the Mutiny may be expressed in a condensed form in two words—bad faith. It was bad faith to our Sipáhis which made their minds prone to suspicion; it was our policy of annexation, of refusing to Hindu chiefs the permission to adopt, with them, a necessary religious rite; of suddenly bringing a whole people under the operation of complex rules to which they were unaccustomed, as in Oudh, in the Ságar and Narbadá territory, and in Bundelkhand, and our breaches of customs more sacred to the natives than laws, which aroused the large landowners and the rural population against the British rule.'—'History of the Indian Mutiny,' by Kaye and Malleson, vol. v., p. 282.

claim for good faith does not dispose of the question. It is perfectly safe to say that there is not an Indian Prince who did not feel his throne shake when the Maharaja of Kashmir was deprived of all power and authority in his State. The arbitrariness of the act made itself felt as a presage of woe everywhere. It is equally safe to say that there are uneasiness and sorrow in the minds of at least nine-tenths of the Indian people at what has been done in Kashmir. And, after all, though Indians have no votes, and are not able to make their feelings known to the authorities in any constitutional manner, account ought to be taken of their feelings; it is only by the contented acquiescence of the Indian people that satisfactory British rule can be continued in our Indian Empire. A policy carried out in face of the discontent and dissatisfaction of the majority of a people is not a safe policy. There is something wrong somewhere when an act which is capable of being described in the tone and language adopted by Lord Lansdowne is universally condemned and distrusted, and becomes occasion for growing distrust. It is not difficult to see what the 'something wrong' is in this instance, or to ascertain the reason why it should create suspicion. Until the Maharaja of Kashmir is once more in power, and the British Resident is relegated to the position which such a functionary ought to occupy in a feudatory State, but never does occupy, the distinct danger which has been created will not be removed.

It is, again, no sufficient answer to say that the 'permanent persons' in the Calcutta Foreign Office advised the course which was taken. These estimable persons are bureaucrats; they are not statesmen. One great reason why such noblemen as Lord Lansdowne are appointed to supreme rule in India is that they may at one and the same time bring a fresh and unprejudiced mind to the consideration of great questions and supply the needed measure of statesmanship which Indian modes of rule are not likely to educe. India has produced some of the finest administrators the world has known. Of statesmen—even of the third and fourth class—she has produced none. The most complete failures in English public life are the Anglo-Indians who find their way to Parliament or the School Board. And, yet, those who do get into public life are men who have achieved the highest reputation as Indian administrators. Lord Lansdowne's duty is not done by simply writing 'Very well' at the foot of a minute, or by accepting what the Foreign Office puts before him. His duty, above all else, is to put the statements of the experts in the crucible of a widely-matured and experienced mind, and, having taken heed of all the circumstances—circumstances not stated as well as those stated—then to take action. There is not a bureaucrat in India who, on the Parry-Nisbet fussy visit to Calcutta and the imbroglio which followed, could not have done what Lord Lansdowne did. Something vastly more high-minded, more statesmanlike was expected, and rightly expected, from one of His Excellency's experience and from one occupying his exalted and responsible position. Foresight and wide-sight having been carefully avoided, the Viceroy need not be surprised if his stroke of policy is not regarded by others as he himself regarded it.

The *Patrika's* own justification of the publication of

the Memorandum which so greatly incensed the Viceroy is thus stated:—'The object of the publication of the document was to put before the Viceroy, who is a new-comer, the real facts of the Kashmir case. The Viceroy has brought certain charges against the Maharaja of Kashmir, upon the strength of secret and *ex parte* reports from Mr. Plowden and the Foreign Secretary. Our object in publishing the document was to show that those who had persuaded him to believe in the guilt of the Maharaja and to cause his deposition, were, even before the advent of His Excellency, hankering after "the whole thing".'

An attempt has been made in the House of Commons to procure the publication of an authentic copy of the document, but its production has been refused. Material information, to enable hon. members to judge of the conduct of the Government of India in this matter, has, therefore, been withheld.

The fact is now accepted in India that the reasons announced for the conduct pursued towards the Maharaja of Kashmir were not the whole of the reasons—were not, in fact, the real reasons. Unpleasant similes are used by publicists in discussing these matters, as, for example (see Appendix C), one in which Khiva and Kashmir are connected, and the British Indian and Russian Governments are contrasted. It is made clear that the conduct which most Anglo-Indians and some home-staying Englishmen are never tired of condemning in Central-Asian Russians finds its parallel nearer home.

The Indian Government has had its way. Captain Durand is at Gilgit. The Maharaja, whose deposition was considered necessary, is living a life of seclusion and of utter misery. He is permitted to see no one without leave of the Resident. Lord Cross and his Under-Secretary indulge in utterly meaningless talk about their desire to restore the Maharaja as soon as he gives proof of his willingness to rule his subjects justly and wisely. Meanwhile, he remains degraded. He is suffering for no proven fault, so far as can be seen for no committed fault, but only because it was necessary he should be set aside for more pliable creatures. It is declared he is in his present position as the result of his own voluntary act.

Whether pressure was used, as he asserts it was, or not, his signature was obtained to a paper in which he resigned to the State Council, as approved by the Government of India, for five years, certain only of the powers that rightfully belonged to himself alone. The Maharaja may have wished to give the Council full powers, with limitation of his sovereign rights—and he did, doubtless, hope to improve the administration in this way—but he cannot have intended to efface himself by this consent, or to be absolutely ignored as head of the State. He hoped to have been consulted upon, and to have control over, the Council's proceedings, more especially as three out of the five members were foreigners, ignorant of the language as well as of the wants of his subjects. But the Maharaja has now no power or control; he is an absentee, living almost alone in his palace, moping and brooding despondingly over his position, 'cabined, cribbed, confined,' as though he were to be preserved in this half-demented condition for the day, more distant perhaps than the stipulated five years, when the Viceroy may think proper to restore him to the exercise of his inherited position.

The strained position that the Maharaja fills has been forced upon him. Considerations of importance are involved: first, because a milder and better treatment might have been substituted; and next, because the Government of India is now open to the suspicion of intentionally degrading the Maharaja with the object of maintaining permanently the control it has voluntarily assumed. That a milder treatment could have been adopted must, of course, be admitted. The meaning put upon the resignation by the Maharaja to the Council of certain powers he legitimately holds might, and should have been, that the advice and control of His Highness would be accepted; in this way his rank and position would have been maintained. The humiliation now imposed on him is needless for the furtherance of any rightful claims of the British Government, or for the improvement of the administration.

Is it surprising that in such a condition of things unpleasant surmises should be entertained of what is going on in the Kashmir State? It is supposed that, in order to make the annexation of Kashmir not only an easy matter but a necessity, the obvious plan is to make the world believe that the Kashmirian mode of administration was so hopelessly bad that by annexation alone could it be remedied. One's feeling revolts at such a Machiavellian policy. But how is an objector to satisfy himself as to the honesty and sincerity of the intentions of the Government of India? Lord Dufferin, on October 30 last, in a speech addressed to the London Chamber of Commerce, clearly stated that he had thought, when Viceroy of India, that it might be needful to restrain the powers of the Maharaja of Kashmir. Nevertheless, he did not take any action. Lord Lansdowne, however, before he had had time to become himself acquainted with the true condition of affairs, directed that the Maharaja should be treated as he now is. It is well understood in India that the policy pursued by every Foreign Secretary, since the time when Lord Lytton was appointed Viceroy, is to put a check upon the supposed movements of Russia towards India. The late Afghan war, and all that has been done since to subsidize the Ameer of Afghanistan with the object of purchasing his friendship; the Penjdeh Commission; the frontier railways and fortifications: have all been undertaken with the single object named. The Kashmir State alone remained on the frontier, entirely disconnected with schemes for frontier defence. What has recently happened has been told in these pages. The policy of the Foreign Office in India is shortsighted; it originates in groundless fears, and is opposed to the true interests alike of the Government of India and of the avowed policy of the Home Government, not only as far as regards the people of India, but as to the foreign relations also of the British people. Let it be understood that the Maharaja is not responsible for the misrule which he found when he was put on the *gadi*. Undoubtedly a certain amount of misrule existed; how much has never been proved. Maharaja Pertab Singh has not had the freedom required to introduce permanent changes and reforms; he is a quiet, confiding, simple-minded man, who deserves that paternal consideration for the welfare of the people which the Government of India has the credit of displaying throughout India; but, instead, he is not permitted to exercise the powers conferred on him by the British Government; he is treated with ignominy and left to circumstances which cannot fail to exercise a painful influence upon him.

By way of furnishing you with independent testimony by an eyewitness of the condition of the Kashmirians, and of the treatment meted out to the Maharaja, I may here quote a communication sent to the *Times*. It was written by a gentleman who describes himself as having worked in that country for nearly ten years, and who has had the honour of an intimate acquaintance with the Maharaja and his brothers. He says:—

I feel sure, if not now, it will be admitted in time to come, that great credit is due to Mr. Bradlaugh for his very able address on behalf of H.H. the Maharaja. The Under Secretary of State said it was a curious illustration of the irony of fate to find Mr. Bradlaugh advocating the rights of a Prince; but, instead of its being an irony, does it not give proof of his praiseworthy efforts to advocate the cause of the oppressed be they Prince or people? I may not be credited, but it is true nevertheless, that no case could be cited in the history of British India where greater misunderstanding or perversion of facts has been exhibited than in the present crisis in Kashmir. The recent speeches of honourable members, including the Under Secretary of State, I beg to say, with due deference, are full of errors. Sir John Gorst spoke of the poor Moslem cultivators of Jammu. No such people exist. The inhabitants of Jammu and its district consist almost entirely of Hindus. They are nearly all of the same caste as the Maharaja, and what is more, if they could possibly express their wishes without fear, would to a man declare in favour of their deposed king.

That talented Indian statesman, Sir Richard Temple, was heard to say that the 'sovereignty was transferred from one brother to another'. Is this correct? The brother is as much the Sovereign of Kashmir as is Sir Richard himself. Why, it is due entirely to the failure of the other brother to become king that all this trouble has been brought on Kashmir. The country has been rent asunder for years by the rival claims and factions of the three brothers, all hungry for the crown. The present arrangement is no solution of the difficulty, simply a continuation of the complication in another form, with the addition of disgrace and exile inflicted on His Highness in his own house and his own kingdom.

Then, it is said by honourable members that the Government of Kashmir is now invested in certain capable Indians as Members of Council. Is that a fact? Is it known to the British Government that the so-called Council of Kashmir (all strangers to the country except the brothers) has as much power as a parcel of schoolboys to dictate to their tutor? All that has been done is to transfer the government of Kashmir from one autocrat to another. In the very constitution of the Council, that is, rules made for its guidance, it is ordered that their deliberations can be vetoed by the Resident in Kashmir. They are, hence, careful to pass only such resolutions as shall meet with his approval beforehand. I have heard from *their own lips*, in as emphatic manner as could be expressed, that their independence is a farce and their power barely nominal. Why, sir, the proceedings of the Council are published in English, while the majority scarcely know a word of the language. And, if anybody desires it, I can show original documents issued to me, from which it will be seen that the

Government of Kashmir by the present Council is nothing short of a myth and delusion.

It is further stated, as matter for congratulation, that there is not even a single European member in the Council, and the Government is carried on entirely by natives of India. Will it be believed that the Maharaja in his letter to the Viceroy, of his own accord, *asked* for a European member to be nominated to his Council? He very wisely saw that a set of native subordinates appointed by the Government could only be the tool of the Resident. The fact is well known: the government of the country is vested to all practical purposes in the Resident alone. Indeed, it is not possible for anybody to set foot in that country without a written permission from him. His will is law, he is king, and has surrounded himself with his own friends and *protégés*, and turned out many an old and faithful servant of the State. Nobody dare open his mouth in that country, and, if any one is so bold as to raise the most feeble protest, he is threatened with the 'most serious consequences'—such as were inflicted on me; and, were it not for the kindness and sense of justice of those who surround the Viceroy, I might have been utterly ruined.

As for oppression of his subjects, of which so much has been made, no doubt there has been much misgovernment by incompetent and corrupt officials. But what could the distracted Maharaja do? One change followed another in rapid succession after his father's death. The brothers were in continual feud with themselves and their own ministers. Two of the ablest political officers in India were transferred from Kashmir one after another, the Prime Minister was disgraced, spoliated, and turned out. Affairs became hopelessly entangled. Then came the real 'irony of fate'; in Sir John Gorst's own words, 'a personal friend of the Maharaja, and in whom he had implicit confidence, was sent'. To do what? Why, to depose, disgrace, and very probably ruin, the Maharaja for life.

Is it possible that in a country visited by six to eight hundred Europeans annually, by the Viceroy (the Marquis of Ripon) by the Duke of Connaught, by commanders-in-chief, and other celebrities who have travelled from one end of the country to the other, that grave oppression or misery could exist to any serious or visible extent? Has there not always been an able British Resident with the Maharaja, ready to take serious notice of any misdemeanour? Ask the hundreds of tourists, who visit Kashmir from all parts of the globe, if they have not found the Kashmirians sleek and fat, and as well off as any other Indians of similar position. Has not the second brother, perhaps the most honest-minded man in Kashmir, heaps of documents in his possession from the people of the country in favour of the rule of the Maharaja or his family?

On my works I employed thousands of labourers, yet I had the greatest difficulty in getting local labour or inhabitants of the country to work for me; they were too independent and too well off. And, if it were not for large importations of outside labour, I could never have got through the extensive works I carried out in the last nine years.

Then, it is said Kashmir is of no military importance, that the British Government do not cast 'greedy eyes' on it. Blame me as you will, but record it for yourself, unless there is a decided change of policy before long, Kashmir will soon be as much British India as is now Burma.

And is the country of no military importance? I think the military authorities in India consider otherwise. Why, the first instructions issued to me ten years ago, were to make a 'gun carriage road' through the mountains. Is there not a road being projected now to the utmost corner of the kingdom, with vast sums of money being spent on it, solely for military purposes? Has the Maharaja not been repeatedly threatened with a military cantonment, to be placed in the most favourable situation in the valley?

There is no doubt of the pureness of the motives of the Government either here or in India. Nobody in his senses could doubt for a moment that the Viceroy and Governor-General of India has any other desire than the welfare and prosperity of the kingdom. But is the information given him correct? Are the means employed fair and just to the rightful owner? In a country where false stories are proverbial, where those who know are afraid to speak, what correct information is it possible could reach the Government of India?

By all means make railways, roads, waterworks, and what not.

Everybody knows these are essential for the advancement of any country. But will you go so far as to make that country hopelessly bankrupt? Will you use the savings of a monarch's ancestors, cut up his land and change the very face of the country, and not consult him? Is he to have neither voice nor wish in the matter?

What other means, it may be asked, could be adopted? Why, give him an ultimatum. Lay down distinctly what you want done; give him reasonable time. Let him chose his own officers; help him to procure them. Give him a constitution the same as other Indian Princes possess. At the same time avoid petty interference. Protect him from his enemies and the rivalries of his brothers. If His Highness does not then succeed, let the British Government take a plebiscite and govern the country according to the unanimous voice of the people.

I hope I may be permitted to say that it would have been far better for the Government to have taken the country straight off than created a makeshift as now. The President of the Council has printed on his papers, 'Prime Minister to H.H. the Maharaja'. Which Maharaja? The one deposed and locked up in his private apartments? There is no finality in such an arrangement. It cannot last. It leads to up and down, hope and despair, both in Prince and people.

There is no necessity for the Government here to appoint any committee of inquiry. The Government of India are the best authority to make the required investigation. Let this be done openly, and by competent judges, and I promise you some curious revelations.

The Indians are a humble race; with hands folded they have submitted to the edict of the Viceroy. But justice and humanity cry for redress. The Proclamation of Her Most Gracious Majesty declares equal justice to white and black, and that the rights of her feudatories shall be respected. This is in the mouth of every Indian; they know well what it means, and, if you will infringe it in the case of Kashmir, you may sow such seeds of discontent as will bear fruit when least expected.

I have only to add I have not the honour of acquaintance with Mr Bradlaugh, and that this has not been written at the instigation of H. H. the Maharaja or his agents.

Such is the story of the degradation, the cruel and unmerited degradation, of a loyal and sincere feudatory.

What can be done, and who can do what needs to be done?

As matters stand, a Select Committee of the House of Commons, or a Commission with judicial powers and enabled to take evidence in India, alone can ascertain the facts, and procure, through the Imperial Parliament, to whom its Report should be presented, that justice which has been so conspicuously wanting throughout this unhappy business. Will the House appoint such a Committee or Commission? The division on July 3 is not promising, so far at least as this Parliament is concerned. What a new House, fresh from the constituencies, and with more zeal for righteousness than the present moribund assembly possesses, may do, remains to be seen. The direct result of the intervention of the House, in the sense I have named, would be great; the indirect effect, upon the princes and peoples of India, cannot be fully set forth. British justice would become a reality to Indians of all races, and our connection with that great Empire made strong and lasting.

I pray you, sir, to reconsider the papers laid before you in the light of the facts I have presumed, in the interests of a greatly-wronged Prince and of outraged millions of our fellow-subjects, to lay before you. I have done this with the hope that you, and many of your fellow-members of the House of Commons, will, on a full consideration of the whole circumstances, see that His Highness the Maharaja Pertab Singh of Kashmir is at least entitled to an opportunity to prove his innocence of the charges insinuated, rather than plainly expressed, against him.

I am, Sir,

Your obedient servant,

Wm. Digby.

INDIAN POLITICAL AGENCY,
25, Craven Street, Charing Cross, London,
July, 1890.

P.S.—Since I concluded my letter I have had the opportunity of reading a verbatim report, taken by the Hansard staff, of the debate. This verbatim report I include among my Appendices. My surprise at the course you felt it your duty to take has hitherto been of a mild character; it is now one of utter amazement. That you should have been influenced by the sophistries of the able gentleman who represents the India Office in the House of Commons is surprising. The air of judicial reserve which your official experience would have led one to expect would characterize your observations are, permit me regretfully to say, wholly wanting in your short speech. This feature was, fortunately, not absent from the debate. But it marked the statements of Sir William Plowden, and not those of Sir U. Kay-Shuttleworth. What Sir William Plowden with much dignity advanced is, I repeat, precisely what members of the Liberal Party had a right to expect from the official representative of the late Liberal Government when he intervened in such a debate, and was, in a sense, charged with the fate of the accused Prince. As I show on a previous page (p. 88), that very system of forced labour which called forth Sir John Gorst's sympathy and aroused his indignation has, within the past few months, been made use of by the British Résident himself. As for another complaint of the Under-Secretary of State, namely, that relating to a Moslem population under a Hindu ruler requiring special consideration at the hands of the Government of India, Sir John Gorst at least knows that this is not the only instance in India of alien rule. He will not need reminding that the opposite holds good in the Deccan to a sixfold greater extent. In the Nizam's dominions a Muhammadan Prince rules over a Hindu population. Beyond writing a sensational and inaccurate article for the *Fortnightly Review* in 1884, Sir John Gorst has done nothing to remedy a condition of things analogous to that which, on July 3, moved him to pity. Eight days after, on July 11, referring to some remarks made by Sir John Gorst in the debate, Mr. Bradlaugh asked a question. This is what occurred :—

Mr. Bradlaugh : I beg to ask the Under Secretary of State for India, if he will state the number of cultivating ryots in Jammu : And, how many of them are, respectively, Moslems and Hindus.

Sir J. Gorst : I am extremely sorry that I cannot answer this question. The last return was received in 1873, and no record has been preserved [? received] since.

Mr. Bradlaugh : Does the right hon. gentleman mean to say that he has less information now than he had the other night when he made a statement on the subject?

The question was not answered.

One word more on the debate, and this long epistle to you will come to an end. Sir Richard Temple interposed in the debate. That is a pity. It is more than a pity. It is a calamity—for the reputation of ex-Anglo-Indian officials. Sir Richard, among other things, said that the rule of Kashmir had been transferred from the Maharaja Pertab Singh to his brother. This is entirely incorrect. Yet it was on the side of a cause supported with such knowledge and wisdom as this that you threw the weight not only of your own blameless Parliamentary career, but that of the members of Mr. Gladstone's late Administration, who may be considered to be committed by your action to an adverse view of Maharaja Pertab Singh's case. It is with no little concern I remind you of this, to you, not wholly creditable fact.

W. D.

APPENDIX.

A.

GOVERNMENT PAPERS.

EAST INDIES.

PAPERS RELATING TO KASHMIR.

No. 1.

THE GOVERNMENT OF INDIA to the SECRETARY OF STATE FOR INDIA (EARL OF KIMBERLEY), dated Simla, April 7, 1884.

EXTRACT.

WE have the honour to address your Lordship on the subject of the Kashmir State.

The three principal facts which it is necessary to notice are that the death of the Maharaja Ranbir Singh is apparently near at hand; that the administration of the Kashmir State is so thoroughly disorganised as to threaten a complete breakdown; and that the heir-apparent to the Chiefship is said to be unfitted in character and habits to govern the State. The first two of these facts we have unfortunately been in a position to anticipate for a long time past. The Maharaja has been suffering for years from a mortal disease; while the recent famine afforded convincing proof of the corruptness and inefficiency of the administration of Kashmir. We have also heard from time to time unsatisfactory accounts of the heir-apparent, and it has of late been reported that his father entertained some idea of setting him aside by a testamentary disposition. In our judgment, the time has now come for determining the course which the British Government should adopt on the death of the Maharaja; and we therefore proceed to lay our views before your Lordship.

Turning first to the question of the succession to the present Chief, we are of opinion that the eldest son, Mian Pertab Singh, should be proclaimed at once when his father dies. We do not consider that we can take cognizance of the vices attributed to Pertab Singh unless they have reduced him to a condition of actual incapacity, which does not appear to be the case; nor do we think that in this matter we should be justified in attaching any weight even to the wishes of His Highness Ranbir Singh. For the general interests of peace and good order among the Native States, no encouragement should be given to the idea that an eldest son can be set aside at the will of his father; and we hold that in practice nothing but the clearest evidence of actual incapacity to rule should be allowed to stand in the way of a regular succession by order of primogeniture. Further, we are entirely opposed to permitting any partition of the Kashmir State, by will or otherwise, among the three sons of the present Chief. Feeling confident that our opinion upon these points are in accord with established policy, we have anticipated your Lordship's orders by issuing the instructions necessary for the guidance of Lieutenant-Colonel Sir Oliver St. John, K.C.S.I., the Officer on Special Duty, in case of an emergency arising. In the meanwhile we do not think it desirable formally to announce to the Maharaja that a will affecting the succession could not be recognised, because this course might raise unplesant discussions. But the Officer on Special Duty will avail himself of any good opportunity for intimating to His Highness that such a will would not be expedient.

On the succession of the new Chief, it will not, in our opinion, be proper to postpone any longer a representation of our views upon the necessity for introducing substantial reforms into the administration of Kashmir. The misgovernment to which the people of that country have long been sujected was some time since prominently brought to our notice by Mr. Henvey. We did not take action at once, conceiving that a more favourable opportunity would present itself on the occurrence of a fresh succession —an event which seemed unlikely to be long postponed. When that event takes place, we consider that it will be our duty to impress upon the Kashmir Government its obligations to its own subjects, and to see that the reforms which are so urgently needed are no longer postponed. With this view we would propose, immediately on the occurrence of the next succession, to inform the Maharaja that we regard the present state of affairs as most unsatisfactory, and that substantial reforms are required. We would if possible lead the new Government to propose the measures necessary to give effect to this altered policy, but we should require that their execution should be entrusted to competent hands. While firmly insisting upon the necessity for a change, we should avoid any direct interference with administrative details.

We are, however, sensible that, if our advice is to be effectual, it may be necessary to alter the present arrangement under which our representative remains in the Maharaja's territory for a portion only of the year. Such a change would probably be welcomed by the people of Kashmir; and as it would not be introduced until after the death of Maharaja Ranbir Singh, his feelings in the matter would be fully respected. It is a measure which may be called for, not merely by the need for assisting and supervising administrative reforms, but also by the increasing importance to the Government of India of watching events beyond the North-

Western frontier of Kashmir. Any disturbances which continued misgovernment might create in Kashmir would be acutely felt on the frontiers of Afghanistan; the connection between Kashmir and its dependent Chiefships would in all probability be severed; and grave political complications might easily ensue. We have therefore to consider the necessity for providing for efficient political supervision, not merely in the interests of the people of Kashmir, but also in the interests of the people of India. Under these circumstances we are anxious to obtain from Her Majesty's Government authority to appoint, if it should appear to us necessary, at any time after the death of the present Maharaja, a Resident Political Officer, who will exercise a general supervision over the affairs of the Kashmir State. We do not propose that this officer, if appointed by us, should hold any actual position in the government of the State, nor do we think that it would be necessary to give him special powers in the Province of Kashmir. It will suffice if he occupies, with regard to Jammu and Kashmir, the position and powers ordinarily given to a British Resident in a feudatory State.

The British Government are not debarred by any engagement, express or tacit, from posting a Political Officer permanently in Kashmir; and we see no reason why an arrangement which has been accepted without demur by such a State as Hyderabad should not be adopted in regard to the Kashmir State. If this view is correct, the only question which arises is, whether existing circumstances do not render it desirable to give us the authority we seek.

No. 2.

The SECRETARY OF STATE FOR INDIA to the GOVERNMENT OF INDIA.

My Lord Marquis, India Office, May 23, 1884.

I have to acknowledge the receipt of the letter of your Excellency's Government, dated the 7th April, relating to Kashmir affairs.

2. In anticipation of the death of Maharaja Ranbir Singh, which is believed to be near at hand, your Excellency in Council has had under consideration (1) the course to be adopted in regard to the succession; (2) the measures which should be taken on the commencement of a new reign, in order to secure reforms in the administration of the State; and (3) the expediency of a change in the existing arrangements for the representation of the British Government at the Maharaja's Court.

3. Your Excellency in Council is of opinion that any attempt on the part of the Maharaja to exclude his eldest son from the succes-

sion should be discouraged, and that Mian Pertab Singh should be proclaimed immediately on his father's death; you propose to require from the new ruler substantial reforms in the administration, and to insist upon their execution being entrusted to competent hands; and you request from Her Majesty's Government discretionary authority to appoint, at any time after the death of Maharaja Ranbir Singh, a British Resident in Kashmir, with the position and powers ordinarily given to such an officer in a feudatory State.

4. While I regret to receive so unfavourable an account of the character of the Maharaja's heir, I agree with your Excellency's Government in regarding as inexpedient any deviation in the case of Kashmir from the regular succession by order of primogeniture, or any partition of the State, by will or ortherwise, among the three sons of the present Chief. I approve, therefore, of the instructions in accordance with this view, which I understand to have been sent to the Officer on Special Duty in Kashmir.

5. As to the urgent need of reforms in the administration of the State, there is, unfortunately, no room for doubt. It may, indeed, be a question whether, having regard to the circumstances under which the sovereignty of the country was entrusted to the present Hindu ruling family, the intervention of the British Government on behalf of the Muhammadan population has not already been too long delayed; but, however this may be, Her Majesty's Government are satisfied that, upon a fresh succession, no time should be lost in taking whatever steps may be requisite in order to place the administration upon a sound footing.

6. The same occasion would, in the opinion of Her Majesty's Government, be a suitable one for introducing a change in the present arrangement under which your Excellency's representative remains in Kashmir for a portion only of the year.

7. In 1846 it was decided not to appoint a political officer to reside permanently at the Maharaja's Court, whilst in 1873, when the measure was recommended by Lord Northbrook's Government, the necessity for it did not seem to Her Majesty's Government to be so clearly established as to justify them in disregarding objections which were expressed by authorities entitled to respect. But in the interval which has since elapsed, circumstances have greatly changed; and whether regard be had to the condition of the country, to the character of the Prince into whose hands the Government will shortly pass, or to the course of events beyond the border, which has materially increased the political importance of Kashmir, the appointment which you request a discretionary authority to make appears to be not only desirable but necessary. Your Excellency in Council is, therefore, at liberty to proceed in the matter as you may think proper at any time after the death of Maharaja Ranbir Singh, taking care meanwhile that strict secrecy is observed as to your intentions.

I have, &c.,

(Signed) KIMBERLEY.

No. 3.

The GOVERNMENT OF INDIA to the SECRETARY OF STATE FOR INDIA (Lord Randolph Churchill), dated Simla, October 19, 1885.

Extract.

We have the honour to forward correspondence relative to affairs in the Kashmir State.

The demise of the late Maharaja Ranbir Singh was announced to your Lordship by telegram on the 12th September; and the papers now enclosed will acquaint Her Majesty's Government with the steps we have taken to carry out the policy approved by Lord Kimberley's despatch, dated the 23rd May, 1884. The succession of Pertab Singh, the eldest son of the deceased Maharaja, to the undivided Chiefship of Jammu and Kashmir has been recognised and confirmed. The position of the Political Officer in Kashmir has been placed on the same footing with that of Residents in other Indian States in subordinate alliance with the British Government. The attention of the new ruler has been drawn to certain measures of reform which we consider essential to remedy the long-standing misrule in His Highness's territories. At the same time the Maharaja has been assured that we desire to leave the initiation of these measures in his hands, to abstain from unnecessary interference in his affairs, and to allow him all legitimate discretion and a liberal period of time for the execution of a work which is as difficult as it is necessary.

Your Lordship will perceive that the change in the Political Officer's appointment has evoked a remonstrance from the Maharaja Pertab Singh. We were prepared for some opposition in this matter on the part of the Durbar, and, as the question has been fully considered and finally settled, we have declined to enter into any further discussion on the subject.

We trust that our proceedings may meet with the approval of Her Majesty's Government.

Enclosure 1 in No. 3.

From the Secretary to the Government of India, Foreign Department, to the Officer on Special Duty in Kashmir, dated Simla, August 1, 1884.

Extract.

I am directed to convey to you the instructions of the Governor-General in Council upon the condition of affairs in Kashmir.

In case of Maharaja Ranbir Singh's death, his eldest son, Mian Pertab Singh, will succeed to the undivided Chiefship; the new Maharaja will be called upon to introduce such reforms as may seem to be necessary; and a Resident political officer will be stationed in Kashmir. It remains to inform you of the precise steps which the Governor-General in Council desires you to adopt for carrying out these arrangements.

So long as Maharaja Ranbir Singh is alive, the Government of India do not propose to make any change in their existing policy. His Highness should be quietly dissuaded. if he refers to you on the subject, from executing any testament in favour of the partition of his territories; but it will not be necessary for you to make any formal communication to His Highness upon this matter; or to travel beyond existing practice in recommending to him administrative reforms, or other desirable measures. You should abstain from any allusions to the subject of changes in the existing position of the Officer on Special Duty in Kashmir, and you should avoid as much as possible anything which is calculated in the Maharaja's present state of health unnecessarily to disturb his mind. It is of course desirable that you should use your influence, as far as you can, even during the life of the Maharaja, for the improvement of the condition of Kashmir; but the Governor-General in Council wishes to treat His Highness with the utmost consideration; and, as any substantial reform would probably involve a very unpalatable degree of interference with his proceedings, it will be sufficient if, during the remainder of his life, you can preserve the administration of the State from any material change for the worse.

If at any time the Maharaja's death should appear to be very near at hand, you should make arrangements to join His Highness at Jammu, or wherever he may then be, and to prevent any disorder occurring. If his illness should unfortunately terminate fatally, you should take the earliest opportunity of announcing that the Viceroy is pleased to recognize the succession of Mian Pertab Singh to the Chiefship, and you should formally instal the new Chief on the *gaddi* of Jammu and Kashmir.

At the same time you should inform His Highness, and the members of his Durbar, of the views and intentions of the British Government in regard to the future administration of the State. You should give them clearly to understand that His Excellency the Viceroy regards the existing condition of affairs in Kashmir as most unsatisfactory; and you should warn His Highness and those about him that substantial reforms must be introduced without delay. You should then announce that, with the view of aiding His Highness in the introduction and maintenance of those reforms, the Viceroy has decided to give His Highness the assistance of a resident English officer, and that for the future the British representative in Kashmir will have the same status and duties as the Political Residents in other Indian States in subordinate alliance with the British Government.

It is important, in order to avoid uncertainty and the risk of disorder, that this announcement of the intentions of the Government should take place without delay, and that they should be clearly and fully understood both by the Maharaja and by all others concerned when he is installed. The recognition and installation of the new Chief should be as prompt and formal as possible, and nothing should be omitted that can have the effect of assuring His Highness of the good-will of the British Government; but, while treating the Maharaja with the utmost friendliness and courtesy, you cannot speak too plainly in regard to the Viceroy's views and intentions.

Immediately after the news of Maharaja Ranbir Singh's death reaches the Government of India, a letter addressed by His Excellency the Viceroy to the new chief will be sent to you for delivery. A draft of this letter is enclosed for your information. When you receive the signed copy of this draft or before you receive it, if the ceremonies connected with the change of rulers should afford you an opportunity of speaking earlier, you should invite the Maharaja to indicate the reforms which he may consider it necessary or desirable to introduce; and you should ask His Highness to inform you of his views with regard to the persons whom he would propose to place in charge of the administration. It will not be expedient to bring in a Minister from elsewhere if a sufficiently well qualified local candidate can be found; and as far as possible the Governor-General in Council would wish to leave the Maharaja free to form his own Government. Any proposals, therefore, which His Highness may put forward on this subject will be tentatively accepted, unless you should see decided reason to object to them as holding out no prospect of success.

You will notice that the draft letter to the Maharaja impresses upon him the necessity for consulting you fully at all times, and following your advice. You should therefore not hesitate to offer your advice freely whenever you may think it desirable to do so; the more particularly because, owing to the peculiar conditions under which the Maharaja will succeed to the Chiefship, it will be necessary that his administration should for a time at least be closely supervised; the condition of Kashmir must be thoroughly reformed; and the Governor-General in Council cannot allow this object to be frustrated by any obstruction or procrastination on the part of the Durbar.

I am now to enumerate, for your information and guidance, the principal measures of reform which appear to the Governor-General in Council to be necessary after any arrangements required for the immediate alleviation of distress, if distress exist, have been adopted and carried out. In the opinion of the Governor-General in Council those measures are: the introduction of a reasonably light assessment of land revenue, collections being made in cash if on examination this seems to be a suitable arrangement; the construction of good roads; the cessation of State monopolies; the revision of existing taxes and dues, especially transit dues and the numerous taxes upon trades and professions; the abolition of the system of farming the revenue, wherever this system is in force; the appointment of respectable officials, if such exist, and their regular payment in coin; the establishment of a careful system of financial control; the removal of all restrictions upon emigration; the reorganisation and regular payment of the army; and the improvement of the judicial administration. In order to afford the Maharaja all possible help in the introduction of such reforms, the Governor-General in Council will if necessary grant His Highness a loan from Imperial revenues, and will also be willing to place at his disposal, for a time, the services of any officers of the British Government who may seem specially qualified to assist the new administration in carrying out the measures contemplated. Such assistance seems to be more particularly required with regard to the revision of the settlement and the construction of roads. The pay of any officers transferred must, however, be found by the Kashmir State.

With reference to the relations existing between Kashmir and the States upon her northern border, the Governor-General in Council does not think it necessary at present to issue any detailed instructions. The question is an important one, and will require your close and constant attention. You should be kept accurately informed of all movements of troops and other noteworthy occurrences in the direction of the frontier; and you should be prepared to advise Maharaja Pertab Singh freely on all matters of frontier policy. But at present the Governor-General in Council has no special instructions to give you on this subject.

I am to add that if the death of Maharaja Ranbir Singh occurs during the Kashmir season, and you find yourself obliged in consequence to leave Srinagar for Jammu, you should on starting hand over the charge of your current duties to the Agency Surgeon or other qualified officer. The Governor-General in Council is willing to leave to your discretion the question of the route by which you should go to Jammu; but he desires me to suggest to you that your passing down by the direct route through Kashmir territory might have a good effect in maintaining quiet and order. And I am to say that it is very desirable not to move any British troops across the border if this can possibly be avoided. If it becomes absolutely necessary to do so, the special sanction of the Government of India should be obtained before any movement is made.

I have only to remark in conclusion that circumstances may evidently occur to which the terms of this letter will not be strictly applicable. The Maharaja Ranbir Singh may die suddenly in your absence, or his life may be unexpectedly prolonged. Mian Pertab Singh may be absent from Jammu at the time of his father's decease, and it is even possible that before that event occurs he may become actually incapacitated for rule. These or similar circumstances may render some departure necessary from the letter of the instructions now given to you. But the Governor-General in Council relies with confidence upon your judgment in the event of any such contingency, and has no doubt that the instructions now given to you will suffice for your guidance in all matters of practical importance. If necessity arises they can hereafter be modified.

Enclosure 2 in No. 3.

From Resident in Kashmir to Secretary to the Government of India, Foreign Department. Jammu, 16 September, 1885.

Extract.

I have the honour to report my arrival here yesterday morning, my journey having been much delayed by the bad state of the road. At Vernag, late at night on the 12th, I received a telegram from Mian Pertab Singh, the heir-apparent, informing me of the death of his father, Maharaja Ranbir Singh, at 4.30 p.m. that day.

From conversation with Dr. Gopal Chander, His Highness's medical attendant, and others, I learn that, about the 29th August, the Maharaja, who was still weak from the effects of the fever from which he had suffered two months ago, had an attack of dysentery, which the medicines given him failed to relieve. He grew rapidly worse, but was under no apprehension of a fatal result till 24 hours before his death, when, finding that the forgiveness and return of a Brahmin whom he had exiled many years ago, and under whose curse he was persuaded by a seer he was labouring, failed to give him any relief, he made up his mind that his end was at hand. He then enjoined his sons to live in peace with one another, and told Pertab Singh, the eldest, to complete the good works he had begun. He also ordered that the contract for the sale of liquor in Jammu, recently sold for 40,000 rupees, should be cancelled. and the sale of spirits forbidden as heretofore; and further directed that the toll levied on persons crossing the Tavi river by ford should be discontinued, and that fire-wood and vegetables should for the future be allowed to enter Jammu free of duty. At four in the afternoon he became insensible, and according to Hindu custom was removed from his bed to the floor, where he breathed his last shortly afterwards.

The next day, the 13th, the Maharaja's body was burned on the bank of the Tavi river with great ceremony in the presence of a large multitude. The corpse is said to have been enveloped originally in forty coverings of shawl and other rich stuffs, interspersed with gold coins and jewels of great value placed there by the women of his harem; but I am told that all but thirteen of the wrappers were taken off by the attendant Brahmins before the body was placed on the pile. The whole of the Maharaja's wardrobe, jewels, riding horses, with seven elephants, and a number of cattle, besides a very large sum in cash, the whole estimated at from five to ten lakhs of rupees, were set aside for distribution among the Brahmins or to be sent to holy men in the neighbourhood. All business was suspended, and all shops ordered to be closed; but the next day this order was so far relaxed as to allow provision dealers to carry on their trade through one leaf of their shop doors. All Government employés, including the soldiers, shaved their heads and faces, excepting only Sikhs, Mussulmans, Brahmins, and those Rajputs connected with the Maharaja by marriage. White garments are worn by all, and ornaments of every description laid aside.

The period of mourning extends over thirteen days, and the Minister, Diwan Anant Ram, whom I saw immediately after my arrival, made some difficulty about my seeing the new Maharaja Pertab Singh before its expiry. The duties of religion, he declared, absolutely debarred the chief mourner from touching or even sitting on the same carpet with any other human being, till its close. Thus my reception in Durbar would be impossible. Under these circumstances it became impracticable to carry out to the letter the instructions conveyed in your letter of the 1st August, 1884, a formal installation of the new Maharaja on the *gaddi* being incompatible with the earliest possible announcement of his recognition, and the delivery of his Excellency's message as to the views and intentions of the British Government. It seemed to me, however, all-important that there should be no delay in these last, and I therefore told the Diwan that it was imperatively necessary that I should see the Maharaja at once. He replied that if I would consent to forego the usual ceremonies of reception, and had no objection to sitting on the floor (it being impossible to admit any article of furniture into the room with the Maharaja), His Highness would be glad to see me.

Accordingly, at five in the afternoon I went to the Palace, where I was received by Mian Amar Sing, the late Maharaja's youngest son. In an inner room opening from the Durbar Hall I found the Maharaja sitting on a small square carpet covered with white cotton. A similar one was placed by its side for my accommodation. After I was seated all present left the room, entirely contrary to custom (I have never had an interview with the late Maharaja without two at least of his Council being present). After a few sentences of compliment and condolence, I told Pertab Singh that I had a message for him from the Viceroy, to be delivered in the presence of his Council. He replied that he had not yet appointed a Council, to which I answered that it was to the members of late Maharaja's Council that I referred. He then called in Diwan Anant Ram alone. It was clear that an unpalatable communication was anticipated, and that it was hoped to confine it to as small a circle of hearers as possible. I therefore said that the message I had to deliver was not private and confidential though very important. On the contrary I had hoped to deliver it to His Highness in Durbar, but this being impossible I begged that he would call in at least Babu Nilambar and Diwan Gobind Sahai, who I knew were waiting outside. On this Pertab Singh ordered them to come in. On their seating themselves I told His Highness that His Excellency the Viceroy had ordered me in the first place to lose no time in announcing that His Excellency is pleased to recognise his succession to the Chiefship. This was received with expressions of gratitude and loyalty, the Maharaja rising and bowing his thanks. I then gave him the message contained in your letter, translating it sentence by sentence into Hindustani, only using the words "Kashmir and Jammu" instead of "Kashmir" only, as it might have been asserted afterwards that the message referred to Kashmir only, and not to the whole State.

The first part of the message referring to the introduction of reforms was received without any mark of surprise by my auditors, but the announcement of the immediate appointment of a Resident was evidently an unexpected blow.

I then took leave of the Maharaja. In the evening Babu Nilambar called on me with reference to another subject, and asked that I would explain, for the Maharaja's information, what was meant by the 'assistance of a Resident'. Did it imply that the Resident would take an active part in the administration of the country? I told him that I could not undertake to define the exact duties of a Resident, but that he would certainly leave all the active work of administration to the Durbar, while claiming the right to be made acquainted, should he require it, with all its details. He would give advice if asked for, and on any point he thought proper unasked; and in this latter case would expect his advice to be followed.

To-day Babu Nilambar called on me again, accompanied by Diwan Anant Ram. They brought a message from the Maharaja, begging me to use my influence to obtain for him a short delay before the appointment of a Resident, in order that he might get the credit for the reforms he had long made up his mind to introduce if ever he got the opportunity. It is unnecessary to detail the long conversation that ensued. Babu Nilambar finally acknowledged that the main objection was to the name 'Resident'. To this I replied that at the present juncture, putting aside other arguments, the name was all-important. The Maharaja and his councillors appeared to me to underrate vastly the difficulty of the task before them. It was one thing to order reforms and another to carry them out. In remedying the abuses which were ruining the country, they would have opposed to them the entire army of employés, high and low, who had been fattening on the land for years. The public appointment of a Resident would show these officials that there was something beyond caprice or the zeal of a new ruler in the reforms initiated at Jammu, and they would soon recognise that they must be carried out. At the same time the people at large would welcome the appointment of a Resident as an assurance of substantial reforms to come. Under these circumstances, while anxious to do all in my power to meet the Maharaja's wishes, I regretted that I could not recommend to his Excellency any delay in the formal appointment of a Resident.

The state of affairs seems to be somewhat as follows:—The death of Wazir Punnu (who fell down dead in Durbar on the 6th instant) was a stroke of extraordinary good fortune for the opposite party, represented by Diwan Anant Ram and Babu Nilambar. It not only removed their most powerful adversary, and the man who had the greatest influence with the present as with the late Maharaja, but it also keeps the country quiet without any effort on their part. The name of Punnu was a bye-word and a reproach among the people, and all the tyranny and oppression from which they suffered was invariably laid to his door, not always with justice. Had he survived his old master, he would have been the leading spirit in the Councils of the new Chief, and the people, hopeless of improvement, would probably have made rebellious demonstrations, which, with an army eighteen months in arrears of pay, would not have been easy to suppress. But Punnu died six days before Pertab Singh succeeded to the Chiefship, and the people, overjoyed at their deliverance from the man whom they believed their sole tyrant, are probably indifferent to the change of rulers, and will remain quite in confident anticipation of early relief from their burdens.

Another fortunate circumstance for the new Chief is the general prosperity of the country, as far as it can be prosperous under such a Government. The late spring rains caused some loss in the low country and the outer hills, as did the summer floods in Kashmir, but the agricultural out-turn for the last year has everywhere been exceptionally high, and the prospects of the crops now in the ground are excellent. Commerce is shown by the Punjab trade reports to be steadily improving in spite of the vexatious restrictions placed on it. Thus, as far as the country itself is concerned, Maharaja Pertab Singh and his councillors have everything in their favour. At present he is looking for advice to Babu Nilambar and Diwan Anant Ram. The first is clever and well-intentioned, but without practical experience of administration and deficient in force of character. The Diwan is perhaps well meaning, but his bringing up inclines him to lean to the old way of managing the country, and he is weak and cunning. They are, I fear, wholly unable to cope with the difficulties which will meet them in improving the administration, should they make any real effort to do so. Certain simple reforms, such as the abolition of obnoxious imposts and export dues and the more regular payment of officials, they may effect, but it will, I fear, be hopeless to look for any serious improvement in the administration generally, without constant and heavy pressure, and material interference in details.

A probable early source of trouble will be the influence possessed over the new Maharaja by his personal followers. These, who are mostly men of the lowest class, are already beginning to assert themselves, and to offer to help their friends to lucrative employment. It can hardly be long before they and the party of Nilambar and Anant Ram come into conflict. The latter will not have the courage to lean on the Resident, and govern as Salar Jang did in Hyderabad in spite of the Chief, but will try to trim with the usual consequences. On these points I will write more fully as the situation develops itself. For the present I have only pointed out to Anant Ram and Nilambar the urgent necessity for paying the troops, and for relieving the export trade of the country from its burdens. They will not, or cannot, give me any information of the actual state of the finances, except that the public treasury is practically empty. I have every reason to believe, however, that the late Maharaja regularly diverted the revenue of certain districts to his private chest. Some of this was devoted to religious purposes, but popular report has it that he has left large sums hoarded in obscure forts in different parts of the country. It is also said that he solemnly enjoined that this money should never be used to meet the current expenditure of the State, and no doubt, if it exists, every effort will be made to keep it intact, or at all events to spend it on no useful object. The annual customs contract expires in the course of a month or two, and this will be a favourable opportunity for a revision of the tariff, which should entirely free the woollen and metal trades of Kashmir from the heavy export duties to which they are now subject. This will give an impulse to production in Srinagar, which should tide the artisan class over the winter, of which the prospects are exceptionally bad owing to the final collapse of the shawl trade in Europe, and the paucity of visitors in the valley this year.

The Maharaja ends his mourning on the 26th, when he will take his seat in the Durbar. This will be the proper opportunity for the delivery of the *kharita* from his Excellency the Viceroy, of which a copy was enclosed with your letter of the 1st August, 1884.

KHARITA, dated Simla, the 14th September 1885, referred to in last paragraph of above Enclosure.

From His Excellency the VICEROY AND GOVERNOR-GENERAL OF INDIA to the MAHARAJA OF JAMMU AND KASHMIR.

I have received with deep regret the news of the death of your father, Maharaja Ranbir Sing: and I wish to assure you without delay of my most sincere sympathy.

Maharaja Ranbir Sing rendered valuable service to the British Government. I feel that his loss is the loss of a friend; and I wish that it had not fallen to me, during the period of my Viceroyalty, to consider the measures rendered necessary by this unfortunate event.

It is now my duty to inform you, on behalf of the Queen-Empress of India, that I recognise and confirm your succession to the Chiefship of Jammu and Kashmir. I trust that Your Highness's life may be long and prosperous; and that, in all difficulties, of whatsoever kind, you will rely with confidence upon the good-will of the British Government, which will never fail you so long as you are loyal to the Crown and earnest in the desire to rule your State with justice and moderation.

Your Highness has before you a difficult task. During the illness of your father the administration of the State became seriously disorganised, and it will be necessary for you to introduce many reforms. But my Agent, Sir Oliver St. John, will remain with you and help you to the utmost of his ability; and I feel confident that with his aid all your difficulties will be successfully met and overcome. I request your Highness to refer to him for a more detailed explanation of my views regarding the future administration of the Kashmir State; and I hope that your Highness will not fail to consult him freely at all times, and to be guided by his advice in carrying those views into execution.

Enclosure 3 in No. 3.

From MIAN PERTAB SINGH to His Excellency the VICEROY AND GOVERNOR-GENERAL OF INDIA.

Jammu, September 18, 1885.

YOUR MOST ESTEEMED EXCELLENCY,

I beg to offer my heartfelt thanks for your Excellency's kind message of condolence on the demise of my father, whose devoted loyalty to the British Crown won for him those assurances of personal friendship from your Excellency which he valued so highly, and of which he felt so very proud.

I have also to present my grateful thanks to your Excellency for the most welcome message conveyed to me on the 15th instant by Colonel Sir Oliver St. John, the officer on Special Duty in Kashmir, that your Excellency has been pleased to recognise my succession to the *gaddi* of this State, and I hope by the blessing of God to let your Excellency have the satisfaction of learning before long that I am as fully alive to the undoubted and immense importance of conscientiously discharging my duties towards my subjects by doing all in my power to secure their best happiness, as I am awake to the supremely important duty of giving renewed proofs of loyalty to the British Government by following in the footsteps of my father and grandfather.

I do not hesitate to admit that the existing state of affairs in Kashmir and Jammu urgently requires immediate introduction of substantial reforms into the administration of the country, and now that I have power commensurate with my responsibilities, I beg to assure your Excellency that nothing shall be spared on my part, and no time will be lost to prove beyond any possibility of doubt that it is my ambition to succeed in making my country a model of a well-governed State in alliance with the Government of India.

It has, however, pained me extremely to learn that exactly at the time when I have made up my mind to deserve and win your Excellency's approbation and encouragement by proving myself equal to the onerous and responsible duties of a good ruler, your Excellency has been thinking of changing the status of the British Officer on Special Duty in Kashmir to that of a Political Resident, and thus lowering me in the eyes of my subjects and in the estimation of the public. It is fully known to your Excellency that I have only just now acquired the power of showing to the world that, without any interference from any quarter or any, the smallest, diminution of long-enjoyed rights and dignity of this State, I am able and willing of my own accord to introduce and maintain such reforms as are calculated to entitle a ruler to the lasting gratitude of his subjects, and encouraging approbation of the paramount power as well as the public at large.

I may submit to your Excellency that I am fully aware of the wise and benevolent principles which guide the Supreme Government of India in its relations with the Native States, and I have not the least doubt that your Excellency will estimate me not by the splendour of my Court, nor by the pomp of my retinue, but by my conduct towards my subjects and by the only standard of good government combined with sincere and active loyalty.

I am confident, also, that I have only to convince your Excellency of the purity of my intentions, the earnestness of my purpose, and the firmness of my determination to govern well, to win your Excellency's sympathy with me in my desire to see the position of the Officer on Special Duty in Kashmir unaltered in his relations with this State.

I have sufficient confidence in the unbiassed justice of your Excellency's Government to hope that your Excellency will not form any unfavourable opinion of my abilities, intentions, and character, till the result of my administration for a sufficient length of time should justify a definite conclusion, and that your Excellency will see no necessity for altering the status of the Officer on Special Duty in Kashmir, and that, therefore, there will be no occasion now for my waiting personally on your Excellency at Simla, to give your Excellency the trouble of taking into serious consideration the sanads of Her Imperial Majesty's Government, securing to the Chiefship the full enjoyment of all the rights of my father and grandfather, and to submit to your Excellency the grounds on which I attach so much importance to the credit of earning the reputation of a just and benevolent ruler without any meddling[1] from any quarter, and of preserving intact in all its relations the integrity of the State as inherited from my father as well as of endeavouring to exalt its dignity in the estimation of the paramount power by doing exactly what the ruler of a large and important State should do.

Requesting your Excellency to excuse the trouble I have given you, I beg to subscribe myself, etc.

Enclosure 4 in No. 3.

From Resident in Kashmir, to Secretary to the Government of India, Foreign Department, dated Jammu, Sept. 27, 1885.

Extract.

In continuation of my letter of the 16th, I have the honour to report that Mian Pertab Singh, eldest son of the late Maharaja Ranbir Singh, formally took his seat in the Durbar on the afternoon of the 25th instant.

The previous day and the morning of the 25th had been occupied in distributing gifts to Brahmins by the river side, at the place where the late Maharaja's body was burnt. In addition to a large sum of money, these gifts consisted of 13 sets of everything that had been used by the Maharaja in this world, including horses, cows, and other domestic animals, but only one elephant. The total value is estimated by public opinion at two lakhs of rupees, but was probably less. The remainder of the Maharaja's

---

[1] The Persian version renders this word by "dastandazi".—J. A. C.

effects, with a sum of five lakhs from his private treasury, are retained to be added to the fund consecrated by him to the perpetual use of the temples, which fund last year already amounted to 15 lakhs.

On concluding the distribution of the gifts destined to facilitate his father's passage to Paradise, Maharaja Pertab Singh returned to the Palace, and performed the ceremony of "dastarbandi," *i.e.*, tying on of the turban, which marks the close of the period of acute grief.

At 5 p.m. I paid the Maharaja a formal visit to congratulate him on his accession. The *kharita* of his Excellency the Viceroy had already been delivered to him privately, to put an end to further useless argument on the question of the "Resident," and to avoid mention of the topic in Durbar, which would have been very distasteful to the Chief. Instead therefore of reading the *kharita*, I made a short speech in Urdu, of which a translation is attached (Enclosure A.).

Babu Nilambara Mukerji then read a manifesto in English, a translation[1] of which in Urdu was subsequently read by Diwan Anant Ram, followed by the proclamation alluded to.

The imposts and customs mitigated or abolished are as follows:—

(1.) The custom of "khodkasht." This is a system by which the State farms a part of the village lands itself. Advances are annually made to the persons employed for the purpose, but it is notorious they they embezzle the money, and cultivate the land with forced labour, and seed extorted from the villagers.

(2.) The custom of "leri". This is a system of paying sepoys and others by remission of rent, instead of in coin, and, for some reason not easily explained, is much disliked.

(3.) Each group of ten houses in Jammu territory will no longer, as before, be obliged to supply one Sepoy or other Government servant; forcible enlistment generally is abolished; and the rule of obliging families to provide substitutes for deserters is done away with.

(4.) The customs duty on rice and other provisions brought into Srinagar for sale is reduced from two annas in the rupee to half an anna, in other words from 12½ to 3⅛ per cent.

To understand the severity of this tax it must be explained that Government itself is the principal grain dealer, and fixes a permanent rate at which grain is sold. Thus the rate for unhusked rice is Rs. 1-4 (English) per kharwar, equivalent to about 10 annas a man. If a Zemindar sends rice to market, he can ask no more for it than 10 annas a man, and has in addition to pay the customs contractor 1¼ anna before he can offer it for sale. Under these conditions it is clear that the remission of three-fourths of this tax will benefit the producer, and not the consumer, who will pay the same price for his rice as before.

---

[1] Enclosure B.

(5.) The next impost remitted is also in favour of the Zemindar. Every large village community in Kashmir comprises a "Zillahdah," or "Harkara," whose business it is to report the misdeeds of his fellows. The Durbar affect to look on these officials as rural police; but as they are occasionally women, and have no powers beyond reporting, spies would be a better name for them. They are paid by a cess of 1½ per cent. on the gross produce of the land. Some years ago it occurred to Wazir Punnu that the Zillahdars were making too much money, and he therefore made their chief, the Harkara-Bashi (head-bringer of news) pay an annual sum to the treasury. This has been raised till it now amounts to 60,000 Chilki rupees (37,500 English), a great deal more than the estimated total value of the cess from which it is supposed to be paid. This most obnoxious impost is now abolished, but the Zillahdars are warned that they must continue to send in reports, and that if found extorting anything beyond the legitimate 1½ per cent. they will be punished.

(6.) The tax on the sale of horses in Kashmir, called "Zar-i-nakas", which at one time amounted to 50 per cent. of the purchase money, is abolished.

(7.) The tax on "Ekhas" plying for hire to Sialkot, which amounted to Rs. 1-11 on a total of Rs. 2-10, is abolished, and some other minor dues are remitted.

On the whole the above consititute a valuable boon to the people, especially to the cultivating classes of Jammu, whose main grievances are now removed. Sensible relief is also given to the Kashmir peasant; but the artizan of the towns, whose needs are greater, gets nothing but a slight possible reduction in the price of fruit and vegetables.

Yesterday afternoon I had a private interview with the Maharaja, at which only Diwan Anant Ram and Babu Nilambara Mukerji were present. According to my instructions I asked him to let me know what reforms he proposed to initiate, and to what persons he proposed to entrust their execution. As regards reforms he would only refer me to the manifesto (Enclosure B), repeatedly declaring with reference to both reforms and ministers that he required time to reflect. At last he said that he entrusted Babu Nilambara with all business connected with finance, while Diwan Anant Ram would continue as before to conduct foreign affairs, which he defined to be those of Ladak and Leh, and correspondence with myself. I told the Maharaja that I was going back to Kashmir for the present, but that I should return before long, and hoped that by that time he would have matured his schemes for reform. I could not, however, leave without doing my utmost to impress on him the imperative necessity of relieving the manufacturing classes of Kashmir from the present burdens on trade. I then tried to explain the question to him, but the only answer to be obtained was that he would think it over. I should here remark that I had previously discussed the question with Babu Nilambara, who tried to argue that the Government of India should do something in return for concessions on this point. Of course I replied that our only object was to benefit the Kashmir Government and the people, who are the only sufferers from the insane policy of imposing crushing duties on their own manufactures. I fear that much pressure will be required to bring about this most essential reform.

As mentioned in my former letter, Maharaja Ranbir Singh is said to have left considerable private wealth. Babu Nilambara tells me that this is certain, but that neither he nor anyone outside the household have any idea of the amount. The public treasury, or rather treasuries, for there are many in Jammu itself, are empty, but money has been produced from the Palace (2¾ lakhs) to pay the troops up to the end of the last Hindu year, for which they had as yet received nothing. This leaves them only five months in arrear. The troops in Kashmir have already been paid.

My impression as regards the new Maharaja is that, though entirely wanting in the quick wit of his father, he has inherited a full share of his obstinacy and cunning. He will consent to certain surface reforms, but on the cardinal points of delegating real power to his ministers, freeing trade, improving communications, and making a proper land settlement, he will, I fear, offer as much opposition as he dares.

Babu Nilambara and Diwan Anant Ram, freed from the fear of Wazir Punnu, seem to think themselves strong enough to go on alone without the support of a Resident, which they formerly declared to be essentially necessary. They will soon find themselves mistaken, but in the meantime had better be left to themselves. On this account I am glad to return to Kashmir, for which I start to-morrow, inspecting the cart-road *en route*. On this work, the completion of which is an essential preliminary to the greatest of the reforms required in Kashmir, a proper land revenue settlement, I will submit a full report at the earliest opportunity. I will also, while in Kashmir, ascertain the exact burdens now imposed on the export trade which are constantly varying.

I have seen with regret that His Highness keeps his younger brothers, Ram Singh and Amar Singh, and his cousin, Raja Moti Singh, of Poonal, at a distance. I have let him know that I think this a mistake, and have exchanged visits with them for the first time. During the late Maharaja's reign overtures to this effect met with no response.

Enclosure A.

Your Highness! I beg to offer you my congratulations on your accession to the place occupied by your father and grandfather, whose loyalty and devotion to the British Crown you will, I feel sure, do your utmost to emulate.

No Chief in India has ever succeeded to the *gaddi* with more opportunities for doing good. The State of Jammu and Kashmir has fallen behind the majority of the States of India in that progress which is necessary to the welfare of the people and the good name of their rulers.

It is your Highness' good fortune to have it in your power to remedy these shortcomings; and, though the task will be a difficult one, I feel assured that you will address all your energies to it. The Government of India will take the warmest interests in your efforts to improve the administration of your State and the condition of your subjects of every class; and the eyes of all enlightened persons in India will be fixed on you to see how you perform the duties for which you are now responsible.

It is my earnest hope to be able before long to congratulate you on ruling over a country foremost in India for good government and happy subjects as it is for loyalty and devotion. May your Highness' reign be long and prosperous, and may your name be handed down to posterity as the Nowshirwan of Jammu and Kashmir.

ENCLOSURE B.

SIR OLIVER ST. JOHN, SARDARS, AND GENTLEMEN,

My hearty and cordial thanks are due to his Excellency the Viceroy, and his worthy representative and my sincere friend, Sir Oliver St. John, for the *kharita*, recognising my succession to the Chiefship of this large and important State, and I take this fitting opportunity to declare publicly, that of the many arduous and responsible duties which I shall have to perform as the ruler of this State, the foremost under all circumstances will be the duty of following in the footsteps of my illustrious grandfather and his lamented Highness, in giving substantial proofs of unswerving and devoted loyalty to Her Imperial Majesty's Government, and, when the necessity will arise, of placing all the resources of my country at the disposal of his Excellency the Viceroy, and of personally joining the British army with the whole of my military force.

2. Next in importance to my obligations to the paramount power, but next to those only, will be the duty of governing my country with justice and moderation. The responsibilities which I am going to undertake will be high and heavy indeed, but I believe God will grant me firmness and strength enough to discharge them with credit to the family of my renowned ancestors, and benefit to the lakhs of subjects, whom it has pleased Providence to place under my care.

3. I have before me the difficult task of introducing substantial reforms in the administration of the country, but I believe I have only to look the difficulties boldly in the face and show a determined front, to achieve complete success and earn the reputation of a just and good ruler. Armed with purity of intentions and firmness of purpose, I may reasonably entertain the hope of being able to clear

the administrative agency of all corruption and incompetency, and impart to it the maximum of honesty and efficiency. I now warn my officials of all ranks that I have fully made up my mind to put down corruption and intrigue wherever they may be found, and I hope they will do all in their power to help me in making my administration a blessing and a source of unmixed good to my people.

4. I know that the paramount power as well as the public will watch with interest the progress and development of my measures of reform, and I am fully alive to the fact that they will estimate me not by the pomp and splendour of my court and retinue, but by the amount of happiness that I may secure to my subjects.

5. I need not trouble you now with minute details of what I intend to do, but I think I can declare without committing myself to any particular measure the policy and the general principles that will guide me in the conduct of my affairs. I shall adopt such measures only as are calculated to secure to my subjects their greatest good and the fullest enjoyment of their rights and privileges, and shall conduct my administration so that the tiller of the soil will enjoy a fair share of the produce of his labour, and the manufacturer the fruit of his skill and industry, that every facility will be given to commerce by improving the means of communication and removing unnecessary and vexatious restrictions, that every encouragement will be offered to get all the resources of the country properly developed, that adequate measures will be taken to give my subjects the benefits of sound and useful education, that ample provision will be made for the relief of the sick and the suffering, and that real merit and worth in my subjects will be recognised and fostered without any distinction of race or rank, creed or colour.

6. To commemorate this auspicious accession with a few acts pointing to the character of the policy I am going to follow, I do now abolish and reduce certain duties and taxes, and remove certain restrictions detailed in the proclamation[1] which my Diwan will read out to you.

No. 4.

The SECRETARY OF STATE FOR INDIA to the GOVERNMENT OF INDIA.

India Office, London, 27th November, 1885.

My Lord,

Para. 1. I have to acknowledge the receipt of the letter of your Excellency's Government, dated the 19th ultimo, reporting the measures which have been taken in reference to the State of Kashmir, in consequence of the death of Maharaja Ranbir Singh on the 12th September.

2. When in the spring of the year 1884 the death of the

[1] This proclamation was not received from India.

Maharaja was supposed to be imminent, Her Majesty's Government, in accordance with recommendations submitted by the Government of your Excellency's predecessor, decided that, upon the occurrence of that event, His Highness's eldest son should be recognised as successor to the undivided State, but that he should be required to introduce substantial reforms into the administration, and to entrust their execution to competent hands. The Government of India was also authorised, at its discretion, to substitute for an Officer on Special Duty in Kashmir a Resident with the same position and duties as Political Residents in other Native States in subordinate alliance with the British Government.

3. The papers now received from your Excellency's Government show that, the contingency contemplated in 1884 having arisen, the utmost consideration has been shown to the susceptibilities of Maharaja Pertab Singh in giving effect to the policy then determined upon. His Highness has been informed that, within reasonable limits, he will be allowed full scope and ample time to introduce the requisite administrative reforms, and will get the full credit for initiating them, while it has properly been pointed out to him, in reply to his objections to the proposed change in the status of the representative of the Government of India at his court, that an arrangement, which is considered suitable in the cases of the other great Princes and Chiefs of India, cannot be regarded either as derogatory to the dignity of the Kashmir State, or as indicating a desire on the part of the paramount power to interfere unnecessarily in its internal affairs.

4. I have to express my full approval of the proceedings of your Excellency's Government in this matter. Having regard to the condition of the country, to the character of the new ruler, and to the aspect of affairs beyond the frontier, in reference to which Kashmir occupies so important a position, I entertain no doubt as to the necessity for the measures now reported, which will, I trust, conduce to the material well-being of the people of the State, and tend to the better security of imperial interests.

I have, etc.,

(Signed) RANDOLPH S. CHURCHILL.

No. 5.

The GOVERNMENT OF INDIA to the SECRETARY OF STATE, dated Simla, August 18, 1888.

EXTRACT.

In March last Mr. Plowden thought the time had come when, for the sake of the State, it was essential to effect some reduction of the Maharaja's authority. There is no doubt some justification for Mr. Plowden's estimate of His Highness's capacity for rule; but, on the other hand, the condition of the State does not seem to demand at present such decided action as Mr. Plowden has suggested. We have, therefore, determined not to resort to measures which would have the effect, directly or indirectly, of taking the power out of the Maharaja's hands, and His Highness will now have another opportunity of showing under favourable circumstances whether he is capable of carrying on the administration.

Enclosure 1 in No. 5.

REPORT on the Affairs of the STATE of JUMMU and KASHMIR by the RESIDENT in KASHMIR, dated Sialkot, March 5, 1888.

EXTRACT.

I have had more opportunities of studying the Maharaja's character than perhaps any other officer in the country. My intercourse with him, official, private, and social, has been frequent; my relations with him have been always friendly; there has never been any friction or tension between us. He has never failed in personal courtesy to me, nor ever refused to see me at any time or on any occasion; therefore, I can fairly say that I am not actuated by any feelings of personal dislike towards His Highness.

I think, however, that the Government of India should be under no illusion as regards Maharaja Pertab Singh. From first to last I have failed to discover in him any sustained capacity for governing his country, or any genuine desire to ameliorate its condition, or to introduce those reforms which he has acknowledged to be necessary. More than two years have passed since his accession, but not only has he achieved nothing, but he has opposed beneficial measures proposed by others. The progress made has been in spite of him. I do not believe he is loyal, but fortunately he is powerless to carry his country with him. And I am convinced that the Government will commit a serious mistake if it believes that the reforms which the country urgently needs will ever be effected by Maharaja Pertab Singh. He will never, of his own free will, establish a capable and honest administration; nor, if any power of interference is left him, will he permit any administration appointed by the Government of India to carry on the business of the country. He will thwart and oppose it in every way he dares; the only restraint will be the limit of his powers and his fears; therefore I do most earnestly advise that the Maharaja be made plainly to understand that he has had his chance, and that he will not be allowed any longer to stand in the way. I would assign him a liberal income, to be placed at his absolute disposal, and treat him with full honour as titular Chief; but I would exclude him from all real power. He may reign, but not govern. A great danger with the Maharaja is that his notorious weakness of character and purpose render him an easy tool in the hands of an unscrupulous adviser, and therefore it is essential that he should be controlled by some agency upon which the Government of India can place confidence. I consider that a reduction of the Maharaja's authority on these lines is an essential condition precedent to all other necessary measures.

Next, as to the form of Goverment. One plan is to appoint Raja Amar Singh Prime Minister, on condition of his undertaking to carry out in all respects the policy of the Government of India. He has not got sufficient experience or solidity of character to execute a task of this magnitude without the aid of a resolute and experienced adviser, and it would be necessary to constitute some such office as "Secretary to Government," and to nominate to it a suitable British Officer—Native or European. I have great doubts whether Raja Amar Singh can be trusted, and, unless he has a strong officer at his elbow to keep him straight, I do not think it would be safe to employ him. He has never forgotten his father's intentions on his behalf, and the object he is working for is to become Maharaja of Kashmir. Once he gets power into his own hands, he will use it without scruple to attain this end. At present the Maharaja is friendly to Raja Amar Singh, because he wishes to break the bond which unites the two younger brothers and Diwan Lachman Das, but there is no genuine affection or confidence between them; and the well-known fact that the late Maharaja would have liked to supersede Pertab Singh in favour of his youngest brother is a special cause of jealousy. And I should expect that, after a short time, all the influence which the Maharaja possesses, especially Zenana influence, would be brought to bear against Amar Singh. Another probable result of his elevation would be a feud between him and his brother Ram Singh, thereby raising against him another hostile party.

Another plan is to bring in a Prime Minister from elsewhere. There is no one in the Maharaja's employ fit for the post, and the selection would need particular care. The situation is this: no Native could administer the affairs of Jammu and Kashmir unless he is not only of exceptionally strong character but also exceptionally honest; and, in any case, he would require besides the full support of the Government of India. If a weak man is chosen he will succumb to local intrigue, notwithstanding all the support which the Government may give him; and, if he is not honest, he will yield to the temptations with which the place abounds, and go with the swim. But, if a Native Minister is brought in from outside, I recommend precautionary measures being adopted with the young Rajas. I should order each of them to take up his residence in his own jigar, and so occupy the same position as Raja Moti Singh, of Punch. It is not right that these young men should be given large jigars which they never visit. It ought to be a condition of the grant that they reside on their property and be personally responsible for its administration. They might pay yearly visits to Jummu just as Moti Singh does. Another good result of this measure would be to lay the foundation of a class of Sardars such as exist in the Rajput States. As long as Raja Ram Singh continues to command the State Army there is no hope of any serious re-organisation; and, if Raja Amar Singh were to remain at Jammu, he would not leave a stone unturned to render the Prime Minister's position untenable.

A third plan is to continue the existing Council, making the

Resident its temporary head, and strengthening it by the addition of two selected Natives. An administration so constituted would probably be strong enough to introduce all needful reforms, and to set the country in order. Three years would suffice to set things straight, and the Resident might then withdraw from the headship of the Council, and an administration be established on ordinary Native lines.

I believe that, sooner or later, the Government will have to choose one or other of these three plans or some modification of them. But, whatever plan is adopted, there is one measure which must under any circumstances be prescribed. This is, first, the immediate removal of the band of incompetent, corrupt, and mischievous men who are at the bottom of most of the intrigues by which this unfortunate State is torn; and, secondly, the appointment of an adequate number of trained native officials on reasonable salaries who can be trusted to carry out the orders given to them. Until the entire Kashmir establishment has been recast, and honest and competent servants substituted for the fraudulent and incapable men now employed, no reforms can be carried out, nor can any mere alteration of the form of Government be of any use.

I will endeavour to anticipate an objection which I foresee is likely to be raised. The action suggested in this report brings forward the question of the amount of interference in the affairs of a Native State which may be rightfully and expediently exercised by the paramount Power. It is the settled purpose of the British Government to avoid unnecessary and improper interference in the affairs of Native States. And the basis of this policy is respect for the rights of others, because our treaties with the principal Native States are founded upon their general independence in internal affairs. But, notwithstanding these treaties, cases must from time to time occur in which the Government of India as paramount power is forced to interfere in a radical manner, and it does habitually interfere in a lesser degree. A reluctant interference which circumstances have rendered unavoidable does not, however, infringe the general principle of non-intervention. The question is whether in the case of Kashmir an instance of unavoidable interference has arisen. I submit it has. First, because mis-government producing evil consequences to the people has admittedly existed for many years, and, though a wide margin of time and opportunity has been allowed, there seems no hope whatever that the State, unaided, will be able to settle its own affairs. Secondly, the condition of Kashmir affects countries on its northern border beyond its limits, and thus becomes an injurious and disturbing element in the Imperial scheme of frontier defence. I advocate interference only so far as is indispensable for the accomplishment of the object aimed at, but I would interfere decidedly and effectually for this purpose. A strict adherence to the principle of non-interference implies that Government must also tolerate the local disorder and mal-administration which are bound to ensue.

Enclosure 2 in No. 5.

From RESIDENT IN KASHMIR to the SECRETARY TO THE GOVERNMENT OF INDIA, Foreign Department, dated April 21, 1888.

EXTRACT.

I have the honour to enclose a kharita from His Highness the Maharaja to the address of His Excellency the Viceroy. I am not aware of the contents of the kharita, but I understand that it gives cover to a scheme for the reorganisation of the State Council.

I should be glad to be informed what is the rule in other native States in respect to the transmission of kharitas, *i.e.*, whether or not the Resident is entitled to be furnished with a copy of the kharita or to be informed of its contents. The precedents in this State appear to show that the Resident is not informed in the first instance, but that the Government of India furnishes him with a copy together with the reply. But so short a time has elapsed since a Resident was first appointed in Kashmir that it can hardly be said that any binding usage has yet been established.

In the present instance I have asked His Highness to give me a copy of the kharita not only because the Maharaja expressed his intention of informing me of his proposals and of availing himself of my assistance, but because that both under the instructions of August 1884 and under subsequent instructions the Resident is bound to offer his advice on all important matters, while on his part the Maharaja is required (kharita of 14th September, 1885) "to consult the Resident freely at all times and to be guided by his advice in carrying his views into execution".

KHARITA, dated Srinagar, the 13th April 1888.

From His Highness PERTAB SINGH, Maharaja of Jammu and Kashmir, to his Excellency the VICEROY AND GOVERNOR-GENERAL OF INDIA.

Your Excellency is already aware that circumstances obliged me to dismiss Diwan Lachman Das, Prime Minister and President of the Council. As I think that the Council which was formed with your kind advice should be continued, I have prepared a scheme for its reorganisation which I beg to forward herewith to your Excellency.

I beg to express the high consideration and esteem I entertain for your Excellency and to subscribe myself, etc.

JAMMU AND KASHMIR COUNCIL.

Constitution.

1. The Council shall consist of a President, a Vice-President, three Members, and a Secretary.
2. His Highness the Maharaja shall be the President.
3. His Highness shall appoint a Vice-President, Members, and a Secretary.
4. Three shall form a quorum.

5. The Vice-President, Members, and the Secretary may be removed and substituted by majority of votes of the Members of the Council, for reasons to be recorded.

6. The Council shall be a consultative one.

Appointment of Members.

7. Raja Amar Singh is hereby appointed Vice-President, and Raja Ram Singh and Babu Nilambar Mukerji, Members, with Diwan Janki Prasad, Member and Secretary.

8. The Members shall represent the following branches of administration:—

1. Military.—Raja Ram Singh.
2. Judicial and Foreign Department.—Raja Amar Singh.
3. Revenue.—Babu Nilambar Mukerji.
4. Miscellaneous.—Diwan Janki Prasad.

9. The Vice-President shall also be the Prime Minister with executive powers.

10. The Vice-President and Members shall take the following oath:—

> "I solemnly declare that in giving my opinion as a Member of Council, I shall keep in view the best interests of the State, and shall freely express my honest convictions, without fear or favour, and I shall not divulge any secrets of the State."

Business.

11. The Council shall sit three days in the week, authorised holidays excepted, and any extraordinary meeting shall be held, on the requisition of the Prime Minister.

12. It shall be the duty of the Council to legislate and hear and pass opinion on all subjects that may be brought forward by the Members.

13. The Council shall, on meeting, frame rules for its guidance, which may be removed or modified by it only.

14. All matters shall be decided on majority of votes.

15. Besides the matters which may be brought forward in the Council by the Members, the Prime Minister, who is the head of the Executive Government under His Highness, may refer to the Council for opinion all important questions affecting the administration in all its branches.

16. The respective opinions of the several Members shall be recorded and signed.

17. When a Member brings forward, or the Prime Minister refers, any special matter to the Council, it shall be the duty of the Secretary to furnish all the Members with a written statement of the subject-matter.

18. The office establishment shall be considered and settled by the Council or meeting.

Enclosure 3 in No. 5.

From the SECRETARY TO THE GOVERNMENT OF INDIA to the RESIDENT IN KASHMIR, dated Simla, July 25, 1888.

EXTRACT.

THE Government of India have decided to accept in principle the scheme which His Highness has put forward, and your own alternative proposals have for the present been set aside. In coming to this conclusion the Governor-General in Council has not overlooked the fact that the Maharaja's scheme is open to many objections, and that partly on account of His Highness's personal character and partly for other reasons, it is not unlikely to prove a failure. But before sanctioning any measures which would have the effect, directly or indirectly, of taking all power out of the Maharaja's hands, the Government of India have felt that it would be just and right to allow the Maharaja a further opportunity of showing whether he is competent to discharge the duties of a responsible ruler. If after full and fair trial it becomes evident that he is wholly incapable of conducting the administration of the State the proposals which you have submitted will be reconsidered.

In the meantime I am to ask you to afford the Maharaja every assistance in your power with regard to the reorganisation of his Council and all other matters upon which he may consult you. The Governor-General in Council does not desire you to press upon him your own views as to these matters. You should understand that the responsibility for the success or failure of the present experiment will rest upon the Maharaja; and your aim should be to meet his wishes in every possible manner, not refusing your advice when His Highness asks for it, but avoiding any course of action which might prevent him from feeling that the Government of India desire to allow him the fullest opportunity of proving his fitness. You should help His Highness as much as possible in doing this, but you should not insist upon the advantage of any measure which he disapproves, however desirable it may seem to be in his own interests.

You will notice that the Government of India have declined to permit the employment of Babu Nilambar Mukerji as member of council in charge of the revenue administration. If the Maharaja should raise the question of employing him in any other capacity, you may inform His Highness that the Government of India do not consider it desirable that the Babu should return to Kashmir. With reference to the question of principle whether the Maharaja is at liberty to employ Native British subjects without the consent of the British Government, you should give His Highness to understand that the interpretation of the treaty of 1846 with regard to this point is no longer open to discussion. The Government of India desire to give the Maharaja all possible assistance, and he will always find them willing to place at his disposal the services of competent British officials; but they must maintain their right to be consulted before any British subjects receive employment within the State.

The enclosed kharita points out to the Maharaja the urgent necessity for a thorough examination into the condition of the Kashmir finances. This is evidently a point of the greatest importance, and you should use your influence to bring it to the special notice of His Highness and his advisers.

The Governor-General in Council does not consider it necessary to give you more detailed instructions with regard to the course which you should pursue. He has no doubt that a consideration of this letter, and of the terms of the enclosed kharita, will suffice to show you the principles upon which he desires you to act, and he hopes that with the aid of judicious and sympathetic advice on your part the Maharaja may, before you leave Kashmir, have succeeded at least in laying the foundations of an efficient scheme of Government.

KHARITA, dated SIMLA, the 25th July, 1888, enclosed in above.

From His Excellency the VICEROY AND GOVERNOR-GENERAL OF INDIA to His Highness the MAHARAJA OF KASHMIR.

I HAVE received your Highness's letter of the 13th of April, informing me of the dismissal of Diwan Lachman Das, and forwarding, for my consideration, a scheme which you have prepared for the re-organization of your Council.

Your Highness's letter has received my most careful attention, and I have now to inform you of the conclusions at which I have arrived with regard to the very important questions which you have been good enough to refer to me.

In the first place, I cannot avoid informing your Highness that the news of the sudden removal of Diwan Lachman Das was received by me with some surprise. Your Highness appointed him to your council after consulting me, and I hoped that your Highness would, before making another change of Government, give me some previous intimation of your views. However, this point has already been brought to your notice by Mr. Plowden, and I do not now desire to dwell upon it any further.

With regard to your Highness's scheme for the future administration of Kashmir, I would ask you to consider the following observations.

Your Highness proposes that the administration should be conducted or assisted by a council consisting of a president, a vice-president, three other members, and a secretary. The presidency you would retain in your own hands. You would appoint your brother Raja Amar Singh to be vice-president, and you would also make him Prime Minister with executive powers. The other three members of the Council would be Raja Rama Singh, Babu Nilambar Mukerji, and Diwan Janki Prasad; and they would be charged respectively with the control of affairs in the millitary, revenue, and miscellaneous departments. The Prime Minister would have special charge of the judicial and foreign departments.

Diwan Janki Prasad would be secretary in addition to his other duties. It is proposed that the Council should be consultative.

It appears to me that a Government constituted in this manner is open to some criticism. In the first place, I am inclined to doubt whether it is altogether in accordance with your Highness's dignity to be president of the Council. Secondly, your Highness's brothers are still young, and have had little opportunity af acquiring practical experience in administrative work. Babu Nilambar Mukerji has no knowledge of revenue matters, and is altogether unfit to take charge of so important a department of the administration. Of Diwan Janki Prasad I know little, but I understand that he is not a man of marked character and ability. Under these circumstances your Highness's scheme does not appear to me to hold out any certain promise of success.

Nevertheless, I do not desire to raise any objection to the principle of the proposed arrangements. I regard your Highness as the responsible ruler of the State, and I wish to meet your views as far as possible, and to afford you every assistance in carrying them out. If, therefore, your Highness prefers to maintain a Council and to assume the presidency yourself, I am ready to assent to your views in this matter, and also with regard to the nomination of your brothers and Dewan Janki Prasad. On one point only I feel that in your Highness's interests I must ask you to modify your proposals. I cannot think that the appointment of Babu Nilambar Mukerji as revenue minister would be desirable. I am of opinion that for the charge of revenue affairs, your Highness should secure the services of some thoroughly competent official with practical experience of administration. I also think that at least one other official of similiar qualifications should be appointed to direct, either as member of Council or in some other capacity, the judicial and executive branches of your Government. If your Highness can name any Native officials in the British service who seem to me to possess the requisite qualifications I shall be glad to place them at your disposal. If your Highness cannot suggest any names I shall be ready and willing to make inquiries, and to supply you with the best men available either in the Punjab or elsewhere. I have learnt with pleasure that your Highness has already asked for the services of some four or five officers to be employed in the accounts and forest departments. But your Highness's government seems to require something more than the loan of a few subordinate officials. What is wanted is that you should associate with your principal officers two or three thoroughly trained and capable persons, who will be able to give your Highness effective aid in directing and controlling the main branches of the administration. I trust that your Highness will consider these suggestions and will take such steps as may have the effect of strengthening your government from an administrative point of view. I need hardly add that, with regard to this question and to all other questions of importance, Your Highness should freely consult the Resident, who will give you every assistance in his power.

In making these observations I do not overlook the fact that, since the appointment of the Council of which Diwan Lachman Das was a member, considerable progress has been made in the direction of reform; useful work has been done with regard to the revenue administration, and in the reorganization of the Public Works and Medical Departments. But much remains to be done, and it is because I am deeply conscious of the importance of the Kashmir State, and of the responsibilities of the British Government in regard to it, that I have so carefully examined the proposals which your Highness has put forward.

I would particularly urge upon your Highness's attention the necessity for a careful investigation into the condition of your Highness's finances, and of the executive and judicial services. Until these are placed upon a thoroughly sound footing it will be impossible to hope for any material increase in the prosperity of the State.

I desire to express the high consideration which I entertain for your Highness, and to subscribe myself your Highness's sincere friend.

(Signed) DUFFERIN,
Viceroy and Governor-General of India.

No. 6.

The SECRETARY of STATE to the GOVERNMENT of INDIA.

India Office, London, October 12, 1888.

MY LORD,

I HAVE perused with deep interest the papers regarding Kashmir affairs which accompanied your Excellency's letter of the 18th August, 1888. From them I learn that the instability of the several administrations to which Maharaja Pertab Singh had entrusted the management of the affairs of his State since his accession in 1885 has much retarded the execution of the various reforms which have been repeatedly pressed on the attention of the Maharaja, and that, after the abrupt dismissal of the President of the Council, Diwan Lachman Das, in March last, by the Maharaja, His Highness submitted for the consideration of your Excellency a scheme for the reconstitution of the State Council, in which the Maharaja proposed to assume the post of President.

2. Though this scheme of administration is open to many objections, partly on account of the Maharaja's personal character, and for other reasons, and is not unlikely to prove a failure, your Excellency's Government have determined to allow His Highness a further opportunity of showing whether he is competent to discharge the duties of a responsible ruler.

3. Judging from the reports of the Residents in Kashmir, I

can have little expectation myself that the experiment of a Council presided over by the Maharaja will be successful; but, on the other hand, the objections to any radical change in the government of the province at the present juncture are such that I am willing to sanction your proposal to give the Maharaja another occasion of proving whether His Highness possesses either the capacity or the will to introduce and carry into effect those administrative measures which are essential to the prosperity and security of the Kashmir State.

I have, &c.,
(Signed) CROSS.

No. 7.

The GOVERNMENT OF INDIA to the SECRETARY OF STATE FOR INDIA, dated Fort William, April 3, 1889.

EXTRACT.

In 1888 the condition of Kashmir was by no means satisfactory; and the Resident, Mr. Plowden, had come to the conclusion that so long as the present Maharaja was maintained in power there could be no hope of better things. He therefore urged the Government of India to interfere and exclude His Highness from all concern with the administration. There was much to support Mr. Plowden's view, and we were by no means confident as to the result of any further abstention from interference; but on the whole we decided that the Maharaja should have another opportunity of showing, under favourable circumstances, whether he was capable of ruling the State. He was accordingly continued in power; and Mr. Plowden, who soon afterwards left Kashmir on promotion, was succeeded by Colonel Parry Nisbet, C.I.E., a personal friend of the Maharaja, and an officer of large administrative experience. It was hoped that Colonel Nisbet might succeed in establishing a strong influence over His Highness's mind, in freeing him from the domination of certain unprincipled persons about him, who took advantage of his timidity and superstition, and in gradually bringing him to a proper sense of his position and its responsibilities.

This hope was disappointed, and, after four months in the Kashmir Residency, Colonel Nisbet has come to the same conclusion as his predecessor. The immediate cause which led him to re-submit the matter for our orders was the discovery of some letters, said to have been written by the Maharaja, which were of such a nature as to present his character and conduct in a very unfavourable light. We were not disposed to attach any excessive importance to these letters, because we had received a number of very similar documents a year before, and were not ignorant of the Maharaja's failings. But in this instance the discovery of the letters was immediately followed by a voluntary resignation of power on the part of the Maharaja; and, taking into consideration this and all the other circumstances of the case, we felt that the time had come when some measure of interference could be no longer deferred. We have, therefore, determined that the Maharaja's resignation shall be accepted, and that we should avail ourselves of the opportunity in order to effect a thorough re-organisation of the Kashmir Government.

The form in which our interference is to be exercised will be seen from the terms of our instructions to Colonel Nesbit. To sum these up in a few words, the administration of the State will be handed over to a Council, consisting of the Maharaja's brothers and certain selected officials in the British service. This Council will have full powers, subject to the condition that they will take no important step without consulting the Resident, and that they will act upon the Resident's advice whenever it may be offered. This is the arrangement established in Gwalior, where it is working well. The Maharaja will be excluded from all interference with public affairs, but will retain his rank and dignity as Chief of the State, and will receive from the State revenues an adequate, but not extravagant, allowance for the maintenance of his household and any other necessary expenditure.

These arrangements will not be exclusively based upon the Maharaja's edict of resignation, which was an attempt to save his dignity and secure better terms than he could otherwise expect. This edict contains some inconvenient stipulations, and it would be embarrassing to agree to it as it stands. We prefer to treat it as a confession of incapacity for the rule of the State, and to base our further proceedings upon general grounds.

Your Lordship will observe that our instructions to Colonel Nesbit deprecate any interference in the affairs of the State beyond what is necessary for the reform of the administration. We greatly regret the necessity for any interference at all. But we are now convinced that in the interests of the people of Kashmir, and of the ruling family itself, it is no longer right or possible to leave the affairs in the hands of the Maharaja; and we trust that Her Majesty's Government will concur in this opinion.

Enclosure 1 in No. 7.

From Colonel R. PARRY NISBET to Sir H. M. DURAND, dated Sialkot, February 27, 1889.

EXTRACT.

The day before yesterday I had placed in my hands such reliable evidence as I have said invariably to those who have talked to me, would alone satisfy me of the disloyalty or utter imbecility of the present Ruler of Jammu.

This consists of a batch of thirty-four letters, in the Maharaja's own handwriting, some of which are so compromising as to leave, I submit, no course open save his removal from the State, unless the alternative theory be accepted of his being a half-witted individual, irresponsible for his own acts.

Of their authenticity I have, myself, no doubt, and they are admitted to be in the Maharaja's own handwriting by his brother, Raja Amar Singh; besides, a mass of letters like this are not likely to be forgeries in the way one or two might be.

But, side by side with these treasonable letters in this packet, there are others in an utterly foolish strain, thereby confirming me in the conclusion I have unwillingly come to, that, though with lucid intervals of good sense and propriety, the Maharaja is utterly incapable of being left in charge of his own affairs. The gist of these other letters is that the Maharaja offers large sums of money to certain individuals on condition that they will murder, or cause to be removed, Plowden, the late Resident, his own two brothers, Ram Singh and Amar Singh, and one of the Maharanis, who, for some reason, is personally objectionable to him.

These acts are not those of a man in such possession of his intellect as would justify Government in leaving him in uncontrolled charge of the most important frontier State.

The conclusions the letters lead me to are confirmed by certain rather extraordinary acts of the Maharaja in appointing unworthy and incapable persons to important offices of the State, even since I took over charge, without consulting the proper counsellor, or, in fact, any one at all. The thing is the Maharaja is a timid and very superstitious man at the entire mercy of a set of unscrupulous scoundrels who take advantage of his fears and imbecility to plunder the State to any extent, and there appear to me weighty reasons for advising the practical setting aside of the Maharaja's authority.

It surely is politically dangerous to leave the actual administration of this great State in the hands of an individual who may play us false at any moment, without, perhaps, appreciating the disaster that would follow, and, I believe, any steps Government may take short of annexation will be right and necessary, and generally approved by the Princes and Chiefs of India.

Under the circumstances stated I think it is necessary for me to come to Calcutta at once on hearing from you, to talk the matter fully over with you, so that you may be in a position definitely to settle the future policy of Government towards the State.

Enclosure 2 in No. 7.

From the RESIDENT IN KASHMIR, Sialkot, to the FOREIGN SECRETARY, Calcutta.

TELEGRAM.

March 8, 1889.

I start to-morrow for Calcutta. I have been last two days at Jammu, and Maharaja has himself proposed what will, I think, solve the difficulty of the existing situation of affairs. He asked to be allowed to form a new Council of State, constituted of his two brothers, with Pandits Suraj Kaul and Bhag Ram, and an English officer selected by the Government of India, the Maharaja surrendering entire control of public affairs to such Council for five years.

Enclosure 3 in No. 7.

From Colonel R. PARRY NISBET to Sir H. M. DURAND.

Kashmir, March 13, 1889.

I send you the original edict (with translation) and the official letter handed to me by the Maharaja of Kashmir containing His Highness's application to be relieved of the management for a time of State affairs in order to redeem the past.

I trust this voluntary offer on his part may afford, with perhaps further conditions, an acceptable way out of no doubt a very acute difficulty.

As the Government of India have carefully refrained as long as was possible from any sort of interference in the direct management in the affairs of the Kashmir State, so I think now a direct appeal to do so cannot be ignored, and that there should be no hesitation in adopting the best and most complete measure likely to bring about the reforms necessary.

Sub-enclosure.

From RAJA AMAR SINGH, President of Council and Prime Minister to His Highness the Maharaja of Jammu and Kashmir, to Colonel R. PARRY NISBET, C.I.E,, Resident in Kashmir, Jammu.

March 8, 1889.

I HAVE the honour to submit, for information of yourself and the Government of India, the original Irshad of His Highness the Maharaja by which he abandons his direct management of the Jammu and Kashmir State for a term of five years, and desires that it may be performed by a Council of State consisting of his brothers, Raja Ram Singh and Raja Amar Singh, and three other members, one of whom to whom to be an English officer of special experience and qualifications selected by the Government, and other two members will be

Pandit Suraj Kaul and Pandit Bhag Ram.

2. I am directed to request that you will kindly furnish me with a certified copy of the Irshad, if you want to keep the original in your office.

3. I am further directed to request that you will move the Government of India for early nomination of an English officer to serve on the Council of State as proposed in the Irshad.

Sub-enclosure.

MY DEAR BROTHER RAJA AMAR SINGH,

In the interests of the 'State' and for better administration of the country, and with a view to remodel it, as near as possible on the English system, I hereby authorise a Council, the members of which, for period of five years, will conduct all the public affairs of the State as they think best. The members will be as follows:—

Raja Ram Singh and Raja Amar Singh,

An English member, specially selected by the Government of India on a salary Rs. 2,000 or 3,000 per month.

Rai Bahadur Suraj Kaul and Rai Bahadur Bhag Ram.

This Council will have full and sole powers in all the Public Departments of the State for a period of five years.

In the event of a vacancy occurring among the three last members during the prescribed period of five years, the Government of India will be asked to nominate a new member.

After the expiration of the said period of five years the Maharaja will have the power of re-organising the administration if he finds it necessary to do so.

This period of five years will count from the date of this edict.

The Council will not interfere in any way with the private affairs of the Maharaja.

The Maharaja will continue to draw his monthly allowance for his privy purse as hitherto, no change whatever being made.

The jagirs and other grants of immovable, movable property hitherto made by the Maharaja will hold good and the Council will not interfere.

All usual expenses connected with marriages and other family customs will be provided by the 'State'.

Of my two brothers I will myself appoint one as President of the Council.

During the said period of five years the Maharaja will not interfere and will have no voice in the administration of the public affairs of the State, but he will continue to enjoy the honorary rights and position of Maharaja.

The Council have no power to alter existing treaties without the previous approval of the Maharaja.

The Council will have no power to assign jagirs or immovable property of the State or to make new rules on such subjects without the consent of the Maharaja.

Signed and sealed by His Highness the Maharaja on 27th Bhagan, 1945=8th March, 1889.

Seal of the 'State'.

Enclosure 4 in No. 7.

INSTRUCTIONS from GOVERNMENT of INDIA to RESIDENT in KASHMIR, dated April 1, 1889.

EXTRACT.

I am to request you to inform the Maharaja that for a time at least he will be expected to refrain from all interference in the administration. He will retain his rank and dignity as Chief of the State; but full powers of government will be vested in a Council consisting of the Maharaja's brothers and three or four officials selected by the Government of India. It is not thought desirable that one of these officials should be an Englishman. The President of the Council will be Raja Amar Singh. Besides retaining his rank and dignity the Maharaja will receive from the revenues of the State an annual sum sufficient to maintain his household in due comfort, and to defray any expenditure which may rightly devolve upon him; but he will have no power of alienating the State revenues, and the sum placed at his disposal, though adequate, must not be extravagantly large.

I am further to request you to make the Maharaja and the Members of Council thoroughly understand that, although the Council will have full powers of administration, they will be expected to exercise those powers under the guidance of the Resident. They will take no steps of importance without consulting him, and they will follow his advice whenever it may be offered.

In communicating to the Maharaja and others concerned the decision of the Government of India, you should be careful to avoid basing that decision exclusively either upon the letters or upon the Maharaja's resignation. The letters are repudiated by the Maharaja, and as I have said before they are not of a very novel character; while on the other hand the Government of India are by no means prepared to make the present settlement a matter of compact with the Maharaja, and to accept all the conditions laid down by his edict of the 8th March, for example the five years' limit. You should therefore base the decision of the Government upon a full consideration of all the circumstances, the letters and the Maharaja's wish to retire from the control of affairs being considered amongst other things, but only as portions of a difficult and complicated case, which it has been necessary to settle on broader grounds of general policy.

You should now proceed to work out fresh proposals upon the lines I have indicated. It will be necessary in the first place to define exactly the future position of the Maharaja, the amount of his annual allowance, the expenses which it is intended to cover, the extent of his powers over his own household, and generally the conditions which he will have to conform. It will also be necessary to show the proposed constitution of the Council, the duties falling upon each of its members, and the method of transacting business. You should also ascertain the requirements of the State in the manner of subordinate officials, and should submit for the approval of the Government your view as to the steps to be taken for re-organising the administrative services. In forming those views you should remember that the Government of India has no desire to turn Kashmir into the semblance of a British district, or to place all administrative posts in the hands of Punjabi foreigners. The want of good native officials makes it necessary to import some trained men from the outside, but the number so imported should be kept as low as possible, and your object should be to form with their help a class of Kashmiri officials who will be capable hereafter of administering the State themselves. It is altogether against the wishes and policy of the Government to interfere unnecessarily with the customs and traditions of a Native State, or to force upon it the precise methods of administration obtaining in British territory. Administrative efficiency is not the only object to be attained in such cases, nor, indeed, the principal object.

The Government of India will be glad to know, as soon as possible, the true facts as to the financial position of Kashmir. A separate report should be submitted on this point, and in submitting it you should inquire into the question of the jagirs and allowances given by the Maharaja, and should make proposals as to the manner in which such grants should be treated.

Finally, I am to request that the new arrangements may be introduced as quietly as possible. There should be no ceremonial, and nothing that can be regarded as the public degradation of the Maharaja, who should simply retire from the conduct of affairs. It is desirable that the change should attract no more attention than necessary, and above all, that it should not be regarded as the punishment of a great native Chief for proved disloyalty to the Crown. Rumours to the effect that the Maharaja has been convicted of treasonable practices have already been in circulation, and such rumours do harm both in India and elsewhere.

No. 8.

The SECRETARY OF STATE FOR INDIA to the GOVERNMENT OF INDIA.

MY LORD MARQUIS, India Office, London, May 24, 1889.

From the papers transmitted with your Excellency's letter, dated 3rd April, 1889, I learn that the further opportunity which was given to His Highness the Maharaja of Kashmir of proving whether he was capable of conducting the administration of his State has once more established his unfitness for the position of ruler.

2. You have, therefore, decided to accept the Maharaja's voluntary resignation, and to effect a thorough re-organisation of the Kashmir Government.

3. In accordance with this determination, the administration will be entrusted to a Council, consisting of the Maharaja's brothers and certain selected Native officials in the British service. This Council will have full powers, subject to the condition that they will take no important step without consulting the Resident, and that they will act upon the Resident's advice whenever it may be offered. The Maharaja will be excluded from all interference with public affairs, but will retain his rank and dignity as Chief of the State, and will receive from the State revenues an adequate, but not extravagant, allowance for the maintenance of his household and any other necessary expenditure.

4. Her Majesty's Government fully approve your proceedings, and share your conviction that in the interests of the people of Kashmir, and of the ruling family itself, it has become impossible to leave the control of affairs in the hands of the Maharaja.

I have, &c.,

(Signed) CROSS.

From the GOVERNMENT OF INDIA to the SECRETARY OF STATE FOR INDIA, dated Simla, July 26, 1889.

EXTRACT.

IN continuation of our despatch of the 3rd April, and in further reference to the condition of affairs in Kashmir, we have the honour to enclose copies of the papers noted in the margin.

Demi-official letter from Colonel Nisbet, dated the 19th April, 1889, and enclosure.
From His Highness the Maharaja of Kashmir, dated the 14th May, 1889.
To His Highness the Maharaja of Kashmir, dated the 28th June, 1889.
Report of the Settlement Operations in Kashmir and Jammu by Mr. A. Wingate, C.I.E.

We take this opportunity of expressing the satisfaction which it has given to us to be made aware that the course which has been adopted in dealing with this question has met with your Lordship's approval. The events which have taken place since our decision was arrived at have not led us to modify in any way the opinions which we formed at the time. The Maharaja's allegation that the edict of the 8th March last was signed by him under compulsion is, we believe, entirely unjustified by the facts of the case. The circumstances under which His Highness requested that he might be relieved from active participation in the duties of government are set forth in detail in paragraph 8 of the Viceroy's letter of the 28th June, 1889.

We have, on the other hand, no doubt that His Highness's action in requesting the permission of the Resident to retire from the management of public affairs for a term of years, may have been due to fear of the consequences which he, at that time, apprehended from the discovery of the correspondence, of which copies have been already laid before your Lordship.

Now that His Highness has ascertained that the action of the Government of India has been justified upon other grounds, and that the correspondence in question has been treated with comparative indifference, it is quite possible that His Highness regrets the somewhat precipitate proposal which he made to the Resident. The fact that he should have preferred such a request, and immediately receded from it, affords, in our opinion, further proof of the slight amount of reliance which can be placed upon his character as a ruler.

We are glad to report that we are receiving from the Resident satisfactory accounts of the progress which is being made by the new Council in improving the administration of the State. A large portion of the arrears due to the army have already been paid. We need scarcely dwell on the danger which was likely to arise to the public safety from the existence of a large and ill-disciplined military force, which had, for some months past, been allowed to remain without the pay which was due to it.

We learn that, in the same way, heavy arrears of salaries have been made good in all the departments, a condition indispensable to honest and diligent service of a kind which for many years past has, we fear, been too rarely rendered by Kashmir officials. Public works, the progress of which was seriously threatened owing to want of funds, are being actively pushed on. Much unnecessary expenditure has been curtailed, and the Resident expresses his belief that if the next harvest should prove to be a good one, and suitable measures be taken for the recovery of the land revenue, the close of the year will see the establishment of a financial equilibrium in the accounts of the State.

It is in our opinion scarcely possible to overrate the importance of the results likely to be produced by a period of upright and efficient administration in a country circumstanced as is Kashmir, and with its antecedents. It has been the painful duty of the Government of India from time to time to call the attention of the Secretary of State to the chronic misgovernment to which the people of Kashmir have been subjected by the present Maharaja and his predecessors. It had become evident before the accession of the present Maharaja that the only hope for the State lay in a vigorous attempt to remove the most flagrant of the abuses under which, in spite of the great natural resources of the country, its population had steadily dwindled, and its people had become impoverished to the point of chronic scarcity. At the time when the death of the late Maharaja was imminent, the Government of India entertained the gravest doubts whether the present Maharaja, then heir-apparent to the throne, was fit to succeed to it.

The circumstances under which it was determined to give him an opportunity of proving his fitness are within your Lordship's knowledge. Our experience of him has shown that neither his abilities nor his inclinations are likely to bring about any appreciable improvement in the condition of the people committed to his charge.

In this connection we may refer your Lordship to the report of the Settlement Operations in Kashmir and Jammu, submitted by Mr. A. Wingate, C.I.E., C.S., Settlement Officer, to the Maharaja in 1888. This report, of which a copy is attached to this despatch, contains abundant evidence to show that most of the abuses continued to prevail unchecked. Under the system of assessment in force the cultivator of the soil had, as Mr. Wingate points out, been pressed down to the condition of a coolie cultivating the State property at a bare subsistence allowance, while the population continued to diminish, and the former occupants of the land were being steadily ousted from its possession, which was passing into that of the official classes, who have been enriched at the public expense. This transference of the land from the cultivating to the non-cultivating classes had, in Mr. Wingate's opinion, been proceeding with increased rapidity since the death of the late Maharaja, from which date the central authority appears to have become weaker. The artisan classes, whose skill and industry are well known, appear to have shared the ruin of the cultivating classes.

We have thought it our duty to dwell briefly upon this subject, because the supersession of the Maharaja appears to have been regarded in many quarters as the result of a selfish desire on the part of the Government of India to extend its influence in Kashmir, and possibly to prepare the way for the ultimate annexation of the State. We have, we trust, said enough to satisfy your Lordship that the consideration which has had most weight with us has been the responsibility, from which we cannot divest ourselves, of securing for the people of Kashmir a form of government less intolerable than that to which they have been subjected for many years past. The circumstances under which the destinies of Kashmir were handed over by the British Government for political considerations to an alien dynasty, increase, in our opinion, our responsibility for the condition of the country, and impose upon us an obligation, which we cannot ignore, of taking effectual steps in order to terminate the long period of suffering, mismanagement, and wasted opportunities through which the State has passed.

Enclosure 1 in No. 9.

From Colonel PARRY NISBET to Sir H. M. DURAND.

(Demi-Official.) Kashmir Residency, Srinagar, April 19, 1889.

After arrival here on the 13th, I paid a visit of ceremony on the 15th to His Highness the Maharaja, which he returned on the 16th, but I refrained from discussing any business at these interviews.

On the 17th instant, accompanied by Captain Ramsay, I proceeded to the palace at 11 a.m., and met His Highness the Maharaja in private Durbar. Those present besides the Maharaja were his brothers, Rajas Ram Singh and Amar Singh, the two members of Council, Pandit Suraj Kaul and Pandit Bhag Ram, Diwan Janki Prasad, an old official of the State, and Sardar Bup Singh, Governor of Kashmir. I informed His Highness the Maharaja without comment of the orders of the Government of India, dated 1st April, 1889, and that he might be under no misapprehension, I, at the same time, handed to his Prime Minister, Raja Amar Singh, these orders in writing in the form of a letter, copy of which is annexed, as an answer to his No. 159, dated 8th March, 1882, which is in the correspondence.

His Highness the Maharaja said—'I will consider the letter and return an answer.' After some few minutes conversation the interview closed. In leading me down the Durbar room the Maharaja again said—'I will think it over and give you an answer to what you have told me.' I replied kindly 'an answer is not required, as what I have communicated to you are the orders of the Government. I will always come and give you any further explanation you may wish,' and we parted. I subsequently repeated to the brothers of the Maharaja that they should let him thoroughly understand that the communications made to him were the definite orders of the Government of India, which it was not necessary for him to answer.

On the 18th instant there was a first meeting of the new Council.

Sub-enclosure.

From the Resident in Kashmir to Raja Amar Singh, Prime Minister, Kashmir.

April 17, 1889.

With reference to your No. 159, dated 8th March, 1889, I beg to inform you that the letter with its enclosure was laid before his Excellency the Viceroy and Governor-General in Council, who, after full consideration of the circumstances and the general condition of affairs in the Kashmir State for a long time past, has ordered me to inform His Highness the Maharaja that for a time at least he will be expected to refrain from all interference in the administration. He will retain his rank and dignity as Chief of the State, but full powers of government will be vested in a Council consisting of the Maharaja's brothers and three or four officials selected by the Government of India. It is not thought desirable that one of these officials should be an Englishman. Besides retaining his rank and dignity, the Maharaja will receive from the revenues of the State an annual sum sufficient to maintain his household in due comfort and to defray any expenditure that may rightly devolve upon him, but he will have no power of alienating the State revenues, and the sum placed at his disposal, though adequate, will not be extravagantly large.

His Highness the Maharaja and the Members of Council should thoroughly understand that, although the Council will have full powers of administration, they will be expected to exercise those powers under the guidance of the British Resident. They will take no step of importance without consulting him, and they will follow his advice whenever it may be offered.

Such are the orders of the Government of India, and, on my own part, I beg you will assure His Highness that it will be my endeavour to assist in carrying them out in the way I trust that may be most conducive to the happiness and benefit of His Highness and the State.

Enclosure 2 in No. 9.

From His Highness the Maharaja of Kashmir to the Marquess of Landsdowne.

Kashmir, May 14, 1889.

It is after great suffering and distress, and undergoing greatest contempt and taunt at the hands of my inferiors, that I have, with fear, decided to send the special message to your Excellency per bearer. Necessity and feelings of loyalty have obliged me to seek advice from your Excellency and take shelter under your Lordship's fatherly care. As advised by my late-lamented father from my very childhood, my heart is full of loyalty to the paramount power, and I am always ready to do all that can be desired by the blessed Government. Your Excellency is authorised to consider me as one of your Lordship's most faithful and humble servants. When my late father always considered it an honour to serve the Government loyally and faithfully, I should, and I do, consider it greater honour still to follow his example. All my country, treasury, army, even my life and blood, are at the disposal of the British Government and our Mother-Sovereign, the Queen-Empress.

I know very well that I have been extremely misrepresented before the Government of India through sources which had a show of reliableness, but this, alas! I have come too late to know, when my internal enemies, who are envious of my position, have succeeded to drive me to a very mean and pitiable position, and I implore your Excellency to release and save me from it, taking my destitute position in consideration. The recent allegations brought against me about secret correspondence with Russia, conspiring with Dalip Singh, attempt to poison the British Resident, Mr. T. C. Plowden, and lots of stupid stories, did not affect my mind in the least, for I was under the impression that some special officer will be deputed by your Excellency's Government to inquire fully into the false charges, and thus I shall get the best opportunity of disclosing everything fully, and, through this source, be able to bring all facts to the notice of your Excellency, and have my secret enemies brought to book through your Excellency's kind sympathy. But to my greatest pleasure no notice was taken of those false letters, and all other stupid stories were taken as nonsense by the supreme power. After this was over, the following communication was sent by Colonel R. Parry Nesbit, Resident in Kashmir, to Raja Amar Singh, Prime Minister:—

'From the RESIDENT in Kashmir to RAJA AMAR SINGH,
'Prime Minister.

'Kashmir, April 17, 1889.

'SIR,

'WITH reference to your number 159, dated 8th March, 1889, I beg to inform you that the letter, with its enclosure, was laid before his Excellency the Viceroy and Governor-General in Council, who, after full consideration of the circumstances and the general condition of affairs in the Kashmir State for a long time past, has ordered me to inform His Highness the Maharaja that, for a time at least, he will be expected to refrain from all interference in the administration. He will retain his rank and dignity as Chief of the State; but full powers of government will be vested in a Council consisting of the Maharaja's brothers and three or four officials selected by the Government of India. It is not thought desirable that one of these officials should be an Englishman. Besides retaining his rank and dignity, the Maharaja will receive from the revenue of the State an annual sum sufficient to maintain his household in due comfort and to defray any expenditure that may rightly devolve upon him, but he will have no power of alienating the State revenues, and the sum placed at his disposal, though adequate, will not be extravagantly large.

'2. His Highness the Maharajah and the Members of the Council should thoroughly understand that, although the Council will have full powers of administration, they will be expected to exercise these powers under the guidance of the British Resident. They will take no step of importance without consulting him; they will follow his advice whenever it may be offered.

'3. Such are the orders of the Government of India, and, on my own part, I beg you will assure His Highness that it will be my endeavour to assist in carrying them out in the way I trust that may be most conducive to the happiness and benefit of His Highness and the State.

'I remain,

'Yours truly,

'(Signed) R. PARRY NISBET.'

And now your Excellency can judge what my position at present is, and how much I am slighted in the Durbar, my enemies staring with pride and triumph into my eyes very often and showing all possible contempt.

My chief enemy, and in the present circumstances enemy of the State, who has taken a fancy to become the ruler of the Kashmir State, and who envies my position since long time, is, I am sorry to say, my own youngest brother, Raja Amar Singh. It is only now that I have found him out in his true colours, and all doubts as to his ill-motive have been removed. Since the very day I succeeded to the throne, he caused to set afloat all sorts of rumours against me about my incapacity, insanity, &c., &c.

Many a time he was directly caught in conspiring against me. He encouraged, pecuniarily and otherwise, people connected with the press with the only object of their writing against my person, vilifying me, and causing to circulate the worst rumours against me. Having convenient access to Europeans, &c., &c., and the Residents, to which I never objected, having no suspicion regarding his doings, he filled their ears, as often as possible, with such black stories about me, directly and indirectly, thinking very well that his doing so will, in the long run, set the Government of India against me, and he will be proclaimed Ruler of Jammu and Kashmir territories in that case. To almost every Resident, and specially to Colonel R. Parry Nisbet, he appeared to be the most reliable and intimately connected informant, and all should have believed in what he said; and I have every reason to believe that all rumours which reached the Government against me must have been through this, and this source alone.

Being disgusted with this unworthy conduct, and having ample proofs to silence him in his very face, I twice resolved to order him to remove himself to his jagir, and have nothing to do in the capital. On both these occasions, being informed of my resolution against him, he entered my room, where was no one except him and myself, shedding childish tears, throwing his turban on my feet, imploring for mercy, promising all goodwill and hearty loyalty for the future, and asking for pardon as my dear brother, humblest slave. After all, he was my youngest brother, very dear to me; his lovely young face is still liked by me, and on both these occasions my blood was naturally warm for him, and I was completely moved by his entreaties, and pardoned him after all. To prove to him that my heart was quite in sympathy with him—and I truly loved him as my dear brother—I, at his request, bestowed upon him the rich jagir of Bhadderwa, in exchange to the comparatively poor Bisoli which he had got during the time of my late father, and again made him Prime Minister of all. But, as was known afterwards, he was never slow in conspiring against me, even then. Regaining my confidence twice, and knowing I was quite confident and entirely at ease from his side, he possessed redoubled power and influence in the State, which is natural, and every State official was made to believe and look upon him as my powerful assistant and adviser. All these advantages he brought in force against me for the gain of his one sole object in view above mentioned, and he was able enough to create a strong party of his own among my officials, giving them all hopes of future success and prosperity, in case they remained faithful only to him and join with him in overthrowing me and mine. This promise he has fulfilled now in promoting those who joined him, and degrading those, my sincerely faithful servants, who stood by me amidst all temptations.

Colonel R. Parry Nisbet, as soon as he was installed as British Resident at my Court, I looked upon him as my safe friend, and thought that my difficulties were at an end, because I knew him to be one of the sincere friends of my father and good supporter to myself. I must also confess that for some little time in the beginning he was my sympathiser to some extent, but it is very difficult to say what made him entirely change his motives towards me and to fall in the very clutches of the very same secret and powerful enemy of mine, Raja Amar Singh. This sudden change must be as astonishing to all others as it was to me, so it is the most difficult task to investigate fully into the cause of this sudden change of his policy.

To overcome such difficulties as I was labouring under, at the hands of powerful intriguers who were using all sorts of influence within and without, I asked for the loan of two well-experienced officers from the Government of India to act as my councillors, and I must express my deep and heart-felt gratitude for the kindness with which the Government of India conceded to my request. But excellent men as these were, they also changed their former attitude at once as soon as the Resident changed his, and I believe that they must have done so naturally, as they are more dependent upon the good-will of the Representative of the British Government, under whose employment they have spent almost all their life, and to whom they owe all they have got, than myself, whom they are only lent to, so I was soon being made powerless.

At this juncture the brewing plot of the much-talked-of-letters, alleged to have been written by me, was brought into force. Almost all the rumours about the source from which they are purported to have reached the Resident are false, and without any foundation whatever. Solely Raja Amar Singh was at the bottom of the whole thing. These letters are nothing but most daring forgeries, and there was none more daring than my blood relation, the Raja Amar Singh. I have every reason to thank heartily your Excellency's Government for considering and treating them beneath notice, &c. This news, when it reached Jammu, gave much joy to all but to my brother Raja Amar Singh, and his party fellows, as, for instance, Sardar Roop Singh, the present Governor of Hakim-ila of Kashmir, Diwan Janki Prasad, his Secretary, ex-Governor of Hakimala, Wazir Shibsaran, and Diwan Shibsaran, his own Prime Minister, and who has full power to do anything in the State, and many others to whom it gave excessive pain. I am sure, if the Government of India would have required witnesses, Raja Amar Singh had been the first to swear against me. He was even ready to accompany Colonel Nisbet to Calcutta to complete my disaster for ever. When he came to inform me of his intention, made according to order of Colonel Nisbet, to leave for Calcutta with the Resident at his desire, I questioned him as to what opinion he expressed about the letters before the Resident. In reply he admitted to have said only that the etymological letters resemble those of the Maharaja's handwriting, but the signatures are not quite so. Being startled and heartily pained at this his reply, I simply told him, "All right, Raja Amar Singhjee. You can go to Calcutta with the Resident, if you like, but this was not expected from you. In your admitted deposition you have left nothing to destroy me." On the other day he, I believe, with the consultation of the Resident, decided not to go, and told me—"As your Highness is not favourable to the proposal I won't go, not to displease your Highness".

With the information of these letters, and with the full confidence and strength of being supported by my own brother and his now strong party, Colonel R. Parry Nisbet dashed into my room at a fixed time and brought such a great and many-sided pressure in all solemnity and seriousness that I was obliged to write what was desired, rather demanded by him, in order to relieve myself for the moment, having full faith that your Excellency's Government will not accept such a one sided view of the case, and that full opportunity will be given to me of defending myself. I never admitted the genuineness of these letters, and even an ordinary sense can find out that I could never write such nonsense as the letters are purported to contain. Do I not know the dangers of the change of Government? Do I not understand the value of a peaceful Government presiding over us all? Do I not know what security all the Native Princes of India now are enjoying from internal and external dangers? Do I not understand that my dominions are most safe under the benign British Government? Do I not understand that what then on earth can induce me to correspond with Russia? Who is in Russia to read Dogra Vernacular? Having been in possession of high honours and all regards from the British Government, and having got everything from being loyal to it, what more can I expect, or aspire to get, from a foreign power, where tyranny and despotism are well known to all? As to Dalip Singh (God forbid), if he ever happens to come here, who is in a more dangerous position to suffer from his wrath? That I would conspire with him, is to hit the axe at the very foot of my own existence. About the attempt to poison Mr. T. C. Plowden, I think Mr. Plowden himself must be the best witness. My administration in those days was veste din the Council composed of Diwan Lachman Das, President, Raja Ram Singh, Military Member, Raja Amar Singh, member of all the civil affairs; and let them all sincerely say if they know anything about it. Raja Amar Singh, who was the chief adviser and general controller of all affairs, and under whose cunning guidance Diwan Lachman Das used to act unknowingly, may support this charge—I cannot say but none other, not even one single soul in the whole State will ever stand a witness to this charge. Moreover, who is the fool in the world to commit such base conspiracies to writing? Suppose there was such foul conspiracy on my part, would not the whole thing have been managed orally? But I assure your Excellency with all sacredness that such an idea never occurred to me, in dream even. Although your Excellency's Government treated the letters as *beneath notice*, my cruel enemies have got the fullest advantage that they expected. They are now full conquerors over my head, and under their feet trample me. What is my position now? Simply that of a dead body: even worse than that, for I am taunted every moment by some sort of disgrace and disregard or other. These inferiors and traitors, who only yesterday showed me every respect and bowed down before me, pass me now with contemptuous smile, and I constantly bear the destruction and degradation of all those, my faithful and old hereditary servants, who stood by me. Of course a dead body is unconscious of all these troubles, of which I am unfortunately not.

In his communication, dated 17th April, 1889, to Raja Amar Singh, above quoted in full, the Resident says: "His Excellency the Viceroy and Governor-General in Council, after full consideration of the circumstances and the general condition of affairs in the Kashmir State for a long time past, has ordered me to inform His Highness the Maharaja that, for a time at least, he will be expected to refrain from all interference in the administration. He will retain his rank and dignity as Chief of the State, &c., &c." Now, to put it very plainly, I have never, up to this time, enjoyed complete independence of action in State affairs. Under such circumstances it has been very cruel indeed to hold me personally responsible for any maladministration and to punish me severely as a criminal. By the above order of your Excellency it is plain enough to understand that matters have been so represented as to prove that only *my* interference has brought about the state of affairs for which the Government of India has been obliged to pass such strictures upon me; whereas the case is quite the contrary. The man whose disloyal interference is the chief cause of all mismanagement, and who should have been severely punished, has got not only scot-free, but has been placed over my head, enjoying perfect satisfaction of having been successful in his wicked design. Had there been any other loyal and faithful Prime Minister of mine than Raja Amar Singh, he would have been expected to send in a suitable reply to the Resident's communication and saved me from the deadly disgrace which I have been subjected to; but my brother, Raja Amar Singh, quietly submitted to it, and was extremely satisfied to see me thus disgraced, as it was really his own hearty intention to see me so.

What rank and dignity can I retain under such circumstances? My condition is worse than a deposed ruler, inasmuch as he is taken out to some other place where he does not witness the most insulting scenes. And as regards the stipend that I am allowed at the mercy of the Council and the Resident, such is given even to the treacherous enemies of the British, who massacred their regiments and are now imprisoned or kept safe as political prisoners in the hills. Certainly, if the alleged letters had been proved genuine still no worse fate would have befallen me. The present Council, not content with reducing me to such a state of distress, have now fallen upon all those who remained faithful to me. Not to go into full details, I will only say that Pandit Mahanandjee, Governor of Jammu, Pundit Zankak, Assistant Governor of Kashmir, Pundit Shibkak, Officer of Timber Department, Dussoundhiram, an honest Chief Judge of Jammu, and Pundit Paralal, officer of deciding the old balance accounts, and many others, have all been dismissed, with exception of Dussoundhiram, by one stroke of pen, on one plea and pretence or other, but really simply because they were sore in the eyes of Raja Amar Singh, and did not hear to his illegal recommendation and stood on my side. Their places are now being filled with such men who are notorious for their show of contempt to me.

If your Excellency really wants to make me responsible for the administration of the State (and I am very glad and quite ready to take such responsibility over my head), I would ask to be made responsible ruler. In spite of what has been represented against me about my incapacity, etc., etc., I would ask your Excellency to give me a fair trial in order to see what I am capable of doing for the furtherance of the interests of the Supreme Government and prosperity of my State. From three to five years' time, as I think it quite sufficient for me to put everything into order from the date of holding responsibility, provided I am allowed full strength and independence to choose my own councillors and ministers, and British Resident, instead of throwing obstacles in my way like Colonel R. Parry Nisbet, supports and strengthens my hands. This just Resident should be chosen by the Government of India. I shall always be glad and ready to seek his advice and sympathy, but in all matters concerning the State, &c., the Resident will have to consult me solely. For the present I would like to take Raja Ram Singh, Pundit Suraj Kaul, and Pundit Bhag Ram as my councillors (and remove Raja Amar Singh to his jagir), with full powers to add or diminish any one. If after a fair trial being given to me, I do not set everything (excepting the Settlement Department, which is under the guidance of Mr. Lawrence, and which will not be settled within five years) right, and am found not to rule to the satisfaction of the Supreme Government, and my people within the prescribed time, your Excellency's Government is at liberty to do anything that may be considered advisable. In case this liberty is not allowed to me by the Supreme Government, and I have to remain in my present most miserable condition, I would most humbly ask your Excellency to summon me before you—and I will be most happy to obey such summons—and shoot me through the heart with your Excellency's hands, and thus at once relieve an unfortunate prince from unbearable misery, contempt, and disgrace for ever.

Awaiting your Excellency's commands, &c.

P.S.—The papers on which I write do not bear my official seal, and the reason is that my English Office is in the hands of the Prime Minister, Raja Amar Singh. The English clerks have been detained by him, by the advice of the Resident, to write for me, and thus I write in my own handwriting, and do not think it advisable to use the sealed papers. I hope your Excellency will excuse me for my bad handwriting. The bearer of this petition is authorized to answer any inquiries or refer them to me.

Enclosure 3 in No. 9.

From His Excellency the VICEROY AND GOVERNOR-GENERAL OF INDIA to His Highness the MAHARAJA OF KASHMIR.

Simla, June 28, 1889.

I have received your Highness's letter of the 14th May. It was brought to Simla by a person, deputed by your Highness for that purpose, who appears to have taken advantage of your confidence in order to publish in the newspapers part of a confidential document which should not have been made known to the public at such a moment. I shall always be glad to hear from you should you desire to make me aware of your views, and I hope that you will, in future, forward your letters to me by the ordinary post, through which they will be safely delivered without the risk of any such indiscretion as that which has taken place in the present instance.

It is satisfactory to me to learn from your Highness that you are loyally disposed towards the paramount power, and that it is your desire to be guided by my advice. I shall give it to you frankly, and without any attempt to conceal my thoughts.

Your Highness has stated in your letter that your conduct has lately been completely misrepresented by your secret enemies; that Colonel Parry Nisbet, the British Resident in Kashmir, has dealt unjustly with you, and that your chief enemy has been your youngest brother, Raja Amar Singh. You suggest that the letter to Raja Amar Singh, signed and sealed by your Highness on the 8th March of this year, was written without due consideration, and in consequence of pressure put upon you by the Resident; you urge that you have never enjoyed sufficient independence of action in regard to the affairs of your State to enable you to give satisfactory evidence of your ability as a ruler; you beg that you may now be given a further trial, and, with this object, you virtually recede from the proposals contained in the letter to Raja Amar Singh, of which I have just spoken; and, in conclusion, you express, in the strongest language, your inability to submit patiently to the position in which you now find yourself.

I must point out to your Highness that the decision of the Government of India to relieve you of an active share in the government of your State was arrived at not only in consequence of recent events, but of circumstances which must be within your Highness's recollection, and which occurred some time before my arrival in this country. During the last years of the administration of my predecessor, the Marquis of Dufferin and Ava, extremely unfavourable reports had been received by the Government of India of the manner in which the affairs of Kashmir were administered by your Highness. The finances of the State were in disorder, a disorder which, there could be little doubt, was increased by your own extravagance, while your Highness had surrounded yourself by persons of the worst reputation, whose influence over you had produced the most unfortunate results. These complaints, which were made not only by the then Resident, but also by certain of the Princes and Sardars of the Kashmir State, were borne out by papers which were placed in the hands of the Government of India. These contained, amongst other matters, ample evidence to show that you were squandering the resources of your State in a most reckless and improvident manner, and in the encouragement of the most unworthy persons.

At this time the Government of India anxiously considered the course which it should adopt in reference to your Highness, and its decision was conveyed to you in the kharita of the Marquis of Dufferin and Ava, dated the 25th July of last year. In this letter Lord Dufferin pointed out to you the impropriety of your dismissal of your Prime Minister, Diwan Lachman Das, who had been appointed after consultation with the Government of India without reference to that Government. He strongly urged upon your Highness the necessity of a careful investigation of the condition of the finances of Kashmir, and of the executive and judicial services, and he intimated to you that he was prepared to accept, with certain modifications, a scheme which had been proposed on behalf of your Highness for the formation of a reformed Council, of which you were to be the President. The constitution of this Council appeared to Lord Dufferin to be open to certain objections, but, in deference to your Highness's wishes, he determined not to press these. He, moreover, expressed his readiness to supply you with a certain number of trained native officials who might be of assistance to you in strengthening your administration.

About this time, in order to meet your Highness's wishes, advantage was taken of the appointment of Mr. Plowden to another post, in order to appoint, as Resident in Kashmir, a gentlemen well known to you, and regarded by you with feelings of friendship and confidence.

Looking back at these events, it is surely not too much to say that the result of the action of the Government of India in 1888 was to give your Highness, in the fullest sense of the term, a fair trial, such as that for which you now so earnestly ask. I am, however, constrained to tell your Highness distinctly that the results of that trial appear to have been of a most unsatisfactory kind. In the spring of this year my attention was called to the documents referred to in your Highness's letter; many of these had every appearance of being genuine, and they have, moreover, a striking resemblance to those other papers, of which I have already spoken, and which came into the possession of the Government of India at a previous time. Your Highness is correct in expressing your belief that the action subsequently taken by my Government was not justified merely by the disclosures contained in these letters. Even if the whole of these had been unquestionably genuine, I could not bring myself to believe that they had been written deliberately, or with a full appreciation of their meaning. There were, however, other circumstances which the Government of India could not do otherwise than take into consideration. The reports from the new Resident of the manner in which your Highness had administered the State had been not less unfavourable than those submitted, from time to time, by Mr. Plowden. Notwithstanding the ample resources of your State, your treasury was empty; corruption and disorder prevailed in every department and every office; your Highness was still surrounded by low and unworthy favourites, and the continued misgovernment of your State was becoming, every day, a more serious source of anxiety.

This however was not all. A meeting had taken place between your Highness and Colonel Parry Nisbet at Jammu on the 7th March, and upon that occasion your Highness had distinctly stated that it was your wish to have no more to do with public affairs, and had asked the Resident whether he was prepared to assume, in conjunction with a Council, the management of the State. You repeated several times to the Resident that you were tired of the trouble which had been occasioned to you by official affairs, and that you would prefer to go away and to live in peace privately. At the termination of the interview you stated that you would send your brother, the Prime Minister, Raja Amar Singh, to discuss the matter further with Colonel Parry Nisbet, and Raja Amar Singh, on the following morning, assured the Resident that you had made up your mind to give up interference with public affairs during the next few years. A further conference between yourself and the Resident took place on the following day. You still adhered to the language which you had used on the previous day, only stipulating that the Council was not to interfere with your private affairs. In the afternoon the Prime Minister brought to Colonel Parry Nesbit your edict constituting a Council of State, which was to include an English member, and which was to have 'full and sole powers in all the public departments of the State for a period of five years,' during which it was provided that 'the Maharaja will not interfere, and will have no voice in the administration of the public affairs of the State, but he will continue to enjoy the honorary rights and position of Maharaja.' This proposal, emanating directly from your Highness, could not be treated by my Government otherwise than as embodying your deliberate intentions and wishes; nor can I admit that you are now justified in describing the edict to which I have referred as having been hurriedly written under pressure from Colonel Parry Nisbet, who, your Highness will remember, throughout these conversations, expressly pointed out to you that it would not be practicable for him to undertake the management of the State in the manner which you had suggested.

When your letter to Raja Amar Singh was laid before the Government of India, I felt that, in view of the circumstances which I have recapitulated, no other course was open to me than to accept in substance the proposal which you had made. In so doing, however, some important modifications were made in the original scheme. Amongst these I may mention my refusal to take advantage of your suggestion that an Englishman should be appointed to serve upon the new Council; such a step seemed to me to be unnecessary, and I determined not to take it. Again, instead of requiring that the new arrangement should last for at least five years, it was stipulated that it should continue for a time, of which the length was not specified. I may also remind you of the consideration shown to your Highness by the stipulation that your Highness should receive a suitable income from the State revenues, and that your rank and dignity should be reserved to you. That this has been done, has been amply proved by the respect shown to you by His Excellency the Commander-in-Chief on the occasion of his recent visit to your State.

What I have written will show to your Highness how it has come to pass that the Government of India felt itself obliged to introduce these changes for a time into the Government of Kashmir. The arrangement was arrived at after careful consideration, and with a full knowledge of facts, of which your Highness is well aware. I may add that, by last week's mail from England, I have received a letter from the Secretary of State for India, informing me that Her Majesty's Government fully approve the measures taken by the Government of India in April last, and share their conviction that, in the interests of the people of Kashmir, and of the ruling family itself, it has become impossible to leave the control of affairs in your Highness's hands.

It is idle to contend that all this has been the result of a conspiracy against you, in which the Resident, your brother, and the officials of the State, have all had a part. In your letter to me, you admit that you knew the Resident to be "one of the sincere friends of my father, and a good supporter of myself". You had yourself designated your brother, Raja Amar Singh, towards whom you felt the greatest affection, for the office of Prime Minister. The officers lent to you by the Government of India were, you tell me, excellent men, and they were supplied to you at your own request. If, however, I am to accept the statements now made by your Highness, it would be necessary for me to believe that Colonel Parry Nisbet, Raja Amar Singh, and the officers referred to, must all of them have changed their nature as well as their disposition towards your Highness within a few months. All these men were, I believe, ready to be your friends, but they have found that your conduct in public and private life was such as to render it impossible for them to co-operate cordially with you.

What I have said has reference to the past. For the future, let me earnestly entreat your Highness to show to the people of Kashmir, as well as to the Government of India, by bearing in a dignified manner the loss of power which you have sustained, and above all, by not associating yourself with local intrigues and conspiracies, or attempts to obstruct the Government, that you have not entirely lost the qualities of a wise and prudent ruler. The settlement announced in Colonel Parry Nisbet's letter of the 17th April to the Prime Minister is, as I have already pointed out to you, not necessarily a permanent one. Time will, however, be necessary if the finances of the State are to be restored to order, and the results of past maladministration effectually removed. Until this has been done, the present arrangement must certainly remain in force. When these good results have been achieved, it may be possible to give your Highness a larger share in the control of the public affairs of Kashmir. Much would, in such a case, depend upon your own conduct in the meanwhile. You cannot, therefore, govern yourself too cautiously, or be too careful in selecting your associates and confidants.

I would also ask you to inform Raja Ram Singh, who has, I understand, accompanied your Highness to Jammu, that the Government of India cannot regard with indifference his continued absence from the Council of State. He holds the important post of Commander-in-Chief in charge of the Military Department, and his failure to attend to the business of this cannot do otherwise than produce the most serious results. Unless therefore, he returns shortly to Srinagar and resumes the discharge of his duties, it will be necessary to make some arrangement for the transfer of those duties to other hands.

I will add only one word to what I have said above. Should your Highness at any time desire to address me in connection with this, or other matters, it will always be agreeable to me to learn your wishes, or your opinions; and should you, at the present time, seek an opportunity of hearing from my own lips my views in regard to these questions, I shall at any convenient time be ready to receive you and to converse with you in a friendly and confidential spirit.

Enclosure 4 in No. 9.

PRELIMINARY REPORT of SETTLEMENT OPERATIONS in KASHMIR and JAMMU by A. WINGATE, Esq., C.S., SETTLEMENT OFFICER.

From A. WINGATE, Esq., C.S., Settlement Officer, Kashmir, to His Highness the MAHARAJA OF KASHMIR AND JAMMU.

Srinagar, August 1, 1888.

Para. 1.—History of Appointment.
,, 2.—Preliminary arrangements.
,, 3.—Character of former survey.
,, 4.—Rejection of the previous measurement.
,, 5.—System of measurement adopted.
,, 6.—Area measured in first month.
,, 7.—Local Weights and measures.
,, 8.—Forms of Settlement Records.
,, 9.—Details of Establishment.
,, 10.— ,, ,, Expenditure.
,, 11.—Budget estimate of current season.
,, 12.—Remarks on the above.
,, 13.—Estimated cost of measuring the Kashmir Valley.
,, 14.—Probable maximum area of Kashmir Valley.
,, 15.— ,, minimum area of Kashmir Valley.
,, 16.— ,, area of measurement.
,, 17.— ,, average out-turn per measurer.
,, 18.— ,, out-turn and work each season.
,, 19.—Estimated cost of the settlement.
,, 20 and 21.—Classification of lands.
,, 22.—Remarks on the grouping of villages.
,, 23.—Difficulty of ascertaining current rates of assessment.
,, 24.—Crop experiments.
,, 25.—Rice cultivation.
,, 26.—Famines, etc.—Variations in the season affect the harvest; for example, a wet spring would injure the young crop, or insufficient snows would diminish the water supply, but famine appears only to be caused by heavy rain and cold at the time of ripening or reaping, and fortunately this is a rare occurrence. It is, however, always important that the *shâli* crop should be cut and garnered with the utmost expedition, and any revenue system which tends to delay that operation must in critical season seriously aggravate the disaster. The rabi crops not infrequently suffer from insufficient spring showers, but, from a famine standpoint, wheat, barley, and the like are of little importance, and therefore

in the following history of the seasons only those calamities are noticed which seriously affect the population:—

A.D.	Samwat.	
1815	1872	Population estimated at 8,00,000.
1824 1828	1881 1885	Severe earthquake, followed by cholera.
1831 to 1833	1888 to 1890	Severe famine, caused by heavy rain in the autumn.
1835	1892	Population estimated at 2,00,000.
1838	1895	Floods.
1842 or 1843	1899 or 1900	Cholera.
1857	1914	Ditto.
1859 to 1860	1916 to 1917	Scarcity owing to short water-supply.
1865	1922	Floods.
1869	1926	Ditto.
1871	1928	Ditto.
1872	1929	Cholera.
1873	1930	Population estimated at 5,00,000.
1875	1932	Poor harvest.
1877 to 1879	1934 to 1936	Severe famine, caused by heavy rain from the end of September, 1877, followed by cholera.
1879	1936	Good rich harvest.
1880	1937	Very good ditto.
1881	1938	Good harvest.
1882	1939	Good ditto.
1883	1940	Poor ditto, too little rain.
1884	1941	Very good harvest.
1885	1942	Poor harvest, spring rains too heavy, and sowings retarded. Severe earthquake.
1886	1943	Fairly good harvest.
1887	1944	Good harvest.

Population estimated at 3,00,000 to 4,00,000.

Para. 27.—Decrease of Population (See p. 67)

" 28.—Chronic Scarcity of Food (See p. 68).

" 29.—Profits on the sale of Cleaned Rice.

" 30.—System of Revenue Collection under the Sikhs.—Coming now to the mode of collecting the *sháli* and the revenue generally, I premise that my remarks are based on inquiries made in two tehsils only. The tehsils of Phák and Lál are called cash-assessed, and that was one of the reasons why I commenced there. Under the Sikhs the State took a half-share of the kharif crop, and in addition four traks per kharwár, and on account of the rice straw and the vegetable-produce of the "*Sagasár*" plots, the whole of which were kept by the Asámi and were supposed to be free of assessment, Rs. 1–9–0 per cent. was added to the total. The patwári and kánungo got ½ a trak per kharwár between them. Inferior village servants got something. Nazaráná was levied four times a year, and "*tambol*" (about two per cent.) was taken on occasions of marriages in the ruler's family, &c., &c. The villagers had also to feed the State watchers of the grain, called "*Shakdár*". Non-resident cultivators paid a little less, and Pandits and Pirzádás only paid two extra traks instead of four. For the rabi and kimiti crops all classes of cultivators were taxed alike, and in addition to the half-share, three traks per kharwár were taken under the names of extra cesses. The "*kimiti*" crops appear to be those that have always had a money-value and are til-gogal, sarson, tobacco, cotton, linseed, saffron, and the like. The distinction is said to date back to the time of Todar Mal, and for these crops money was always required, the assessment being calculated in rupees after division of the produce and the produce being returned to the cultivator. For other crops, whether kharif or rabi, the collection might be in kind, or the villages might be farmed out. But I can find no trace so far of any crop rates. Walnut oil, fruit trees, and honey, have also always been taxed. Under the above the State share was not less than three-fifths of the gross produce, and what the cultivator actually retained was certainly less than two-fifths and probably only about one-third. The abundance of fruits, berries, and nuts, the extensive grazing area, and forest produce, enabled the cultivators to live, but an assessment so heavy as this would extinguish all rights in land, would render land valueless, and would reduce a population forcibly confined within the valley to the condition of tenants-at-will.

Para. 31.—Effects of a Crushing Assessment.—Accordingly, we find that pressure has from time to time been exercised to keep the land in cultivation, and to such an abject condition have the cultivators—naturally a fine race—been reduced that I have been told by the highest and most trusted officials in Srinagar that the Kashmiri cannot be trusted with *shdli* because he would eat the whole of it, that he will not plough unless the tehsildar gives him the seed and makes him, and that without this fostering care of Government he would become extinct. The truth being that he has been pressed down to the condition of a coolie cultivating at subsistence allowance the State property. The Kashmiris are called cowardly, because they have lost the rights belonging to the peasantry elsewhere and tamely submit to be driven like sheep before a sepoy. But it is useless to expect that a small population forming an isolated state that looked only to its hills for protection could withstand powerful neighbours like Afghans or Sikhs, or that so distant and inaccessible a province would not be ruthlessly ground down under the endless succession of governors that have enriched themselves in this valley. The Kashmiri is strong and hardworking, but his spirit is dormant; and he is grudged the quantity of food the climate makes necessary, but which a short-sighted policy considers gluttonous; and consequently he is being closer pressed every harvest. With fair treatment the peasantry would make a great advance in numbers and in prosperity; and if their claim to consideration, which I am now advancing, is met, the happy days when Zain-ul-abdin passed his jubilee among a contented people may be repeated. If that claim is denied, the State, as I shall presently show, will soon have no land left to legislate for, and will have to beg for its revenue from its present servants. These servants foresee that a land settlement must come some day, and meanwhile they are buying up or otherwise getting possession of the land, and to secure a little temporary rest the cultivators are only too ready to take shelter behind any sufficiently influential pandit.

Para. 32.—Revenue Management since A.D. 1846.—Since the times of the Sikhs, the pressure has been undoubtedly relaxed; but it must still be pretty severe when cultivators are found ready to sell whole villages for no other equivalent than the protection of a powerful name. Many of the *Mukaddams*, or heads of the villages, are very intelligent, but when it comes to seeing their children stinted of food, with hearts sickened by deferred hope, they sign away fatuitously day by day such rights as they possess. During Maharaja Goláb Singh's rule (A.D. 1846 to 1857) the Sikh procedure was followed, but some slight relaxations were made in favour of land newly cultivated, for large areas were lying waste. His Highness was fond of horses, and a number of grass-rakhs were reserved from cultivation. Under Maharaja Ranbhir Singh, circles of villages were annually farmed out to contractors called kardars. About 1865 (S. 1922) the extra traks per kharwár were reduced for all Pandits and Pirzádás for a time to only one trak. From about 1869 (S. 1926) the practice of contracting with the Mukaddams or with the Zemindars gradually established itself in place of the farming system, and only two extra traks came to be levied instead of four. In 1873-4 (S. 1930-1) the village contracts seem to have been divided up into "*asamiwar khewats*", or cultivators' accounts, and either produce or cash was taken from each man. In 1875 (S. 1932) the harvest was a bad one, and the State took two shares of the produce and left one only to the cultivators. Next year fresh contracts were entered into either with Mukaddams, Kardars, or cultivators, and two traks per kharwár were again added to the assessment, besides an aggregate tax of Rs. 9-12-0 per cent. if paid in cash, or 9 kharwárs 12 traks per 100 kharwárs if paid in kind. This tax included a number of items, such as support of the palace-temple, the abolished kánungo's share, and so on. In 1877 (S. 1934) the scarcity began, and the new contracts broke down, and so the State collected in kind only; and this practically continued till 1880 (S. 1937), when a new "*asamiwar khewat*" was made, based upon previous years' collections, as estimated in cash, but payable either in produce or cash as the cultivator was able. This "*khewat*" or cash settlement is supposed still to be valid, but after the good harvests of S. 1937 and 1938 the settlement was thought to have been too easy, and so it was raised by Rs. 8-9-0 per cent., the chief item of the increment being Rs. 6-13-0 for a pony tax, which might be paid in ponies instead of money, and in place of the Rs. 1-9-0 per cent. formerly levied for fodder, the cultivators were required to give five *kurus* of rice straw per 100 threshed. This settlement includes all cesses except the "*tambol*" and "*nazarána*". In 1885 (S. 1942) the Rs. 8-9-0 per cent. tax was remitted, and so now the "*khewat*" of S. 1937 is supposed to have been reverted to, with the exception of the five *kurus* of rice straw, which are still taken. In 1886 (S. 1943) one seer per kharwár, formerly payable to the zillahdars, was made payable to the State, who appointed paid chowkidars. If this revenue history is not very correct, it must be remembered that access to the revenue records has been denied me.

Para. 33.—The so-called Cash Settlement of 1880.

,, 34.—Hap-hazard way in which the Settlement was immediately increased.—To find out the mechanism of the winding-up process would be tedious if not impossible, but as an example I cite another village. In S. 1937, the "*khewat*" was fixed at Rs. 617-12-0. In S. 1939, when the villages were practically going by auction,[1] a bidder offered Rs. 107-4-0 increase, and this village was knocked down to him at Rs. 725 per annum.

To this extra taxes, namely:—

	Rs.	A.	P.
Dharmarth	3	10	0
Shafakhana	7	4	0
Nazarána	0	14	6
Palace Temple	0	14	6
Pony-tax	69	5	0
Tambol	2	0	0
	84	0	0
Outstanding balance	1	2	0
Total	85	2	0

were added, making the total Rs. 810-2-0 for S. 1941. In S. 1942, the extra taxes were remitted, as already stated, and so the account stands—

	Rs.	A.	P.
Assessment	725	0	0
Add for cotton supplied for spinning and weaving soldiers' clothing— 2 Kharwárs at Rs. 14 = Rs. 28 + a fine of Rs. 4 for failing to supply the clothing within the year..	32	0	0
Outstanding balance	39	3	0
Total	796	3	0

[1] N.B.—For a crushing example, *see* Asham village, para. 47.

For S. 1943 the assessment is Rs. 725, and with outstanding balance the total is Rs. 741-11-9.

These are the village accounts showing collections. The tehsil accounts showing demands, give for S. 1941 Rs. 787, for S. 1942 Rs. 752, and for S. 1943 Rs. 733. It is difficult to deduce from accounts such as these what proportion of the gross produce the State takes, and more difficult still to find out what a village really does pay, as I have now to show. I enter into this detail because it is absolutely necessary it should be understood that any intelligible comparison between the results of the proposed settlement and either the previous *khewat* or the present demand, or the actual collections, will be impossible.

Para. 35.—How the Revenue is Collected.—It might be thought actual collections could be compared with the results of the settlement, but the custom of applying arbitrary prices to the portion of the revenue collected in kind, and which forms a large percentage of the whole, and the want of certainty either as to the proportion collected in kind or as to the share of each crop which is taken to make up that proportion, will effectually prevent any comparison with anything whatsoever. The *khewat*, or so-called cash settlement, so far from being a boon to the people, has been used as a means for getting rid of the restrictions which are imposed by a division of produce, and is accordingly equally detested by the villagers. This is how it is worked. An order is annually issued from Srinagar for the collection of a certain quantity, say nine lakhs of kharwárs of *sháli*, the demand being based upon the general aspect of the ripening crop, and pitched 20 to 30 per cent. above what there is a likelihood of getting. Each tehsildar is then informed of the amount he is expected to contribute to this total. He finds this amount, converted at Rs. 2 *chilki* (Rs. 1¼ imperial) per kharwár, comes to, say, 10 annas in the rupee of his total revenue. He accordingly gives instructions to collect so many kharwárs from each village, the total collections coming up to the amount named from headquarters, or probably rather more, but varying from 16 annas to nothing, according to the amount of *sháli* he thinks can be secured from any particular village. As soon as the villagers learn they have to pay their *khewat*, say, 10 annas in *sháli*, two annas in cotton, mung, &c., and four annas in cash, bargaining and bribery begin; the village, if a fairly well-to-do one, eventually securing enough *sháli* to live upon; if a poor one, having to look forward to some other means of eking out a livelihood for the winter.

Perhaps an instance will make the system clearer. It is a village I happened to examine; the accounts are for the year S. 1939, and the rupees are *chilki*, or worth 10 annas each.

Amount of Demand.		Amount Collected.	
In Cash..	Rs. 384-7-3	In Cash	Rs. 369-10-9
In Kind	Kh. 191-6¾	In Kind	Kh. 182-2-0

The meaning of the division of the demand into "cash" and "kind" merely signifies that there must be so much *sháli* or *makki*, and that for the rest collections may be in cash or in any other produce. In the following details gross produce is shown for most things in 16-trak kharwárs, and the Government share in 15-trak kharwárs :—

Details of Collections.

Rabi Harvest, Rs. 209-2-6.

Gross Produce.			Government Share.		Standard Price per Kharwár.			Assessment.		
	Kh.	Trak.	Kh.	Trak.	Rs.	A.	P.	Rs.	A.	P.
Jaw	79	0	42	0	2	1	3	88	10	0
Wheat	43	0	23	6	5	2	6	120	8	6
					Total ..			209	2	6

Kimiti Harvest, Rs. 108-8-3.

Gross Produce.			Government Share.		Standard Price per Kharwár.			Assessment.		
	Kh.	Trak.	Kh.	Trak.	Rs.	A.	P.	Rs.	A.	P.
Alsi	13	10	6	13	8	0	0	54	13	3
Kapâs	7	2	3	8¾	14	0	0	49	14	0
Mung	0	14½	0	7½	7	14	0	3	13	0
					Total ..			108	8	3
			Add Akrot Tel (walnut oil) 14 manwatas					7	10	6
					Grand Total ..			325	5	3 cash

Kharif Harvest.

Sháli	305	8½	152	12¼
Makki	26	3¼	10	7¾
			at 2-5th Division.	
		Total =	163	4
Add extra			10	14
Grand Total—*Kh.*			174	2 in kind.

Extra Items.

	Rs.	a.	c.	
Rasadát (for Sagazár plots, &c.)	5	0	0	
Contributions to pay of tehsil establishment..	3	8	0	
Fodder, &c.	3	0	0	
	11	8	0	
Add cash..	325	5	3	as above.
	336	13	3	
Add taxes at Rs. 9-12-0 per cent.	32	13	6	
Total	369	10	9	

Thus we have Rs.369-10-9 set down as collected in cash, but which may have been paid partly in kind, and 174 kharwárs 2 traks compulsorily levied in kind, which, at the standard price of Rs. 2 per kharwár, would amount to Rs. 348-4-0. This account would show that the total collections were valued at Rs. 717-14-9.

The tehsil accounts state the demand was Rs. 699. This village rose from Rs. 449 in S. 1937, the year of the *khewat*. In S. 1940 and 1941 there was a further increase to Rs. 758, and notwithstanding the remission of taxes in S. 1942, the demand still is over Rs. 700. If it is asked why the district officers should maintain complicated weighments and accounts when the cash demand has been fixed at, say, Rs. 700 and they might take Rs. 350 in cash and 175 kharwárs in *shâli*, the answer is that no one can tell me.

Para. 36.—Fixed prices for produce enable a Tehsildar to manipulate the incident of the Assessment.

Para. 37.—Why the price of *Shâli* is fixed so low.
,, 38.—How Cotton is dealt with.
,, 39.—Cost of Transport to Srinagar is borne by the Villagers.

Para. 40.—Introduction of a Landlord class.
,, 41.—Chakdars.
,, 42.—Mukarridars.
,, 43.—Evasion of conditions on which Land was granted.
,, 44.—Instances of Lands held in excess of the Grants.
,, 45.—Chakdars ousting the old Cultivators.
,, 46.—Clandestine possession of Villages.
,, 47.—Instances of Villages ruined by Over-assessment.
,, 48.—The Law Improvement Department.
,, 49.—How Proprietary Titles are manufactured.
,, 50.—Impossibility of annihilating all rights in Land.
,, 51.—Official utterance differs from official practice.
,, 52.—Proposals for dealing with the Land.
,, 53.— ,, with regard to Cultivators.
,, 54.— ,, ,, Chakdars, &c.
,, 55.— ,, ,, Waste Lands.
,, 56.—Importance of regulating the distribution of water for irrigation.

Para. 57.—Self-preservation requires that the Darbar should confer rights upon the peasantry.

Para. 58. —Serious opposition anticipated.

,, 59.—Outstanding Balances.

,, 60.—Forced Labour.—Another matter urgently demanding attention is the manner in which *begar*, or forced labour, is managed. I am not prepared to say that it can be got rid of all at once. For example, for the Gilgit-expedition-transport resort to compulsion is probably necessary. But, were your Highness aware of how orders are carried out, many abuses might cease. At present chakdars' lands, jaghir and other specially assigned villages, villages secretly bought or in possession of officials or influential persons, are all exempt. I rode through a particularly nice village with a little bazaar, and the women and children looking to the trained observer in many little ways better off than the average. I said this village is doing very well, but was answered at once it belongs to so and so, mentioning a well-known official. No coolie can be seized in villages so protected, and that is one of the main reasons that the khalsa cultivators seek to transfer themselves to some nearer shelter. Consequently ths whole burden of providing coolies falls upon the khalsa villagee and mostly on those too small and poor to attract anybody's care. Further, the way of collecting coolies occasions more discontent than is necessary. A requisition is made, say, for 500 coolies. The tehsildar doubles the number. His emissaries quadruple it, and so a village that ought to supply, perhaps, five coolies, is asked for twenty. Fifteen men have to buy themselves off. It is notorious that this year large sums have been illegitimately collected in this way, to the prejudice of the good name of the Darbar. Just as I ventured to recommend that the amount of *shāli* to be taken from each village should be fixed once for all and published, so I would suggest that one coolie per so many rupees of assessment be required to be furnished by each village. A roll would then be made showing how many coolies each village ought to furnish, and this simple expedient would in a great measure stop the oppression and bribery now going on. Eventually, in the Settlement Rules, I should propose to define for what purposes and to what extent, and by whose orders, *begar*, or forced labour, may be required, and to regulate its remuneration. At present an order to collect coolies sends most of the able-bodied population of a tehsil into hiding for a week or two, to the great detriment of agricultural operations, and a settlement could not exist side by side with such disorganization of revenue-paying families.

Jammu.

Para. 61.—Depredations of Game animals.

,, 62.—Out-turn of Work.

,, 63.—Classification of Lands and Soils.

,, 64.— ,, ,, ,,

,, 65.—Difficulty of getting Information.

,, 66.—Land Tenure.

Para. 67.—Previous Settlements.
„ 68.—Obstacles to increased Cultivation.
„ 69.—Necessity of reorganizing the rights of Proprietors.
„ 70.—Proposals for dealing with Cultivators.

„ 71.—I have now laid before your Highness my proposals for dealing with the land in Kashmir and Jammu. Should these proposals meet with approval they will be embodied in a Code of Settlement Regulations and submitted for final sanction before the introduction of the settlement in the first tehsils. My account of what is in progress under your Highness's authority, but against your Highness's interests, has been long because I stand alone, and my mere assertion that the State treasury was being depleted, and the poor were being turned out of their lands, and the staple food of the people had become a monopoly of the officials, would not be believed. I appeal to your Highness with some confidence, because I have been impressed during my interviews with the belief that your Highness has a ready sympathy for the poor, a keen interest in land questions, and a determination to protect the cultivators against the officials. But my heart fails me when I think that there is no one among those who surround your Highness from whom I can venture to hope for a word in support of my prayer, that one and all will use every argument to persuade your Highness that my proposals will be detrimental to the traditions, the policy, or the dignity of the State; that they are impossible, and that neither the rice nor the land ought to be trusted out of official custody. I remember how carefully your Highness had been prepared to be firm on two points, one, that the "*Hak malikana*", or proprietorship of the land in Kashmir, belonged to the Maharaja, and second, that no settlement should be announced till the whole country was measured and ready for settlement on one day or the Government could not be responsible for the rice supply. I remember also with what cordial approval your Highness's remarks on these points were invariably received by the high officials present. The first position, they well knew, secured to them the power of terrorizing over the defenceless cultivators, and, continuing their methods of acquiring the proprietorship of the lands for themselves. And the second position would keep my department from interfering with these practices for years, and as the first papers would grow obsolete before the last were prepared, they knew, that if that condition could only be maintained, the settlement would never come at all. Your Highness, however, was soon convinced that to indefinitely postpone the settlement, however desirable from the point of view of the officials, was a serious danger, and I have since been urged to prepare tehsils for settlement as soon as possible. But the first position is still preserved, and, though your Highness has listened with patience, I cannot hope I have prevailed. Yet, unless the cultivators are guaranteed possession of the lands they till, a cash, or partly cash and partly shâli, settlement is impossible. If the cultivators are to work hard, pay punctually, and keep the treasury fuller than it has ever been before, they must not be the hopeless, discontented, depressed class they are now. The State cannot expect to get everything and give nothing. And behind a strong contented peasantry there must be persons ready to lay out capital when necessary. But who will lend money to a cultivator who may be turned out of his fields any day? Your Highness may think an order not to turn anybody out would suffice. It would be useless when the cultivators themselves are ready to transfer all and any rights they have, to accept any position, any field, so long as they get some shelter, and the officials are eager by every device known to educated and clever men in a position of untrammelled power, and all working with one object, to convert themselves into proprietors, to manufacture prescriptive rights to intervene between the State and the cultivator, to finally arrive at the coveted end when the pandits shall be landlords, the cultivators tenants-at-will, or, rather, coolies who cannot escape, and the State demand limited to a nominal sum per kharwár which lapse of time and ingenious interlarding of words will combine to make permanent.

Para. 72.—Possibility of Leases.
,, 73.—Renewed Obstructions.
,, 74.—A reason why we are objectionable.
List of Zillahs and Tehsils in the Kashmir Valley in 1887.

B.

HOUSE OF COMMONS, July 3.

[*Specially Reported by the Hansard Staff and Revised by the Speakers.*]

Mr. BRADLAUGH said: I beg to ask leave to move the adjournment of the House for the purpose of discussing "a definite matter of urgent public importance", viz., the taking away by the Government of India from the Maharaja of Kashmir the Government of his State and part of his revenues whilst refusing to allow any judicial or Parliamentary enquiry into the grounds for such action against a great feudatory prince.

The SPEAKER having appealed to the House, and considerably over forty members having risen in their places,

Mr. BRADLAUGH said: I am obliged to move the adjournment of the House, because it is the only possible way in which any appeal for the Maharaja of Kashmir can be submitted to Parliament. The Government of India have deprived this chief of his authority and of his property under cover of allegations which are emphatically denied by the Maharaja himself. The Maharaja, as I shall show, has applied for a trial in India. That has been denied him. The Secretary of State here has been asked to sanction an enquiry, and has refused; the leader of the House has been asked to appoint a Select Committee of enquiry, and has also refused; so that neither judicial nor Parliamentary nor Governmental enquiry is being allowed, although this gentleman has been subjected to penalties which in the case of the meanest person in this country would entitle him to have the accusations brought before some tribunal and witnesses against him heard. There is no other manner of bringing this matter before the House than by moving the adjournment. Though I can understand that hon. gentlemen opposite may think it unfair that the adjournment should be moved, they must remember that on Indian matters I have always shown the greatest consideration to the Government; so much so that at the beginning of this Session I did not avail myself, as I might have done, of my right to move an amendment to the Address, and I only now make a motion for the adjournment because there are no Estimates in Supply in which, as in any case affecting any other portion of Her Majesty's dominions, a question of grievance may be raised. It is either in the manner I am raising it to-night that this grievance must be submitted, or not at all. Now on May 14th of last year—that is more than twelve months ago—the Maharaja himself asked the Government of India for a fair trial. I will read to the House presently the touching words in which that appeal for a fair trial was met. From then till now, except in a despatch from which it will be my duty to quote, no kind of answer has been made to that appeal, and the Maharaja has been condemned unheard. I should have pressed this claim for inquiry twelve months ago, but there were then no papers before the House. It would have been open for the Government to say in the fashion in which rumour has said that this unfortunate gentleman had been guilty of crime or was suffering the consequences of vice, because these suggestions could be found embodied in official despatches to which I shall refer, and that there was, therefore, a lack of duty in bringing the matter before the House until the Government had put before it the statements on which they rely. Although this unfortunate gentleman was deprived of his authority and his property at the beginning of last year, the presentation of papers has been delayed until last week. They have been repeatedly pressed for by myself and other members. Until the Government had put their case on the table, any one would have been at a great disadvantage in submitting to this House any matter for its decision. I do not propose to ask the House, in the division I shall challenge, to express any other opinion on the facts I shall submit than that when such a penalty is enforced against a prince with whom we have a treaty—who has recently been regarded as being in the position of a feudatory prince—the man so dealt with is entitled to that which any other subject of Her Majesty, if he be a subject of Her Majesty, is entitled to, viz., a fair trial before condemnation. The Under Secretary must not shelter himself under considerations of State. If considerations of State can justify the Government of India in depriving one man of his authority and property unheard, there is no protection for any one, be he prince or peasant, throughout the whole of our Asiatic dominions. The other day the question was stated as simply as possible in the language of the right hon. gentleman the Under Secretary for India (Sir J. Gorst) in answer to a question put by myself. The right hon. gentleman said, "The action of the Government in Kashmir has been based, not upon grave personal charges made against the Maharaja". I would ask the House to remember that, because this man's character has been rumoured away and lied away with the help of forged letters during the last year and a-half—forged letters used as instruments of political warfare—letters, the authenticity of which has been denied by the Maharaja, letters which have never been produced in his presence and which yet the Government have the face to refer to in their worst fashion in one of the despatches I shall read to the House. I shall be relieved from any question as to the personal conduct of the Maharaja. He may be good or bad. I do not care what he is—he is entitled to justice. If he has been criminal let him be condemned and punished, but do not rob him under cover of a criminality which you dare not bring in evidence against him, and as to which you will allow no inquiry either in India or here. The right hon. gentleman the Under Secretary said the action of the Government was based upon the long-continued misgovernment of Kashmir. Well, this unfortunate gentleman has only been the ruler of Kashmir for about five years, and I will quote, to within a few months of the time he was dispossessed, the testimony of the Government itself that misgovernment did not exist as far as it was in his power to help it. I cannot conceive—I should not be justified in saying before you, Sir, anything more impudent—but I can conceive nothing more cool than the audacity of the confidence that this House would be imposed upon by the statement of the right hon. gentleman the Under Secretary that there had been long-continued misgovernment in Ireland such as justified the dethronement of this man. Vague statements there are here, but not one statement of fact. Misgovernment must be made up of something. You may shadow a man, put him unjustly in prison, or take away his property. None of these things are alleged against this unfortunate gentleman. Well, the right hon. gentleman went on to say that the Government of India have never attached any importance to certain treasonable and criminal correspondence attributed to the Maharaja.

It would have been as well not to have so described the character of the correspondence if no importance was attached to it. Why suggest that it was criminal and treasonable if it was not true, as it was not, that he was responsible for it? I do not suggest that the right hon. gentleman has made an inaccurate statement, but I do say he has been ignorant of the facts. I will read the evidence given by the Viceroy himself with regard to this correspondence which the right hon. gentleman dare not lay before this House, which he dare not put in print, but on which the emissaries of the Government have lied away the Maharaja's character during the last year and a-half. I will dispose of this point at once, because fortunately we have the papers on the Table and are able now to deal with them. So far from its being true that the Government have never attached the smallest importance to the correspondence, the Viceroy himself says the Government were justified "not merely by the disclosure of these letters"—so that they consider themselves in part justified by them (Sir J. Gorst indicated dissent)—The right hon. gentleman shakes his head. It is the Viceroy's head that should be shaken here. I admit that the right hon. gentleman dare not rely on the letters. I admit the right hon. gentleman has too much good sense to use in justification of the position assumed by the Government letters which the man himself declares to be forgeries and which the Government have never dared to produce to his face. But in a long despatch, dated "Simla, June 26th, 1889," I say the Viceroy did say these letters were amongst the things on which the Government acted in condemning this unfortunate gentleman. What did the Maharaja himself say about these letters? In a letter, which unfortunately time will not permit me to read fully to the House, he made a plea for justice first to the Government of India, and then through the Government to the English Parliament. He said, "these letters are nothing but most daring forgeries"; and he suggests that one of the forgers, if not the only forger, is his brother, whom the Government of India has placed in the position of authority of which they have deprived this unfortunate gentleman himself. My allegation will be that it was on those letters—for the papers disclosed nothing else, and further negatives everything else—that this action of the Government was based. (Sir J. Gorst again expressed dissent.) The right hon. gentleman shakes his head, but I have read the papers, which he evidently has not done himself, and I shall read extracts to the House to show that I am within the mark in every statement of this kind I make. Why did the Government of India, twelve months ago, say they did not merely act on these letters? What did that phrase mean if they did not act on them at all? Have the Government since discovered they are forgeries? If so, as they are part of the case on which misgovernment and criminality are alleged against this unfortunate gentleman, the whole story of it does now fall to the ground, at any rate rests on other matters, with reference to which this man demands to be put on his trial, and as to which no evidence has been offered. Lord Cross, speaking last year at Sheffield, used words a little stronger than, and, if I may be allowed to say so, not quite so skilful as the euphemistic language of the First Lord to-night, and of the right hon. gentleman the Under Secretary last week. He said, "we did interfere in the matter of the Kashmir, and why? Because the people of Kashmir were so ground down by the tyranny and misgovernment of the Maharaja that we were bound as the paramount power to interfere for the protection of the interests of the inhabitants." Where in these papers is there one instance of this grinding down? If you want to steal Kashmir, as unfortunately we have stolen State after State in India and other parts of the world, then say so at once, and at least have the merit of honest thieves; don't be hypocritical, by saying you set up self-government where self-government has no real existence. What is the position of Kashmir towards this country? Fortunately the history is not long, so far as it affects this unfortunate man, and I will deal with it as briefly as it is possible to do. The history of Kashmir, for the purpose of to-night's discussion, began with the Treaty of 1846, with the grandfather of the gentleman whose cause I am pleading. Then for a considerable money payment, recorded in the third section of the Treaty, the British Government transferred and made over for ever, in independent possession, to Maharaja Golab Singh and the heirs male of his body, the territory which includes Kashmir and Jummoo. This is not a case of an ordinary feudatory State. So little is it regarded as a feudatory State that in the statistical abstract of this very year you have the evidence of its non-inclusion up to 1881 amongst the feudatory States, and there was never anything to suggest that we had a right or duty to send a Resident there until 1885, on the death of the father of the present Maharaja. I won't trouble the House with what passed until a few days before the commencement of the reign of the present chief. The Maharaja Golab Singh, with whom the Treaty of the 16th of March, 1846, was made, was succeeded by his son about the time of the Indian Mutiny; and Lord Canning, in an official document, gave Maharaja Rumbir Singh, who had succeeded Golab Singh, in 1857, the *Sanad* of adoption, which provided that in case of failure of issue he and his successors would be competent to adopt an heir and thus perpetuate the line. This was given on the ground of the great service rendered by the Maharaja during the Mutiny. The Maharaja Rumbir Singh was ill in 1884, and I am afraid that some fourteen or fifteen years ago, when Jingoism was specially paramount in the making of great military frontiers and things of that kind, we looked with longing eyes upon the property of others, and were disposed to ignore any sense of justice in our dealings with them. It was then said that Rumbir Singh had misgoverned his country. If he had, it was a matter with which, except as being by treaty the paramount power, in which case we might have made remonstrance, we had nothing whatever to do. But, as a matter of fact, we made no remonstrance to him. The Under Secretary of State dissents. Then why is it not in the papers? The papers began in 1884 with a dispatch relating to the alleged misgovernment during the time of the present Maharaja's father. The words of the despatch preclude the possibility of remonstrance having been made. But what happens is that while the Maharaja was dying, the Viceroy of India, looking to the matter, as he says, with a view to his troublesome neighbours on the north-west frontier, suggested certain reforms which on the accession of the son of the then dying man it would be well should be carried out: and I will read to the House in the words of Lord Dufferin himself the admission that many of these reforms had been carried out during the short period that this gentleman sat on the throne. In 1885 the succession of Prapat Singh was formally recognised by the Government. He came to the throne under the treaty which I have read to the House. One new departure there was against which the Maharaja protested, namely, the establishment of a Residency, instead of Kashmir being an independent possession, which under the treaty it was, subject to the supremacy of the Empress Queen. After the appointment of a Resident it is a monstrously unfair thing to spring a mine four or five years afterwards, and allege as an excuse for confiscating property and power that there had been misgovernment where, if there had been misgovernment, it should have been reported day by day, week by week, month by month, and year by year. There are no such reports. If the Secretary of State has got them he ought to have printed them. I am not asking the House to say that this unfortunate man is guiltless, but I am asking them to say that he is entitled to be tried, and to have an inquiry before he is deprived of his rights. In 1889 the Government deprived this gentleman of his chieftainship. By what right? By no right save the right of force. By what law? By no law save the law of force. Upon what charges? Upon charges of the vaguest description. It is clear these papers are delusive papers. There must have been reports made to the Viceroy, which reports ought to be in the hands of the House. If it is said that they are of a confidential character; if it is said they cannot be produced, at any rate the witnesses who can prove the occasions of misgovernment ought to be produced in some court. Is it because this man is rich; is it because his property is in a place where you want to have possession because of frontier considerations, that he is to be deprived of the right which you admit to the meanest person accused within this country, or within the Asiatic dominions of the Empress Queen? It is a monstrous thing, and I ask the House to look at it without consideration of party; because you must remember it is not a question only of this man, but of every feudatory prince whose property you may want to take and merge in our dominions. The papers have not been put on the table in a hurry. They have been in the skilled hands of the Under Secretary. We all know how frank the Under Secretary can be if he tries, and I ask him to tell the House how many papers relating to these important dispatches between the Government of India and the Secretary of State have been kept back, and why. It is clear some have—the language shows it. Why are any kept back? They have been kept back because the action of the Government cannot be defended. I do not know what the charges are against the Maharaja, and I am only asking that this Parliament shall say that the Government of India, however powerful, and whatever the State considerations are, has no right to rob this man. On the 14th of September, 1885, the Viceroy sent a dispatch to which I must allude for a moment. It was sent just on the accession of the present Maharaja to the throne, and I allege to the House it makes a clear bill up to the time, so far as any charges of misgovernment entitled our Government to interfere. The Viceroy says: "I trust that your highness's life may be long and prosperous; and that, in all difficulties, of whatsoever kind, you will rely with confidence upon the goodwill of the British Government, which will never fail you so long as you are loyal to the Crown, and earnest in the desire to rule your State with justice and moderation. Your Highness has before you a difficult task. During the illness of your father the administration of the State became seriously disorganised, and it will be necessary for you to introduce many reforms." I will show you that three years after Lord Dufferin's time reforms had been carried out, and that misgovernment is a pretext for stealing the man's property. The Maharaja wrote in reply protesting against the Residency being placed upon him. He said: "I do not hesitate to admit that the existing state of affairs in Kashmir and Jammu urgently requires immediate introduction of substantial reforms into the administration of the country, and now that I have power commensurate with my responsibilities, I beg to answer your Excellency that nothing shall be spared on my part, and no time will be lost to prove beyond any possibility of doubt that it is my ambition to succeed in making my country a model of a well-governed State in alliance with the Government of India." Having got the Resident at the capital, what do we find? We find that the Resident wants to get rid of the Maharaja, he submits some report to the Government, the particulars of which we do not know, and a report, the particulars of which we do know, dated March 5th, 1888. Let me point out in the first place that in the despatch of the 5th of March, 1888, there is nothing to justify any of the words of Lord Cross at Sheffield, or the words of the Under-Secretary of State last week, as to misgovernment, or the words of the First Lord of the Treasury to-night. Now, what was the decision the Government of India came to in August, 1888? It was that the condition of the State did not seem to demand such action as Mr. Plowden had suggested, and that the Government had therefore determined not to resort to measures which would have the effect directly or indirectlv of taking the power out of the Maharaja's hands. Yet no less than seven months after that dispatch power was taken out of his hands, and taken out solely on these letters. Solely, perhaps, is a strong word to use; but it was immediately after coming into possession of these letters, suggesting the worst of crimes—letters which the Maharaja has always denied, and as to which he is certainly entitled to be heard before a Select Committee of this House or before the Viceroy himself. He had confidence in the British Government, but he had no confidence in the officials who he said misrepresented him. The decision that there should be no interference with the Maharaja directly or indirectly disposes of Mr. Plowden's report of the 8th of March, 1888. I come now to April, 1889, when we had some further action. I will first mention that on the 25th of July, 1888, Lord Dufferin wrote: "I do not overlook the fact that since the appointment of the Council of which Diwan Lachman Dass was a member, considerable progress has been made in the direction of reform; useful work has been done with regard to the revenue administration, and in the reorganisation of the Public Works and Medical Department. But much remains to be done." This is not the language of condemnation of chronic misgovernment and the grinding down of the people. Misgovernment is only on invention—an excuse for having dispossessed this man, and I think I have a right to quote the evidence given by Lord Dufferin in 1888. This unfortunate prince, hampered by the Resident who dictated the policy he should pursue, did make such reforms as entitled him to the praise of Lord Dufferin—a statesman of the greatest eminence, of the keenest judgment, and a man who cannot be charged with being at all partial to the class of man I am defending here this afternoon. Now I come to these forged letters. There is a batch of thirty-four, and the Maharaja says that they are all forgeries. I do not ask you to say whether they are or are not, but I say that if they are used against him he is entitled to go into court and cross-examine the witnesses against him. Other letters on which the Government have relied have been abandoned as forgeries within the memory of many of us in this House. What is the character of these letters as described by the Resident? The character of them is that the Maharaja offered large sums of money to certain individuals on condition that they would murder, or cause to be removed, Mr. Plowden, the late Resident. It is alleged that these letters showed treasonable correspondence with the enemies of England. All these things are denied by the Maharaja. I do not ask you to say whether the Maharaja is right or wrong, but I say that when letters alleging murder are produced against a prince with whom we have a treaty of alliance, immediately after which we take away his property, the commonest and the merest justice demands that he should have an opportunity of being heard before a Select Committee of this House, or some tribunal competent to deal with his offence, if offence he has committed. The Government are not going to stand by these letters to-night, but the Viceroy has stood by them, and I will read you words in which they are so stood by. The Viceroy said "In the spring of this year"—that is last year—"my attention was called to the documents referred to in your Highness's letter. Many of these had every appearance of being genuine, and they have moreover a striking resemblance to those other papers of which I have already spoken, and which came into the possession of the Government of India at a previous time." "Your Highness is correct in expressing your belief that the action subsequently taken by my Government was not justified merely by the disclosures contained in these letters." Where is the report upon which they acted? The man had a right to be tried. The letters are vague statements. The Viceroy goes on: "Notwithstanding the ample resources of your State, your treasury was empty". Well, if you are going to dethrone every Prince whose treasury becomes empty, I do not know how far you are prepared to carry your policy. Does the Government really mean that? If that be so, how is it they took from this man the advance or deposit or loan of a large sum of money, amounting to twenty-five lakhs of rupees? They had this in their hands when the treasury was empty. Why did they take money for Lady Dufferin's admirable fund? Why, if the treasury was empty, did they not reckon the millions of rupees for railway works in the interest of frontier defence? Treasury empty! Why, you and your Resident helped to empty it, and then you tell this unfortunate man it is a reason why he should be dethroned!

Sir J. GORST: Will the hon. gentleman finish the sentence?

Mr. BRADLAUGH: You put on the table what you please, and I have to make the best I can with the House half empty, because every member feels the difficulty when a motion for adjournment is moved. I have, with such knowledge as is supplied, to make what case I can with this far off matter.

Sir J. GORST: I only interrupted the hon. gentleman to point out that he had not read the sentence to the end, and I thought to put the case fairly it should be given to the end.

Mr. BRADLAUGH: I will read it to the end and show that the right hon. gentleman gains nothing by making me read it. "Notwithstanding the ample resources of your State, your treasury was empty; corruption and disorder prevailed in every department and every office; your Highness was still surrounded by low and unworthy favorites; and the continued misgovernment of your State was becoming every day a more serious source of anxiety." Well, there is not a word affecting finance there. I was going to deal with each allegation in turn. "Low and unworthy favourites!" Every prince has these even in his own household; every Oriental prince has such. The whole history of our transactions with native princes shows that when we have hankered to take their money, their land, their position, we have used vices which appeared at the time to suit our purposes and help us to gain our ends. I do not know what the right hon. gentleman means by inviting me to read to the end, as if I had ommitted some allusion to the empty treasury. Why, the Indian Government had then twenty-five lackh of rupees of his, and millions of rupees had been laid out in railway works. Who are these low and unworthy people? It is not enough to make a vague statement: where is the evidence? Let the man be tried. A man complains of a burglary in his jeweller's shop, and you say to him, "Oh but you were misusing the jewels". I ask the House to take at least some tone of dignity in this matter. This despotic government of India; as an Indian Secretary once said, has no public opinion to influence it, no Parliament to control it, no Press to criticise it. The Government of India is a despotism that has in many degrees been well for India, it is a despotism which has brought in its train advantages which many of these poor people would not otherwise have obtained; but it cannot be denied that in many respects that despotism in the past has been tainted with fraud and crime, and I hope it is not left to the present Government to revive these evil traditions in obtaining possession of Kashmir. The Empress Queen, the paramount Power, acting as Judge, has condemned this man unheard. No man should be under menace of this injustice. The grandfather of the Prince bought these lands, and we by treaty declared they belonged to him for ever. (Sir John Gorst expressed dissent.)

The right hon. gentleman does not seem to be acquainted with all these facts in the history of India. Shall I ask him to read and tell us the exact sum paid for the Maharaja's dominions? How do the Government justify their action? They say the Maharaja resigned. He says he did nothing of the kind. I am more inclined to believe him than even the Under Secretary, for whose statements I have always the profoundest respect. Officially, there could be nothing better than the way he answers questions in this House; but when history some fifty years hence comes to deal with him, the comment of the historian will be how wickedly the Government deceived the Under Secretary, making him say as truth the things that were not true. It is said the Maharaja voluntarily resigned. It is true that on March 8th, 1889, the Maharaja issued the following document. I will abridge it; if it is said I am incorrect I will read the whole willingly; but I do not think my abridgement will differ from the exact words. The Maharaja appointed a Council who were to govern the country for five years, he reserving to himself all his princely rights and reserving certain powers, but allowing them much the same authority as, allowing for Oriental position, a Cabinet enjoys here. The Government of India do not accept that, yet they say they accepted a voluntary resignation. What he offered they would not have, what they wanted they took from him. The Maharaja says that even in the decree of March 8th he acted under pressure. I do not ask the House to accede to that, but I do say that he is entitled to a Select Committee here—or he would be even content with an inquiry conducted in India, if Lord Lansdowne will give his personal attention to it. The right hon. gentleman is better acquainted with the Government of India than I am. He knows that Residents are not always perfect, that Residents sometimes quarrel with a prince, and that matters are alleged as facts which do not always bear the test and scrutiny of examination. This man through my mouth appeals to this House, not that you should declare that the Government of India is wrong—he simply asks for an inquiry. He has a right to that inquiry. I regret that the appeal has not been made by an abler tongue, by a better informed man. But I am limited to the information that the Parliamentary papers presented to the House, and such records as the history of India, enables me to present, and I say without fear of contradiction that no case is made out for the action that has been taken. In 1888 the Government of India and the Secretary of State in Council at home came to the conclusion there was nothing for which directly or indirectly the Maharaja ought to be deprived of power; and within seven mouths they take it all away. If you trample on treaties, if your obligations to the Princes of India are to be broken, and the native rulers are not to rely on your word, and English justice in India is a shadow and a delusion, let that be known; but let those who hold a contrary opinion vote for my motion as the means of protest. The government of India is no party question; alike to Liberal or Conservative, Radical or Whig, it is our duty and our interest that our paramount rule in India should be just.

Motion made that this House do now adjourn.

The UNDER SECRETARY OF STATE FOR INDIA (Sir John Gorst, Chatham): I do not for a moment dispute the right of the hon. member to challenge the action of the Government of India, or to ask the House to order an enquiry, if there is anything to enquire into. If the House will give me its attention for a short time I will tell the House why the Government of India has acted in the manner it has, and why it appears to the Secretary of State this is not a subject which can properly be made matter of inquiry, either by Judicial Commission in India or by Select Committee of the House of Commons. I need not take the House back to the early history of Kashmir. The hon. member for Northampton has, in the little history he has given, indicated to the House that after the Sikh war we, by force of arms, placed a Hindu ruler over the Muhammadan people of Kashmir; and by doing this, we incurred, as it seems to me, the responsibility of seeing that these Muhammadan people, who by the action of the British Government were subjected to an alien dynasty, were at least fairly and properly governed. Now complaints of the misgovernment of Kashmir are not so modern as the hon. member for Northampton seems to suppose. I should like to read to the House the observations which were made by the Government of Lord Ripon in 1884, and Lord Ripon was a Viceroy whose error did not at all events lie in over interference with native chiefs. This was what was said by the Government in 1884. The misgovernment to which the people of this country (Kashmir) have long been subjected.—The hon. member for Northampton asks what the nature of the misgovernment was, and I will try before I sit down to give the House some faint idea of the nature and results of this misgovernment.—Lord Ripon said "The people of that country have long been subjected to misgovernment, and this was some time since brought prominently into notice by Mr. Henvey; we did not take action at once conceiving that a favourable opportunity would offer on the occasion of a fresh successor"—the Maharaja Runbir Singh was then suffering from a mortal illness and his death was expected—"when that event takes place we shall consider that it will be our duty to express on the Kashmir Government its obligations to its own subjects, and to see that reforms so urgently needed are no longer postponed." To those remarks of Lord Ripon's Government an answer was returned by Lord Kimberley, Secretary of State, under the right hon. gentleman the member for Midlothian, and Lord Kimberley stated in his despatch his doubts whether the Government of India was justified in hesitating so long as it had hesitated, to interfere in the affairs of Kashmir. It may indeed be questioned whether, having regard to the circumstances under which a Hindoo family were settled as rulers, the intervention of the British Government on behalf of the Muhammadan people had not already been too long delayed. Well, the Government of India waited eighteen months, and in 1885 the late Maharaja died, and the present Maharaja came to the throne. The hon. member for Northampton has already read some of the warnings which were addressed to the present Maharaja of Kashmir on the occasion of his ascending the throne, but he said—and I really was surprised when he made the statement to the House—that until quite recently no complaint was made of his administration, and in fact he quoted a few expressions from some of Lord Dufferin's despatches, which would have left upon the House the impression that upon the whole the Government had been very successfully administered and many reforms had been carried out. Now, what did Mr. Plowden say in March, 1888. He thought it his duty to call the formal attention of the Government of India to the fearful condition of Kashmir under the Maharaja and his associates, whom he calls a band of corrupt and mischievous men. Mr. Plowden says: "I think, however, that the Government of India should be under no illusion as regards Maharaja Pertab Singh. From first to last I have failed to discover in him any sustained capacity for governing his country or any genuine desire to ameliorate its condition or to introduce those reforms which he has acknowledged to be necessary. More than two years have passed since his accession, but not only has he achieved nothing but he has opposed beneficial measures proposed by others. . . . He will never of his own free will establish a capable and honest administration; nor if any power of interference is left him will he permit any administration approved by the Government of India to carry on the business of the country. He will thwart and oppose it in every way he dares; the only restraint will be the limit of his powers aud his fears." Well at the same time that Mr. Plowden made this grave report to the Government of India on the condition of the country and the character of the Maharaja, a proposal was made by the Maharaja himself to appoint a council.

Mr. BRADLAUGH: The right hon. gentleman will pardon me. I stated to the House that on the report of Mr. Plowden the Government came to the decision not to take the power from the Maharaja, and that Lord Dufferin contradicted Mr. Plowden by recognising the fact that since the appointment of the council of which Dinan Lachman Dass was a member considerable progress had been made in the direction of reform.

Sir JOHN GORST: The hon. member is impatient. I am coming to that. I shall have something more to say first. At the time that this report was sent home, application was made by the Maharaja to have a Council appointed, upon which the Government of India decided to give him another trial to see whether by his Council he would govern the country better. I must say, speaking by the light of after events, it was unfortunate that the Government of India accepted the proposal, set aside the report of Mr. Plowden, and gave the Maharaja what in vulgar phrase would be called "another chance". I confess if the hon. member for Northampton instead of attacking the Government of India for having at last relieved the Maharaja of the functions of government had attacked the Government for being so weak in 1888 as to give this second chance, I am sure that I as Under Secretary would have found it difficult to make out a good defensive case. But Lord Dufferin decided on this course. He wrote a complimentary letter to the Maharaja, which the hon. member has read, and no doubt he made use of the expressions the hon. member has quoted as to the success of the Council, since the appointment of Diwan Lachman Dass, under whom considerable progress, he said, had been made in the direction of reform. But will the House believe that the object of that letter, on which the hon. member relies as showing the improvement in the government of the country, was to remonstrate with the Maharaja for dismissing summarily, and without the knowledge of the Government of India, that same Diwan Lachman Dass whose reforms were praised in the passage of Lord Dufferin's letter which the hon. member has quoted as praising the Maharaja for his improvements in the government of his country. The beginning of Lord Dufferin's letter, which the hon. member has not quoted, is as follows: "I cannot avoid informing your Highness that the news of the sudden removal of Diwan Lachman Dass was received by me with some surprise. Your Highness appointed him to your Council after consulting me, and I hoped that your Highness would before making another change of government give me some previous intimation of your views. However this point has already been brought to your notice by Mr. Plowden, and I do not now desire to dwell upon it further." Well, the arrangements for governing the country by means of a Council were made, and in order to give the new scheme the fullest possible chance of success, Mr. Plowden was removed from Kashmir on the occasion of his promotion, and Colonel Nisbet, a a personal friend of the Maharaja and in whom the Maharaja placed implicit confidence, was sent to Kashmir. Now I said I would give the House some little idea of the misgovernment which the hon. member for Northampton made so light of, and of which he said no trace was to be found in the papers before the House. Now if hon. members have read the papers, they will see that they close with the report of a certain gentleman of the name of Wingate. Mr. Wingate was a revenue officer of the Bombay Government of nineteen years' experience, and he had also been employed in the revenue settlement of some of the Native States of Rajputana. He was a highly qualified and experienced officer. He was employed by the Maharaja's Government, and his report well deserves the study of anybody who desires to understand the position of Kashmir, although it is full of technicalities and written in a dry business-like technical spirit, but his narrative is enlivened occasionally by the most horrible statements as to the condition of Kashmir. Let me say this gentleman was eighteen months among the people surveying in Kashmir and Jummoo, and he appears to have gone to work in a dry business-like fashion. In these Oriental States we know that the foundation of the happiness of the people consists in the correct measurement of their land. The first thing Mr. Wingate discovered was that the measurement of the land upon which the ryots paid their rent was altogether measured against the ryots.

Mr. BRADLAUGH: Does the right hon. gentleman represent that in any way that this was done under the direction of the Maharaja?

Sir JOHN GORST: The evil existed under the Government of the Maharaja and it was approved by the Maharaja's Government there.

Mr. BRADLAUGH: Mr. Wingate's report referred to the existing state of things. Part of the condition of things that existed over Kashmir it was no part of the misgovernment of the Maharaja.

Sir JOHN GORST: It was part of the condition of things in Kashmir under a government of which the Maharaja was the head. I do not know whether the Maharaja shields himself under the allegation that all this had happened in the past and that he was not responsible for the misgovernment which he allowed to exist. I don't think this House will take such a view of the limitations of the Maharaja's duties to his subjects. Besides, we have read Mr. Plowden's report, in which it is stated that the Maharaja opposed those reforms he himself considered necessary. Even the assessment of the ryots is arbitrarily fixed, and a divisional official gets the revenue out of the unhappy cultivators in the best way he can—the result being that from one-half to two-thirds of the gross produce of the land was exacted from these unhappy people, mostly in kind and partly also in cash.

Mr. BRADLAUGH: Does not Mr. Wingate say that began as far back as 1874?

Sir J. GORST: I have been reading the report—

Mr. BRADLAUGH: You have not been reading at all.

Sir J. GORST: The hon. member challenged me to say what the misgovernment was in Kashmir.

Mr. BRADLAUGH: I challenged the right hon. gentleman to prove misgovernment on the part of the Maharaja.

Sir J. GORST: I am in the recollection of the House. I appeal to hon. members whether, if the case rested solely on the speech of the hon. member for Northampton, they would not have gone away in the belief that Kashmir was the best-governed country in the world. I am showing what was the state of affairs which compelled the Government of India to take this action. I am going to show the House why the Government in the interests of humanity were peremptorily called upon to take this step. (A laugh.) The hon. member may laugh, but I think it is not a laughing matter. Now let me describe what was done. The assessment was paid at fixed rates in kind: that is to say it was levied on the people in money value and then they were made to give produce at certain fixed and prescribed rates in lieu of paying the assessment in cash. In the case of rice, the main staple which the ryots cultivated, the prescribed rate was extremely unfavourable to the cultivator.—All this is in Mr. Wingate's report, and if I am epitomising it unfairly the hon. member can subsequently correct me. I do not see why he should interrupt me now.—But the prescribed rates for cotton, which is grown by the richer ryots, were very favourable; therefore it came to this: that the officers of the Revenue allowed the rich ryots to pay on the staple bearing the most favourable rate, while the poor ryots had to pay on the staple bearing the most unfavourable rates; and every year, says Mr. Wingate in his report "the bulk of the rice goes into the city", and further he adds, "these poor ryots often have to buy it back at two or three times the price at which it was credited to them in their assessment", and then this dry technical report contains this statement—"In this fertile valley there are women and children actually starving". Further on it says: "It may be easier now to understand why the Kashmiri cares naught for rights in land, why his fields are fallow or full of weeds, and manure and water neglected; why he has, as I can well believe, even to be forced to cultivate. The revenue system is such, that whether he works much or little he is left with barely enough to get along on till next harvest. He is a machine to produce sháli for a very large and most idle city population".

Mr. MACNEILL: Like Ireland!

Sir J. GORST: A city, the population of which consists of officials and of Hindoo pundits who have prepared the brief from which the hon. member for Northampton spoke. These men get their rice cheap, while the ryot who grows it and is forbidden to dispose of it for export, starves. Again, Mr. Wingate says that "the cultivator is compelled to grow rice, and in many years to part with it below the proper market rate in order that the city may be content. If the harvest is too little for both the city must be supplied, and is supplied by any force that may be necessary, and the cultivator and his children must go without. That is the explanation of the angry discontent that filled the valley during the famine. The cultivator is considered to have rights neither to his land nor to his crops. The city population have a right to be well fed whether there is famine or not", and that is not all; the officials of the revenue contractors are gradually in Kashmir converting themselves into landlords. They get grants of waste land, they foreclose upon ryots who are indebted, and they purchase a considerable part of the land, and as Mr. Wingate says: "Since the death of the Maharaja Golab Singh, from which date central authority appears to have been weaker, there has been a steadily, and latterly, rapidly increasing transference of land from the cultivating to the non-cultivating classes, and a landlord element is intruding itself between the cultivator and the state." I earnestly commend this to the attention of some of the hon. members from Ireland. Then, besides this, there exists among the unhappy ryots a system of *begar*, or forced labour. This scourge which is peculiar to the Government villages, and from which the villages which happen to be in the hands of these landlords are free is imposed upon the people with the utmost severity.

Mr. BRADLAUGH: I venture to make an appeal to the right hon. gentleman. I fancy that by the rules of the House I have no right of reply. I wish to ask him, in reference to this forced labour, whether it is not a fact that the system prevailed long before the death of the father of this unfortunate gentleman, and whether the Maharaja did not himself issue a decree abolishing it.

Mr. SPEAKER: Order, order! I may explain that the hon. member will be entitled to reply, and it would be more convenient than to interrupt the right hon. gentleman.

Sir J. GORST: I am glad that the hon. gentleman will have an opportunity of replying, because otherwise he will not wait patiently to hear the end of my argument. He challenged me to show misgovernment in Kashmir. I am telling him what exists there, and presently I will ask him what was the Government of India to do under the circumstances. This forced labour was so unreasonably enforced on the people, that if twenty coolies were wanted it was customary to requisition a hundred. Eighty would buy themselves off with payments to the officers, and twenty of the poorest would be compelled to do the duty. And it was so serious and formidable that they left their homes and hid themselves for days in order to escape the work. I am speaking of matters which are within the knowledge of many hon. members of this House who have served in India. But I am bound to repeat them, when this House is asked to censure the conduct of the Government of India. Mr. Wingate says that the cultivators, under this Hindoo rule, have been pressed down to the condition of coolies cultivating the State property on a subsistence allowance. This has been going on in Kashmir for years, and what has been the result? The population has been reduced by one half, the ryots are deserting the country wherever they can do so, the villages are ruined, the bridges are broken down, the irrigation channels are abandoned, and a population under the protection of a British Government, which boasts of its Christianity and its civilisation has sunk into a condition which I have tried faintly to describe. This, Mr. Speaker, is a description of the condition of the unhappy people of Kashmir which seems to have moved the laughter of the hon. member opposite. I should have thought he would have treated the subject more seriously. Such was the condition of the people—a condition which weighed upon the Government of India and the Secretary of State, who had hoped almost against hope that the new arrangement of the Maharaja would afford some amelioration in the condition of the people. But no: Colonel Nisbett, appointed resident because he was the Maharaja's friend, arrived at precisely the same conclusion as Mr. Plowden, and his conversion to those views was announced to the Government of India at the time of the discovery of the treasonable criminal letters to which the hon. member for Northampton has alluded. These letters in spite of what the hon. member says have never been treated by the Government of India as serious, nor have they been made the ground for the exclusion of the Maharaja from interference in the public affairs of Kashmir. They might never have been noticed had they not been accompanied by the resignation of his own accord of part of his power. The Government of India at the outset said they were not disposed to attach excessive importance to these letters. They also wrote that they did not exclusively base their action upon the Maharaja's edict of resignation, but that edict gave them an occasion—and they would have been criminal if they had neglected to avail themselves of it—for placing the affairs of Kashmir on a more satisfactory basis. The despatch in which their conclusions were announced to the Secretary of State contains these words :—

"We greatly regret the necessity for any interference at all, but we are now convinced that in the interests of the people of Kashmir and of the ruling family itself it is no longer right or possible to leave the control of affairs in the hands of the Maharaja."

In the whole of this business the Government of India have carefully avoided acting upon any personal grounds and I must object to the hon. member for Northampton and those who instruct him trying to make out that this is a sort of personal question between the Maharaja and the Government of India. They insist on making out that the Maharaja has been deposed from his throne because of these letters, or because of some personal vices or because of his own resignation. Not one of these is the real ground upon which the Government of India has acted. As I have stated in this House in answer to questions over and over again the Government of India has acted in the interests of the people of Kashmir, and of their right to better Government. I can only say that in my humble opinion these reforms could not longer be delayed and, if anything, both the Government of Mr. Gladstone and the present Government ought to reproach themselves for the long delay. It is a curious example of the irony of fate that the Radical member for Northampton should be pleading in this House the Divine right of an Oriental despot to deal with his people as he pleaces and that I a humble but reactionary Tory should be pleading the right of these poor Moslems to cultivate their own land. But we have of late been accustomed in this House to strange sights. I ask the House to look at the papers and see how careful the Government of India has been of the rights of this reigning family. Will the House believe that in the Government of this country, tho Government which is the paramount power in Kashmir not an Englishman sits on the Council which is composed exclusively of the natives of the State and includes two members of the reigning family. The Government of India does not and never has in its policy interfered with the personal rights of the Chiefs of India. It has been most careful of all existing rights, of all rights that affect the chiefs. But there is one right which it regards as more sacred than even the rights of Oriental despots to their thrones and that is the right of the people who live under the protection of the power of Great Britain to just and upright Government. I hope that the House of Commons will not stand in the way of justice being done to the people of Kashmir. I hope that the House of Commons to-night will by a large majority approve the conduct of the Government of India in at last interfering in this unhappy State and in allowing the Maharaja of Kashmir and the Chiefs of India generally to know that although their rights are respected it is on the condition that their people are moderately happy and moderately justly governed.

Mr. BRADLAUGH: I will, sir, at once take advantage of the right of reply which you have ruled rests with me. The point I wish to state is so important that I think it better to put it before the House at once. I say that the report of Mr. Wingate refers to no specific act of misgovernment by the deposed Maharaja. It relates a state of things which obtained long prior to the Maharaja's birth, and which he has himself partially remedied since his accession to power. In September 1885 he actually issued a decree abolishing forced labour both in Kashmir and in Jummu so far as he could. For three years this unfortunate man step by step took up reforms, and in one of his despatches he speaks of the settlement of the land question as a task which it would take five years to deal with. I never said that the Government of Kashmir was perfect, on the contrary, I said that, like all Oriental governments, it had many defects, and that the people of Kashmir were in a state of misery and difficulty from which millions of the population of India were not free. I repeat that no specific act of misgovernment has been even pretended to be proved against the Maharaja, and that so far as Mr. Plowden's report is concerned the decision of the Government of India itself was that it did not justify any interference on their part.

Mr. MACNEILL (Donegal Co.); The Under Secretary for India is always interesting and his great abilities add additional charms to what he says. But on this occasion I think it was scarcely fair in accusing me of smiling at the sufferings of these people. I see too much suffering to regard it otherwise than with infinite sorrow and sympathy. What I smiled at was this. Knowing as I do the infamous transactions and secret springs which I intend to expose, I smiled that a gentleman representing a Government guilty of such conduct should claim universal benevolence and pretend to be benefiting the people, whereas they are robbing an ancient prince of his inheritance. The right hon. gentleman was careful to put forward the religious question, and to point out that the Maharaja was an Hindu while his subjects were Muhammadans. But I can tell him that if he would take a plebiscite of the inhabitants of Kashmir he would find that three-fourths of the people favoured the restoration of the prince. We know that forty millions of our subjects in India are in a constant state of starvation, and that during the famine in 1877 the number of deaths from famine exceeded the population of London. Surely our efforts at administration in India have not been so successful as to justify our bringing more of the natives under our system? I heard the speech of the right hon. gentleman, and I must confess I thought it a most shifting defence. I think I shall be enabled to prove that the Maharaja has been deprived of his inheritance simply by the pursuance of an annexation policy, which was the approximate cause of the Indian Mutiny. What has happened is what is called in Ireland "land grabbing". The Maharaja, who was placed in his position many years ago, has displayed nothing but kindness and loyalty to the British rule. He was placed on that throne, and it was reserved to him and his heirs, and in the meantime he has acted well towards this country. With regard to the letters on which so much stress has been laid, none of them have been read to the House.

Dr. HUNTER: Mr. Speaker, the defence which has been offered on the part of the Government does not explain the degradation from his rank of the Maharaja of Kashmir, an act of unjustifiable spoliation. One remark with which the Under Secretary of State wound up his remarks, intended to be eloquent, was an appeal to this House on behalf of the poor Moslem cultivators. Why the Moslem cultivator? Surely a Hindu, if he happens to be a cultivator, is as much entitled to sympathy as the Moslem. But the right hon. gentleman laid stress on the word Moslem, in order to excite those unhappy religious prejudices which unfortunately prevail in India.

We know that in India, unhappily, both Moslems and Hindus are animated by strong fanatical opinions on the subject of religion, leading to collisions and breaches of the peace. And here is the Under Secretary for India in this House pointing his moral by the contrast between the Moslem and the Hindu peasants, and trying thus to fan the embers of religious antipathy. What are the reasons which he adduced why the Maharaja should be deposed. Not one of the reasons had the slightest relation to anything that was done by the Maharaja of Kashmir himself. That I pass by. But what is the state of the country upon which he relies. There were three arguments. The first argument was that in consequence of the mismanagement of the revenue derived from the land, there was a great deal of poverty in the country, and that the population had largely diminished. Well, I was amazed to hear a minister sitting on that side of the House using that as an argument why the Maharaja of Kashmir should be deposed; because the Maharaja has equally good reason for deposing you from the government of Ireland, if that argument has any validity whatever. But that is not the only thing. We are told that the land revenue is extortionate. That is no doubt the reason why you are putting out the Maharaja and putting in yourselves. There is no doubt a margin, a large margin, which excites the cupidity of the British Goovernment, and induces them to take possession of that country. But all this argument simply comes to this point, that according to the view of the Government of India, the ancient, not the recent, mode of collecting the revenue from the land is defective, and that oppressions arise in the exercise of the right; so that, according to the eloquent language of the right hon. gentleman, the people are starving in the midst of plenty. That is precisely the condition of things in Ireland. The case of Ireland is an analogous case. Not a single argument adduced by the right hon. gentleman in reference to Kashmir but is applicable to Ireland, in the eyes of impartial people living outside the latter country. I am afraid the transaction is a very doubtful one, when it has to be supported by such statements as those which have been advanced by the Under Secretary of State.

Sir R. TEMPLE: Mr. Speaker, I feel bound to trouble the House for a very few moments on this subject, because I am one of those members who happen to know this country. I have travelled over every portion of it repeatedly, and for years I was officially connected with it. And though I never had the pleasure of knowing the Maharaja of Kashmir personally, unless I may have seen him as a child, yet I knew his father well, and I knew his grandfather also, and I may say well. Now, sir, much has been said by the hon. member for Northampton and by the hon. member for South Donegal, and again by the hon. member for Aberdeen, who has just sat down, regarding the ambitious or greedy eye which England has cast upon Kashmir. Indeed, in effect, the language used by hon. members implied the charge that England is attempting a theft of territory. Indeed the hon. member for Northampton exhausted the resources of phraseology in order to accuse his country of appropriating the lands of others. But is the House aware that England gains not one rood by the transactions which are now under consideration? All that happens is the transfer of the sovereignty from one brother to another. The power, the wealth, the property, remain in the same family; it is a mere exchange from one person to another. England remains exactly in the same position as she was before, and is in no wise benefitted. She has acted with entire disinterestedness, and whether she is wrong or whether she is right, her sole object has been to benefit the people of Kashmir. What ground has the hon. member for South Donegal for saying that we want a frontier there. I am afraid the hon. member does not know what our frontiers are. We have no military frontiers in that direction. It is not from there that we should be invaded. No, sir, the mighty mountains of the Himalaya constitute an impassable barrier to any enemy, either from Asia or from Europe. Then, sir, the hon. member for Aberbeen seemed to find fault with my right hon. friend the Under Secretary for saying that the Moslem of Kashmir must be protected. The hon. member entirely misapprehended my right hon. friend's meaning. What my right hon. friend meant was this, that the Maharaja of Kashmir was a Hindu potentate, and that we interfered by force of arms to place him over a Moslem population—a population which was not Hindu at all by allegiance or by tradition. They were therefore placed under an alien prince by the action of the British Government. My right hon. friend meant to say that we were bound to see that the Moslem population suffered nothing at the hands of the Hindu masters whom we had put over them. Then the hon. member for Aberdeen spoke of the gratitude which we owe the

Maharaja of Kashmir. I am not prepared to deny that sovereigns of this house have behaved well. The grandfather co-operated with us during the darkest days of the mutiny. But after all the gratitude was due from him to us rather than from us to him. He was our ally. We had placed him on the throne for political reasons of our own, and he was bound to act for us when we required his services. Something has been said of the several British residents. I was grieved to hear the terms of disparagement in which the hon. member for Northampton spoke of those most able servants of the State. At all events, they have no party purpose to serve; they are above partisan considerations. They may, like all men, be liable to error, but they are completely disinterested, and their action is based on perfect impartiality. In this case it was not one or two, but three residents—men of different ideas, but who all come to the same conclusion respecting the Government of Kashmir. Then, sir, regarding the misgovernment, I quite admit that reforms were at one time introduced and carried out to a considerable extent. I myself in former days have been witness to them. But I am afraid those reforms came to a sudden termination. But, sir, much was said, and with great truth, by my right hon. friend with respect to the mismanagement of the land revenues and the gross oppression which was practised upon the ryots. I quite admit that the abuses are not recent, and the report which has been read to-night is only an enlargement of what I used to hear in former years. But I am afraid that the evils have now reached alarming proportions, perhaps even a monstrous development. The hon. member for Aberdeen speaks of the decreasing population. Of all countries, Kashmir is the most favoured in climate. It may be severely cold in winter, but in summer it is fertile and bountiful as any place in the world. That its population is decreasing is a sign of misgovernment. I quite admit that there may have been outbreaks of cholera and other epidemics, but as for famine it is the last place in the world where such a calamity could be expected. The question comes what is the nature of the misgovernment? Well now, I submit that that is a question which should be left to the responsible government on the spot. I submit it is our duty to see that a good government is set up in that Empire. But when that has been set up do not harass it, or interfere with it or try to establish committees of inquiry here to investigate the matters, but accept the advice of the responsible authorities. If you are to havea Government at all we must trust to judge of these questions. There is, we are told, a bad system in this State, that the population is decreasing, property is not secure, that communications are not looked after, that the whole land is going rapidly to ruin, and that all departments are falling to a low level. But how are we to examine into these matters by an inquiry such as is asked for? These are the very things which are within the purview of Government and cannot be tested by judicial process. We all know how that would end. It would end in the acquittal of the charged. All these matters should be left to the Governor-General in Council, and to him we should entrust the responsibility. An inquiry such as is now proposed would have a bad effect in India. The hon. member for Northampton speaks as if this political measure of superseding the Maharaja of Kashmir would have a bad effect; but I can assure him that to have an inquiry of this kind, in which the whole government of Kashmir would be overhauled, would be a measure above all others which would be calculated to alarm and would be repugnant to those very persons whom he proposes to serve.

Sir UGHTRED KAY-SHUTTLEWORTH: In this debate we have been placed under this disadvantage, that the papers relating to Kashmir are not yet in the hands of members. But by the courtesy of the right hon. gentleman (Sir John Gorst), I have had the advantage of perusing these papers for a short time and it is only fair that I should rise to say, that so far as I can judge from a hasty perusal of the papers and following carefully the speech of the right hon. gentleman, he has stated the case as regards the action of successive Viceroys and successive Secretaries of State in their relation to the late Maharaja of Kashmir and the present Maharaja with perfect fairness. I may venture to say one or two words more as to whether the facts which have been laid before us show a necessity for such an inquiry as is asked for. I believe if hon. members will examine these papers they will find that there is nothing in them to call for a review by a Parliamentary Committee of the patient and deliberate action of the Government of India, who seem to have hesitated long before taking any strong step, although the misgovernment of the Maharhja has been, I fear, of a very glaring description. I would only venture to make this one remark. It should be a satisfaction to members on this side of the House to find with respect to the Government of India that it has not been drawn into the annexation policy, which my hon. friend (Mr. Bradlaugh) deprecates, but that it leaves the government of Kashmir under a council of natives of India, guided by the Resident of India; and in concluding a despatch addressed by the Viceroy of India to the Maharaja of Kashmir, the Viceroy treats him with the greatest consideration and courtesy, and expresses a hope that it may be possible to give greater power to him in the future. At present the Maharaja is put in an ornamental position. He is not deposed but simply relieved of the powers of ruler of the country and these powers are confided to a council. I hope therefore the House will pause before voting for this motion.

Sir. WM. PLOWDEN: I will not detain the House for more than a few minutes, but I am not at all satisfied with the statement of the Under Secretary of State for India. The course of the debate has rather taken us from the point we ought to have before us, and I am very much surprised to hear the remarks which have fallen from the hon. member who has just spoken, in face of the glaring case which has been made by the member for Northampton. The member for Northampton is condemning the action of the Government of India, and is asking the House to express its sense of the course taken by the Government of India with respect to the Maharaja of Kashmir, and his complaint is that they have not given this man a chance of clearing himself from the charges which have been brought against him. It is not to a Parliamentary inquiry that this man's chance of clearing himself is to be entrusted. Why should we not have a judicial inquiry, and why is it that the Government are refusing to give this man a real investigation into the charges made against him. From what we have had brought before us there is real reason to believe that not only has considerable misgovernment been going on in Kashmir, now and in previous reigns, but that there has been no reproof administered as to this misgovernment. The right hon. gentleman asks us are we going to stand in the way of justice being done in Kashmir, but is he going to stand in the way of justice being done to the Maharaja? If he asserts that he (the Maharaja) is innocent of the charges brought against him.

Sir JOHN GORST: There are no charges.

Sir W. PLOWDEN: Then if there are no charges why is he

deposed? Evidently there must be some misconduct attributed to this man, in fact we know there is, because the whole defence put up by the Government is that he has been misconducting the government, and because he has been doing so he has been deposed. He says, "I have not misconducted the government. I am not guilty, and I ask to have my case inquired into." If the hon. member for Northampton pressed his motion to a division I shall be bound to support him unless we get a clear assertion from the right hon. gentleman that he will send out instructions to the Government of India to form some judicial Commission which shall inquire into the charges alleged.

The House divided:

Ayes	88
Noes	226
Majority	138

The motion for the adjournment of the House was therefore lost.

DIVISION LIST.

Ayes.

W. Abraham (Glamorgan), W. Abraham (Limerick), J. Austin, W. H. W. Ballantine, J. Barran, M. H. Beaufoy, A. Blane, T. D. Bolton (Derbyshire), Henry Campbell (Fermanagh), F. A. Channing, J. J. Clancy, Dr. G. B. Clark (Caithnesshire), H. P. Cobb, W. J. Corbet (Wicklow), D. Crilly, J. J. Dalton, J. Dillon, L. L. Dilwyn, S. Evershed, J. C. Flynn, Dr. J. F. Fox, T. Fry (Darlington), E. T. Gourley, E. Harrington (Kerry), H. Harrison, L. P. Hayden, G. Howell, J. A. Jacoby, J. S. Keay, D. Kilbride,, D. Knatchbull-Hugessen (Rochdale), R. Lalor, Sir W. Lawson (Cumberland), J. Leahy (Kildare), R. Leake, T. P. Lewis, (Angelsey), W. A. Macdonald, J. G. S. MacNeill, Dr. R. M'Donald (Ross), J. R. Maguire, W. Mather, S. Montagu, A. C. Morton, J. Nolan (Louth), J. F. X. O'Brien (Mayo), P. J. O'Brien (Tipperary), W. O'Brien (Cork, N.E.), A. O'Connor (Donegal), J. O'Connor (Tipperary), J. O'Kelly, C. S. Parnell, J. W. Philipps, E. H. Pickersgill, Sir W. C. Plowden, T. P. Price (Monmouthshire), D. Randell, W. H. K. Redmond (Fermanagh), Sir E. J. Reed (Cardiff), J. Roberts (Flint Burghs), T. Robinson (Gloucester), T. Roe, J. Rowlands (Finsbury), W. B. Rowlands (Cardiganshire), J. Rowntree, C. E. Schwann, T. Sexton, T. Shaw

(Halifax), J. D. Sheehan, F. F. Stevenson (Suffolk), J. C. Stevenson (S. Shields), H. Stewart (Lincolnshire), J. Stuart (Shoreditch), D. Sullivan, (Westmeath), T. D. Sullivan (Dublin), A. Sutherland (Sutherlandshire), A. Thomas (Glamorgan E.), D. A. Thomas (Merthyr), J. Tuite, Captain E. H. Verney, S. D. Waddy, H. Wardel, A. Webb, J. S. Will, A. Williams (Glamorgan), S. Williamson (Kilmarnock), J. Wilson (Lanark), J. Woodhead, C. Wright (Lanc. S.W.), Tellers for the Ayes, Mr. Bradlaugh and Mr. Hunter.

NOES.

W. G. Ainslie, J. Aird, Hon. P. Allsopp (Taunton), W. Ambrose, W. A. T. Amherst, H. T. Anstruther (St. Andrews), Colonel L. Anstruther (Suffolk), E. Ashmead-Bartlett, H. H. Asquith, Sir G. S. Baden-Powell, J. G. A. Baird, Rt. Hon. A. J. Balfour (Manchester), T. C. Baring (London), A. Barnes, A. H. S. Barry (Hunts), G. C. T. Bartley, Sir W. B. Barttelot, Sir E. Bates, A. A. Baumann, Rt. Hon. Sir M. H. Beach (Bristol), W. W, B. Beach (Hants.), E. W. Beckett (Yorks., N.R.), W. Beckett (Notts), W. G. C. Bentinck (Penryn), Commander Bethell, J. Bigwood, A. Birrell, Col. H. B. H. Blundell, G. H. Bond, T. W. Boord, Sir A. Borthwick, Col. Hon. F. C. Bridgeman, Hon. St. J. Brodrick, A. M. Brookfield, Sir W. C. Brooks, A. H. Brown (Salop), G. Bruce (Finsbury), Lord H. Bruce (Wiltshire), W. Burdett-Coutts, J. Caldwell, Sir G. Campbell (Kirkcaldy), Marquis of Carmarthen, Rt. Hon. J. Chamberlain (Birmingham), R. Chamberlain (Islington), Rt. Hon. H. Chaplin, Sir E. Clarke (Plymouth), D. H. Coghill, J. Collings, Sir J. C. R. Colomb, C. W. R. Cooke, J. Corbett (Worcestershire), F. S. W. Cornwallis, Sir J. P. Corry, Col. E. T. D. Cotton, H. H. Cozens-Hardy, Viscount Cranborne, H. S. Cross (Bolton), Hon. W. H. Cross (Liverpool), Sir S. B. Crossley (Suffolk), General Sir W. Crossman, Rt. Hon. G. Cubitt, Hon. G. N. Curzon (Lanc., S.W.), H. J. C. Cust, M. T. S. Darling (Edinburgh), H. T. Davenport (Staffordshire), E. S. W. De Cobain, Rt. Hon. Baron H. de Worms, Baron R. Dimsdale, F. D. Dixon-Hartland, R. S. Donkin, Sir J. E. Dorington, R. W. Duff, J. S. Dugdale, Rt. Hon. Sir W. H. Dyke, T. C. Edwards-Moss, Hon. Art. R. D. Elliot (Roxburghs), G. W. Elliot (Yorks. N. R.), P Esslemont, Sir A. O. Ewing, Col. H. Eyre, Lieut.-Gen. Feilden (Lanc. N.), A. E. Fellowes, R. C. M. Ferguson (Leith), Rt. Hon. Sir

J. Fergusson (Manchester), Admiral Field, G. H. Finch, W. H. Fisher, Sir F. Fitz-Wygram, Sir H. Fletcher, C. Flower, A. B. Forwood, Sir R. N. Fowler (London), Gen. C. C. Fraser, L. Fry (Bristol), S. Gedge, J. S. Gilliat, Major-Gen. Goldsworthy, Rt. Hon. Sir J. E. Gorst, Rt. Hon. G. J. Goschen, G. G. L. Gower, Sir E. Green (Wakefield), E. Greene (Suffolk), Viscount Grimston, F. B. Grotrian, R. B. Haldane, Rt. Hon. Lord G. Hamilton (Middlesex), Gen. Sir E. B. Hamley, R. W. Hanbury, E. Hardcastle (Salford), Sir E. J. Harland, Marquis of Hartington, A. R. Heath, Rt. Hon. E. Heneage, Hon. S. Herbert, Lord F. Hervey, Lord A. W. Hill (Down), Col. E. S. Hill (Bristol), E. B. Hoare (Hampstead), Sir W. H. Houldsworth, J. H. C. Hozier, F. S. Hunt, Sir G. Hunter (Hackney), Rt. Hon. W. L. Jackson, Sir R. Jardine, A. W. Jarvis, A. F. Jeffreys, L. J. Jennings, W. Johnston, Rt. Hon. Sir U. Kay-Shuttleworth, Sir J. H. Kennaway, W. Kenrick, Hon. G. T. Kenyon, Col. W. Kenyon-Slaney, H. Kimber, Sir J. G. S. Kinloch, H. Knatchbull-Hugessen (Kent), L. Knowles, A. Lafone, W. F. Lawrence (Liverpool), E. Lees, T. W. Legh (Lanc.), Lord W. C. G. Lennox, Sir R. Lethbridge, Viscount Lewisham, E. H. Llewellyn, G. W. E. Loder, W. H. Long, J. W. Lowther (Cumberland), Hon. W. Lowther (Westmoreland), L. Lyell, W. G. E. Macartney, C. F. Mackintosh, F. W. Maclean (Oxfordsh.), J. M. Maclean (Oldham), J. W. Maclure, Captain J. M'Calmont, D. H. Madden, W. F. Maitland, Col. J. W. Malcolm, Rt. Hon. E. Marjoribanks, M. H. Story-Maskelyne, Rt. Hon. H. Matthews, Sir H. E. Maxwell, A. R. C. Mayne, F. B. Mildmay, T. Milvain, R. J. More, Hon. F. Morgan (Monmouthshire, Rt. Hon. G. O. Morgan (Denbighshire), W. Morrison, W. G. Mount, R. G. C. Mowbray (Lanc. S.E.), P. A. Muhtz, Viscount Newark, Hon. R. T. O'Neill, Sir R. H. Paget, Hon. F. Parker (Oxfords.), Sir L. Pelly, Captain F. T. Penton, Rt. Hon. D. R. Plunket, W. C. Quilter, J. Rankin, Major F. C. Rasch, H. B. Reed (Bradford), T. Richardson, Rt. Hon. C. T. Ritchie, J. B. Roberts (Eifion), Rt. Hon. J. P. B. Robertson (Bute), Baron F. J. de Rothschild, J. Round, T. B. Royden, T. Salt, G. B. Samuelson (Gloucester), Col. E. J. Saunderson, Captain C. W. Selwyn, M. H. Shaw-Stewart (Renfrew), J. W. Sidebotham (Cheshire), T. H. Sidebottom (Stalybridge), W. Sidebottom (Derbyshire), W. P. Sinclair, J. P. Smith (Lanarksh.), Rt. Hon. W.

H. Smith (Strand), J. Somervell, Rt. Hon. E. Stanhope (Lincolnsh.), E. J. Stanley, M. Stewart (Kirkcudbrightsh.), T. Sutherland (Greenock), J. G. Talbot, T. K. Tapling, F. Taylor, Sir R. Temple, J. Theobald, W. Thorburn, W. E. M. Tomlinson, F. Townsend, Sir H. W. Tyler, Hon. A. H. J. Walsh, Sir R. E. Webster (Isle of Wight), W. C. West, Viscount Weymouth, E. Whitley, H. Wiggin, Hon. R. Winn, Viscount Wolmer, N. Wood, H. S. Wright (Nottingham). Tellers for the Noes, Mr. Akers-Douglas and Sir William Walrond.

C.

Chapter XXI.[1]

KASHMIR AND KHIVA.

The history of the Russian annexation and absorption of Khiva is one of dissimulation and disgrace, and may be told in few words. On the 8th of January, 1873, Earl Granville, wrote to Lord A. Loftus, the English Ambassador at St. Petersburgh, with reference to the then contemplated Russian expedition against Khiva, that he had had a personal interview with Count Schouvalow, by special request of the Czar, who had informed him, that the sole object of the expedition was to punish certain acts of brigandage by the Khan's subjects. '*Not only*,' writes Lord Granville, '*was it far from the intention of the Emperor to take possession of Khiva, but positive orders had been prepared to prevent it.* He gave me,' he adds, 'the most decided assurance that I might give positive assurances to Parliament on this matter.' The despatch goes on to state, that Lord Northbrook, then Viceroy of India had "given the strongest advice to the Khan to comply with the reasonable demands of the Emperor, and if the expedition were undertaken with the object and within the limits described by Count Schouvalow, it would meet with no remonstrance from Her Majesty's Government.' Unfortunate Khan of Khiva, with Russia lusting for annexation, and Great Britain (of all Powers !) counselling submission ! The result is a matter of history. The Russian troops had a 'walk over' into Khiva, and the Treaty which General Kauffman dictated, literally at the point of the sword, to-day gives the lie to Count Schouvalow's pacific assurances. The Treaty commences in this wise: 'The whole of the right bank of the Amou Darya and the lands adjoining thereunto, which have hitherto been considered as belonging to Khiva,

---

[*] "Kashmir Conspiracy; or the truth of the Maharaja's Case." Lahore: Mitra Vilasa Press, 1890.

shall pass over from the Khan into the possession of Russia, together with the people dwelling and camping thereon, etc. In the examination of claims between Russians and Khivans, preference shall be given to Russians. Complaints and claims of Khivans against Russian subjects shall be referred to the nearest Russian Authorities. A fine is inflicted on the Khanate of Khiva of two million two hundred thousand roubles (about £300,000) in order to cover the expenses incurred by the Russian Exchequer in the prosecution of the late war which was *provoked* (??) by the Government of the Khan.' *Und so weiter*. And thus, poor Khiva has been Russianised, at the expense of the blood and wealth of the children of her soil, while Russia has consequently crept up to within a hundred miles or so nearer of her sole perspective aim and design—the Frontier of British India. All the while, Great Britain, the Power most interested, has, according to the despatch of her Foreign Minister, 'offered no opposition' to this wholesale spoliation of one of the outlying bulwarks of defence against Muscovite aggression. On the contrary, she seems rather to admire Russian diplomacy, with its misleading tactics, its false assurances, and its questionable modes of territorial acquisition, and has tried her hand too, *á la Russe*, that is to say employing the same weapons, in the absorption of Kashmir,—the British Khiva.

Consider we now for a while the *modus operandi* employed to anglicanise poor Kashmir, and the intelligent reader cannot fail to be struck with the similarity of the means used by the Russians in Khiva and and the English in Kashmir, and can also draw his own conclusions from the political parallel. *Imprimus*,—of course it was necessary to throw dust in the eyes of our interested neighbours and especially essential was it that England should blind, or try to blind, Russia as to her real intentions regarding Kashmir. Hence, we find both Lord Cross and Sir John Gorst repeatedly and, it appeared to many, unnecessarily, giving the most emphatic explanatory assurances of England's non-intervention,—assurances every whit as unmistakable as those given by the Czar of Russia regarding Khiva. England, we were informed, has not now, nor has she at any time ever had the slightest intention of 'annexing' Kashmir. True, the British Schouvalow did not define his interpretation of the word 'annexing,' and herein lies the key of the whole matter. England might have sought a quarrel with Kashmir, invaded and conquered that country, and then 'squeezed' a war indemnity out of her, thus following the precedent of Russia in Khiva. But, though John Bull submitted quietly to the Khivan aggression which permitted his foes (to use a Russian expression) 'to sit down' almost at his very door, he knew full well, that Russia would make a very positive and practical 'remonstrance' against the *actual* annexation of Kashmir by England. Hence, quite a different line of policy had to be observed. After having satisfied the world at large by repeated and plausible assurances that her intentions towards Kashmir were strictly honourable and purely philanthropic, England proceeds to lay that country at her feet by moral, not military, pressure. First, the Ruler is deposed for no reason except that he was in the way of the Scheme. Then, Rulers, in the shape of a Council, are appointed by England, being controlled and directed by an English Resident. Then, Kashmir is compelled to make a costly military road from the British frontier to her capital. Then, the control of the Kashmir army is obtained, and the troops are placed under British officers, while a military colony, under the guise of post of observation, is established at Gilgit. And, lastly, Kashmir is made bankrupt by forced expenditure and a forced loan, and to-day, as we said before, lies as much at the mercy and under the dominion of England as though she had been formerly and officially annexed by that ever-absorbing Power. When comparing the Russian and English methods of extending their frontier by annexation, the balance to the credit of England lies solely in the fact of non-invasion and consequent saving of bloodshed. The violated assurances, the deprivation of power, the transfer to British rule, the pecuniary requisitions, all remain the same, and, as surely and certainly as the Agent of the Czar of all the Russias rules and controls the destinies of subjugated Khiva, so surely and certainly does the Agents of the Queen-Empress of India rule and control those of the no less subjugated Kashmir.

D.

THE ALLEGED REAL OBJECT OF THE DEPOSITION OF THE MAHARAJA.

(*Indian Union*, Allahabad, June 19.)

The Foreign Office confidential Memo on Gilgit, published by the *Amrita Bazar Patrika*, created a sensation that is far from dead yet. In the controversy that ensued the Editor by no means came off second best, for the honours of war remained with him decidedly. In fact, the dealings of the Indian Government with Kashmir can only be explained on the basis of the Gilgit memorandum. In the March and April numbers of the *Fortnightly Review*, an article contributed by Sir Charles Dilke rather tends to establish the Gilgit memorandum on a yet firmer basis. It seems to show that, as early as the autumn of 1888, the practical deposition of the Maharaja and the annexation of Kashmir had been secretly resolved on at Simla. It must be borne in mind that the cock and bull story of the Jammu forgeries did not originate till the spring of 1889. Sir Charles Dilke landed in Kurrachee in November, 1888, as the honoured guest of Sir Frederick Roberts. January, 1889, saw his return home again. Sir Charles Dilke was sorely wanted to popularize among the public of England the Indian Scientific Frontier Defence expenditure. To this end all the secrets of the Military and Foreign Offices were laid bare to him. At page 474 we find Sir Charles Dilke writing :—'The armies of the Native States are being dealt with by the provision of British Inspection, and a beginning has been made in the Punjab. *It will be possible to make of the army of Kashmir a very useful force for watching the passes on the Kashmir side, to the great relief of our field army;* but I continue to retain the view with which I went to India, that the armies of the great southern feudatory States should be disbanded as such, that is, reduced merely to police guards.' At page 480 Sir Charles Dilke again writes :—'No large Russian army can venture across the mountains of Chitral or descend upon Kabul from Balkh by the Hindukush. Sir Charles MacGregor, who was there writing of what he knew, has proved this to demonstration, although he did not make the allowance that all would who know Russia, for the use of sledges over the passes in winter time. That the attempt would be made by a small force in case of war is certain. *Steps have now been taken to stop any such force descending upon the plains of India without drawing upon our main field army.* Colonel Maurice seems to think that a Russian descent from the North might take us in the flank: a small force no doubt might pass by Gilgit towards Kashmir, a small force by Chitral towards Jellalabad, and a small force by Balkh to Kabul; but until—should this unhappily come about—the Russians have been long at Balkh, no very serious danger is to be apprehended in this direction.' Sir Charles Dilke is here slightly disingenuous, to say the least, for Colonel Lockhardt's mission to Chitral and recent researches have demonstrated that the Hindukush Range is simply honeycombed with easy passes, and the belief now at Simla is that no Russian invasion of India will be attempted by the Candahar route. These extracts show that Sir Charles Dilke was informed in 1888 of what was intended to be done in Kashmir the following year, 1889, when Colonel Nisbet was sent up to force the situation as an *agent provocateur*.